STAR WARS
DARTH MAUL

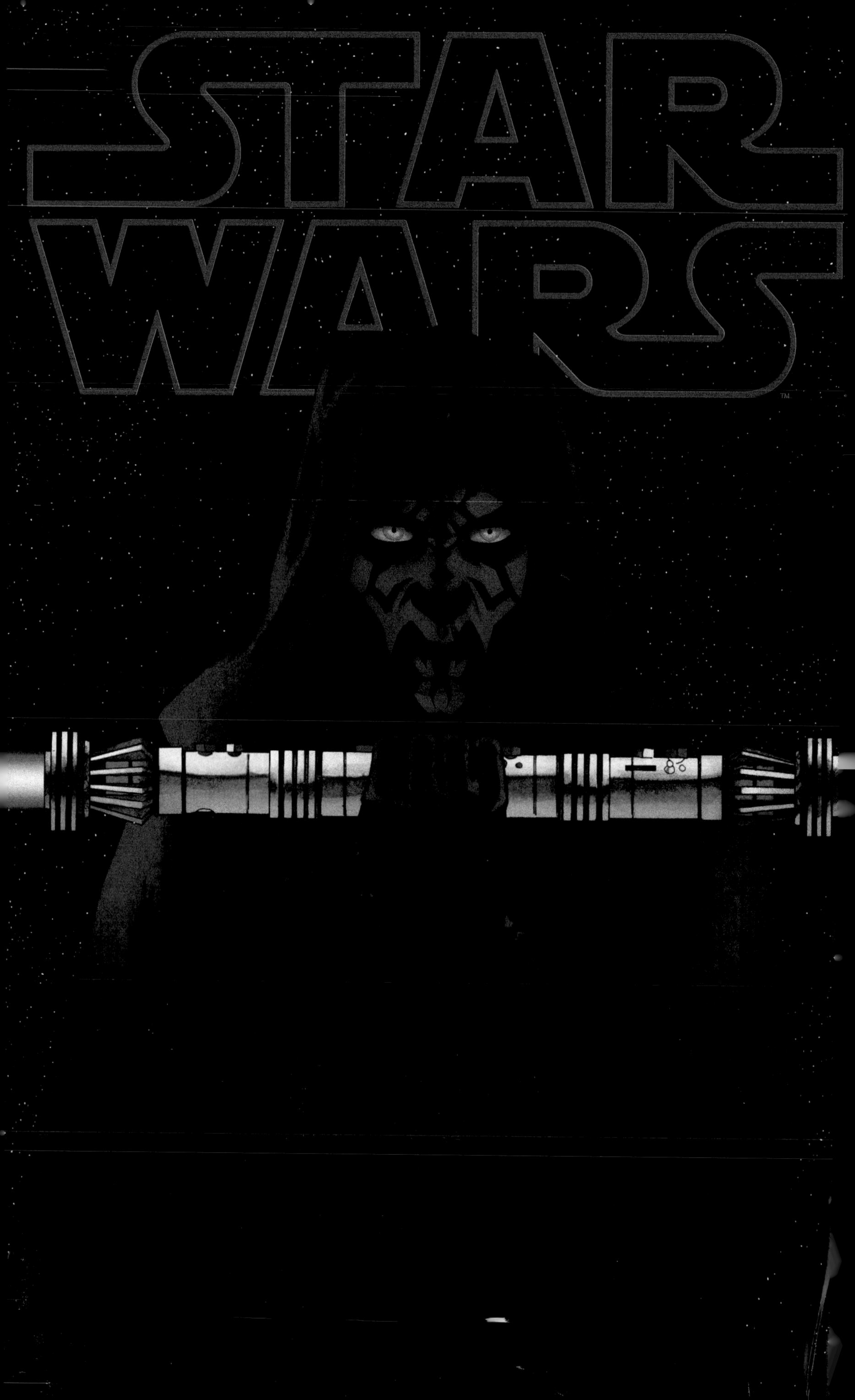
STAR
WARS

DARTH MAUL

Writer CULLEN BUNN
Artist LUKE ROSS
Color Artist NOLAN WOODARD
Letterer VC's JOE CARAMAGNA
Cover Art ROD REIS (#1) & RAFAEL ALBUQUERQUE (#2-5)

"PROBE DROID PROBLEM"
Writer/Artist/Letterer CHRIS ELIOPOULOS
Color Artist JORDIE BELLAIRE

Assistant Editor HEATHER ANTOS
Editor JORDAN D. WHITE
Executive Editor C.B. CEBULSKI

Editor in Chief AXEL ALONSO
Chief Creative Officer JOE QUESADA
President DAN BUCKLEY

For Lucasfilm:
Senior Editor FRANK PARISI
Creative Director MICHAEL SIGLAIN
Lucasfilm Story Group PABLO HIDALGO, JAMES WAUGH, LELAND CHEE, MATT MARTIN

Collection Editor JENNIFER GRÜNWALD
Assistant Editor CAITLIN O'CONNELL
Associate Managing Editor KATERI WOODY
Editor, Special Projects MARK D. BEAZLEY
VP Production & Special Projects JEFF YOUNGQUIST
SVP Print, Sales & Marketing DAVID GABRIEL
Book Designer ADAM DEL RE

STAR WARS: DARTH MAUL. Contains material originally published in magazine form as STAR WARS: DARTH MAUL #1-5. First printing 2017. ISBN# 978-0-7851-9589-4. Published by MARVEL WORLDWIDE, INC., a subsidiary of MARVEL ENTERTAINMENT, LLC. OFFICE OF PUBLICATION: 135 West 50th Street, New York, NY 10020. **Printed in the U.S.A.** DAN BUCKLEY, President, Marvel Entertainment; JOE QUESADA, Chief Creative Officer; TOM BREVOORT, SVP of Publishing; DAVID BOGART, SVP of Business Affairs & Operations, Publishing & Partnership; C.B. CEBULSKI, VP of Brand Management & Development, Asia; DAVID GABRIEL, SVP of Sales & Marketing, Publishing; JEFF YOUNGQUIST, VP of Production & Special Projects; DAN CARR, Executive Director of Publishing Technology; ALEX MORALES, Director of Publishing Operations; SUSAN CRESPI, Production Manager; STAN LEE, Chairman Emeritus. For information regarding advertising in Marvel Comics or on Marvel.com, please contact Vit DeBellis, Integrated Sales Manager, at vdebellis@marvel.com. For Marvel subscription inquiries, please call 888-511-5480. **Manufactured between 6/30/2017 and 8/1/2017 by QUAD/GRAPHICS WASECA, WASECA, MN, USA.**

10 9 8 7 6 5 4 3 2 1

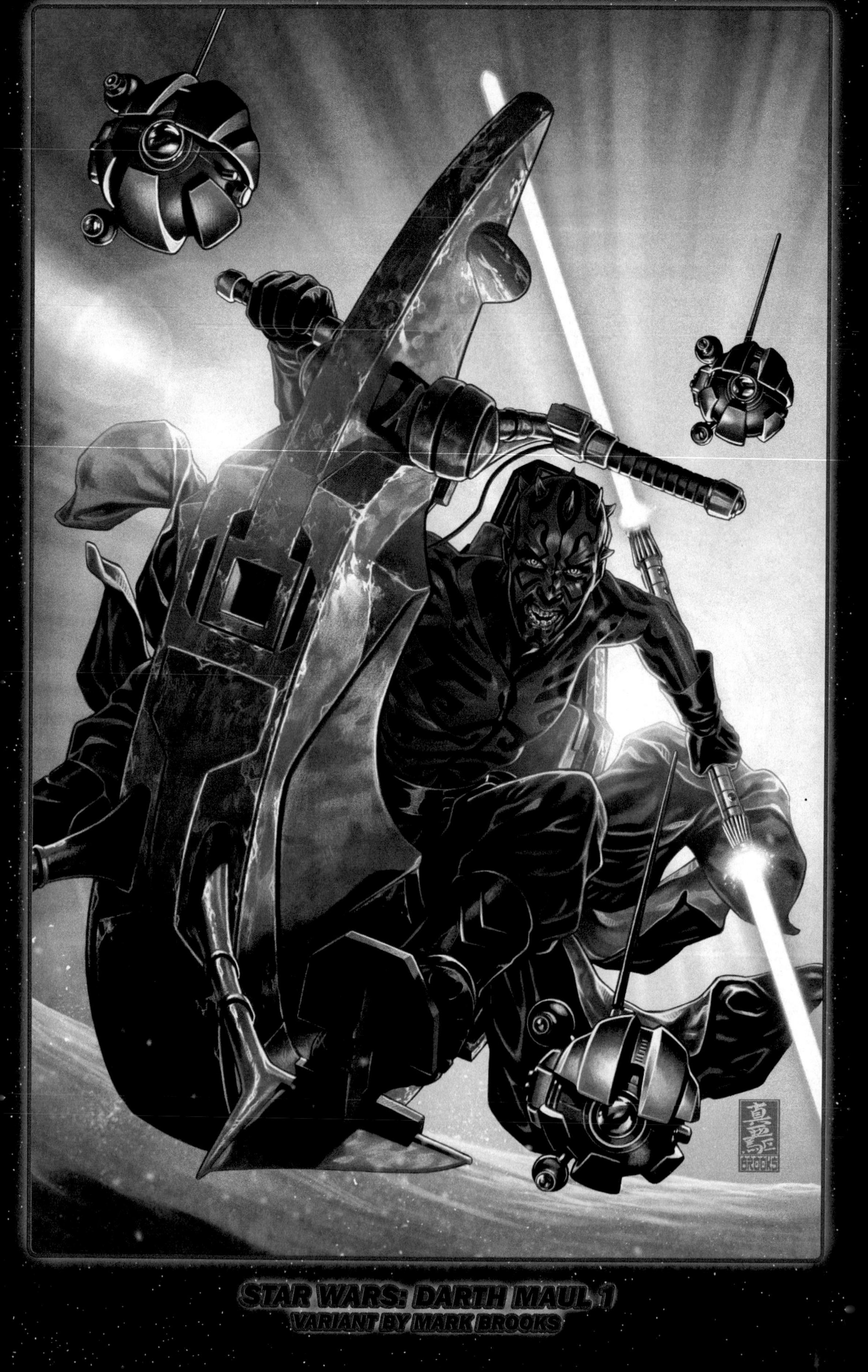
BROOKS

STAR WARS: DARTH MAUL 1
VARIANT BY MARK BROOKS

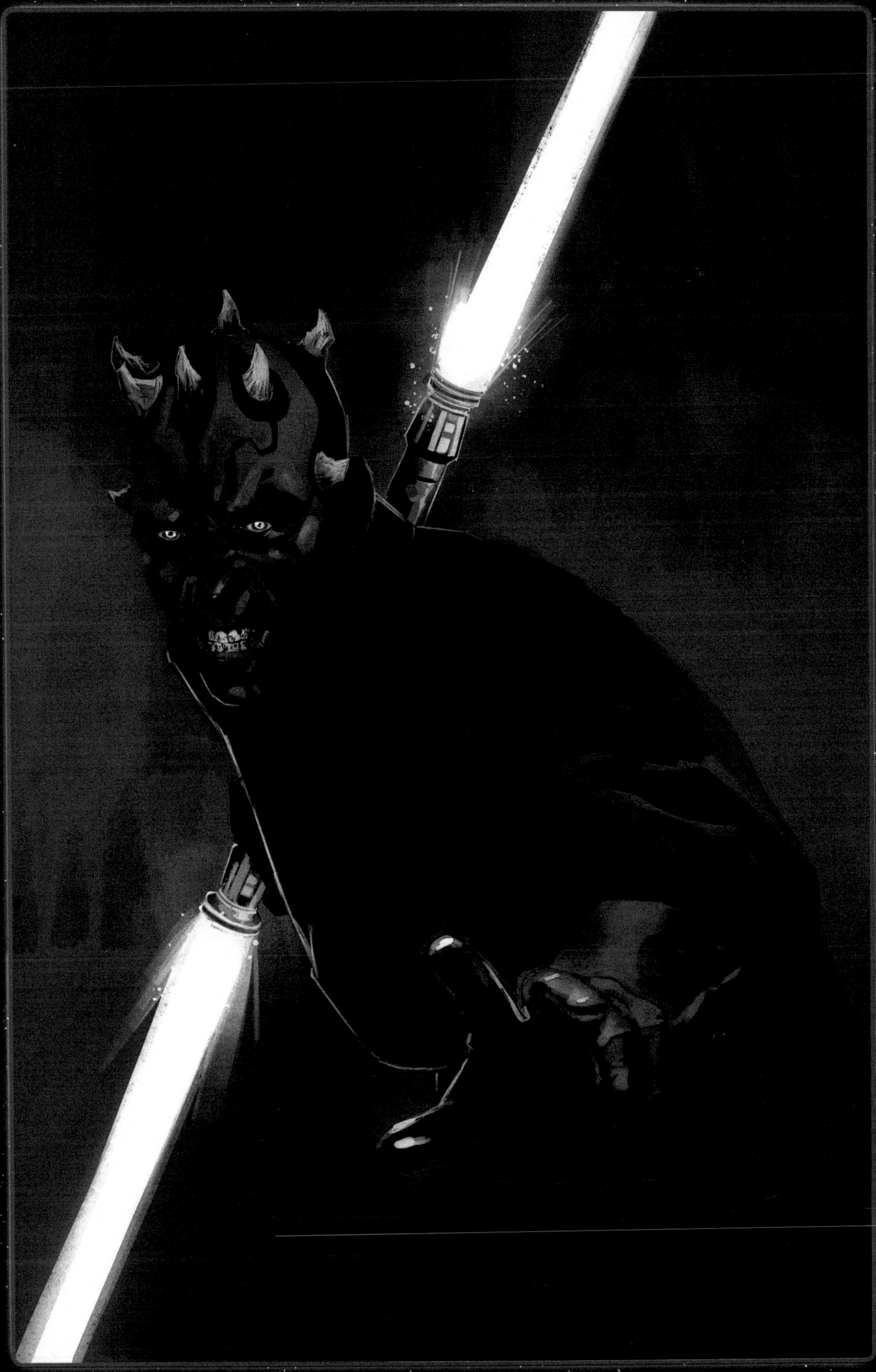

DARTH MAUL

In the shadows, an ancient enemy stirs. The Sith – practitioners of the dark side of the Force long thought destroyed – secretly work to undermine and eventually overthrow the Jedi Order, the guardians of peace and justice in the galaxy.

Two members of the Sith order – Darth Sidious and his apprentice Darth Maul – secretly await their moment to strike. But while Sidious plans an intricate series of deceptions and machinations, Maul grows restless.

The moment of revenge is close at hand, and he is unwilling to wait much longer.....

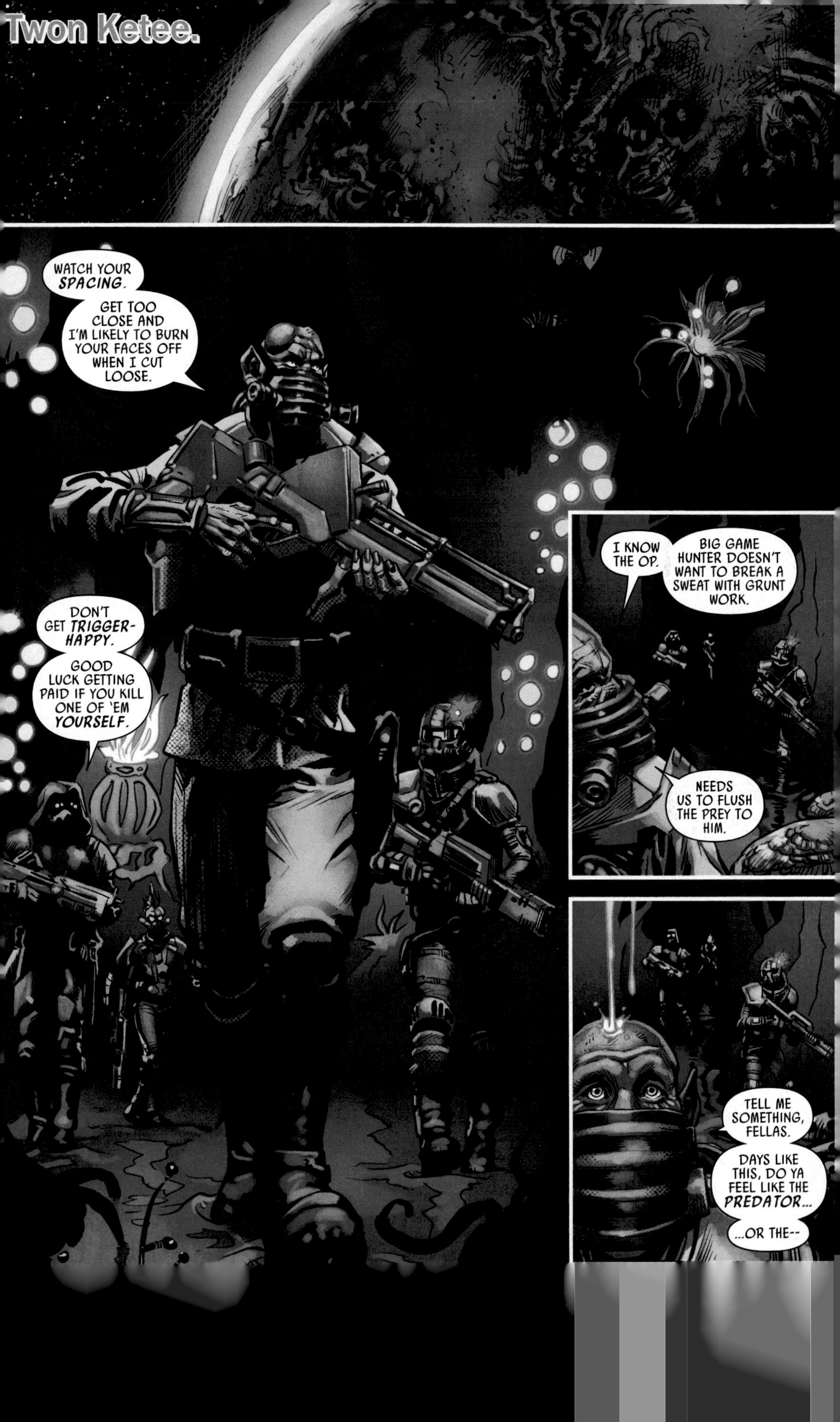
Twon Ketee.
WATCH YOUR SPACING.
GET TOO CLOSE AND I'M LIKELY TO BURN YOUR FACES OFF WHEN I CUT LOOSE.
DON'T GET TRIGGER-HAPPY.
GOOD LUCK GETTING PAID IF YOU KILL ONE OF 'EM YOURSELF.
I KNOW THE OP.
BIG GAME HUNTER DOESN'T WANT TO BREAK A SWEAT WITH GRUNT WORK.
NEEDS US TO FLUSH THE PREY TO HIM.
TELL ME SOMETHING, FELLAS.
DAYS LIKE THIS, DO YA FEEL LIKE THE PREDATOR...
...OR THE--

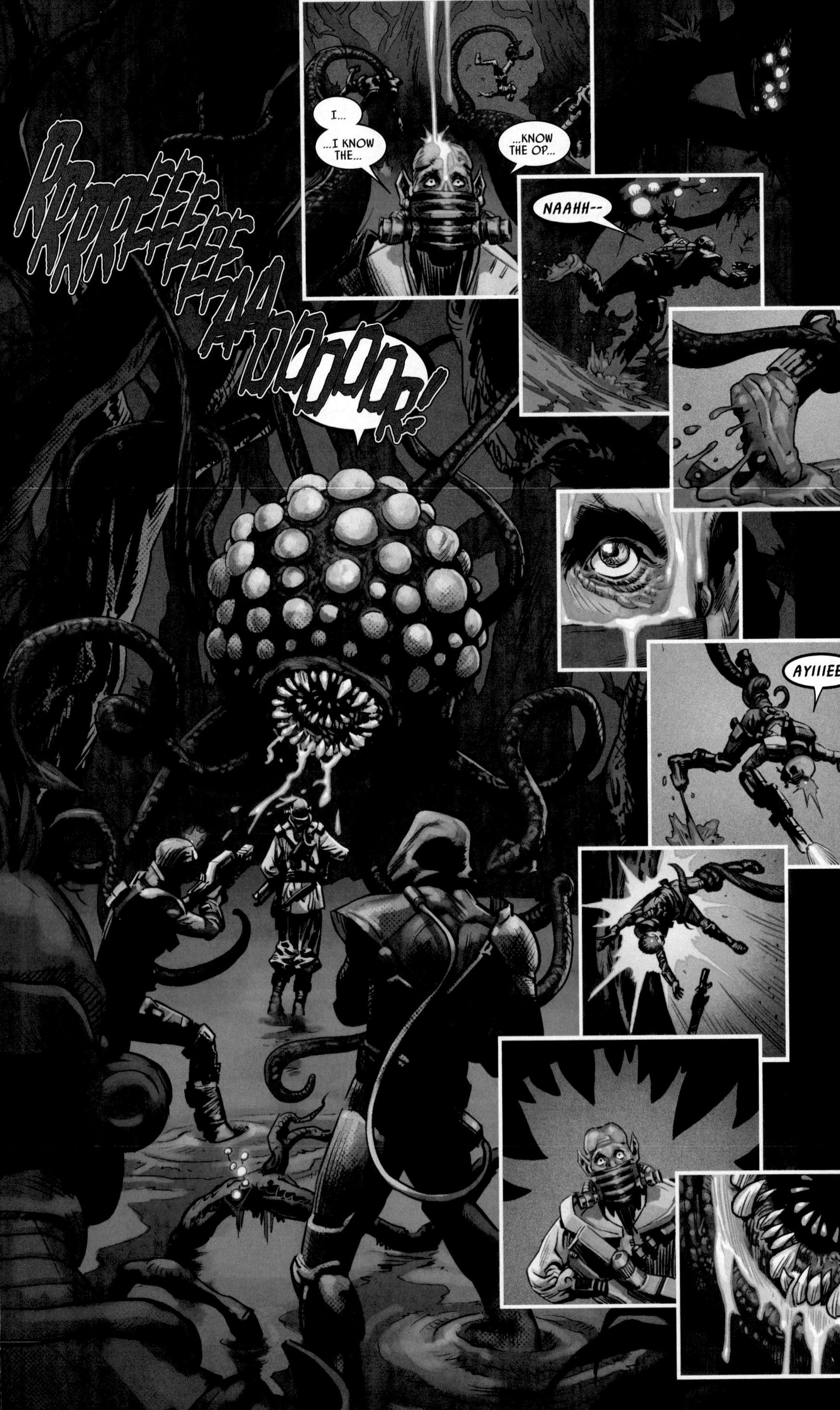
RRRRREEEEEAAOOOOOR!
I...
...I KNOW THE...
...KNOW THE OP...
NAAHH--
AYIIIEE

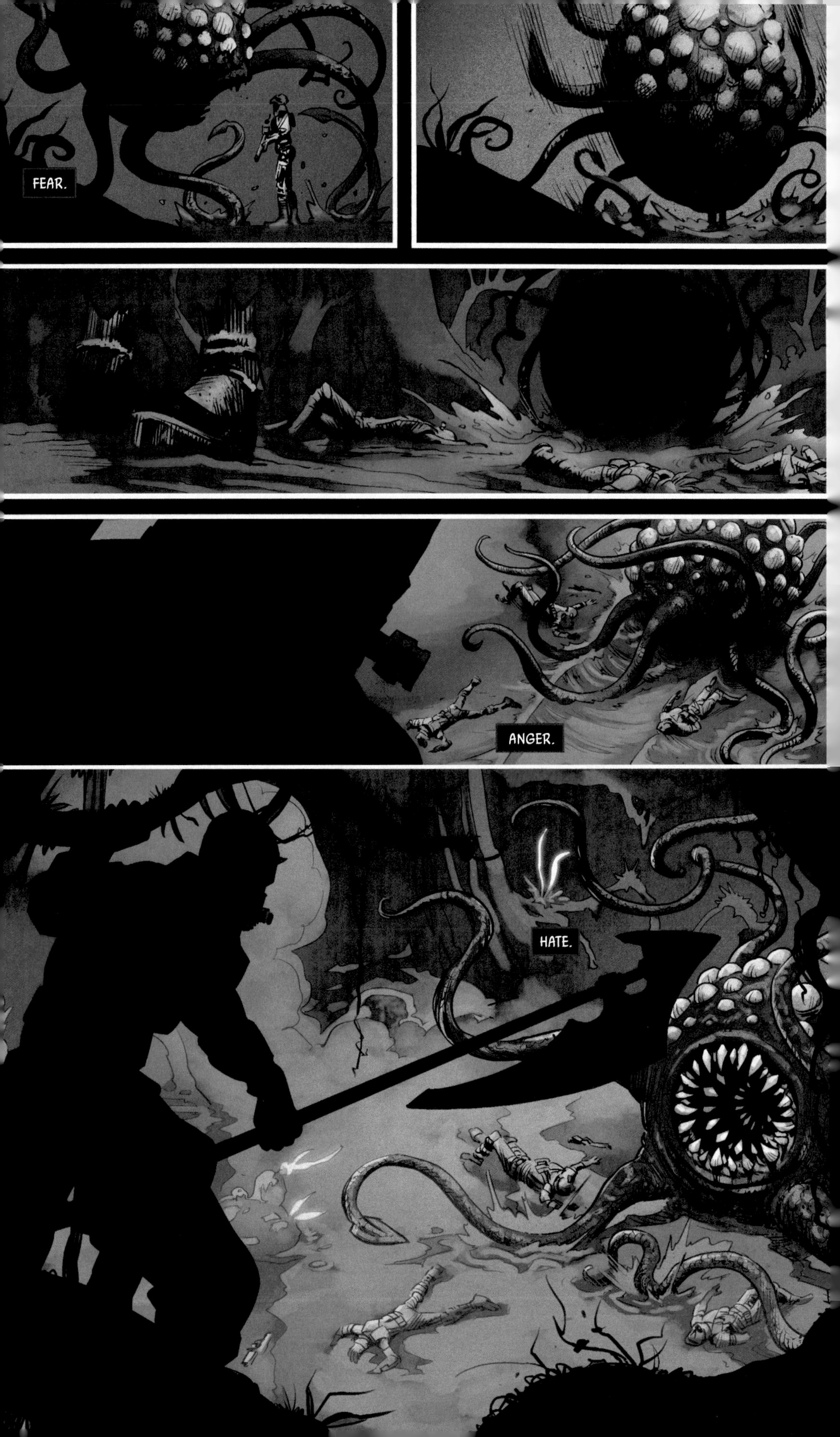
FEAR.
ANGER.
HATE.

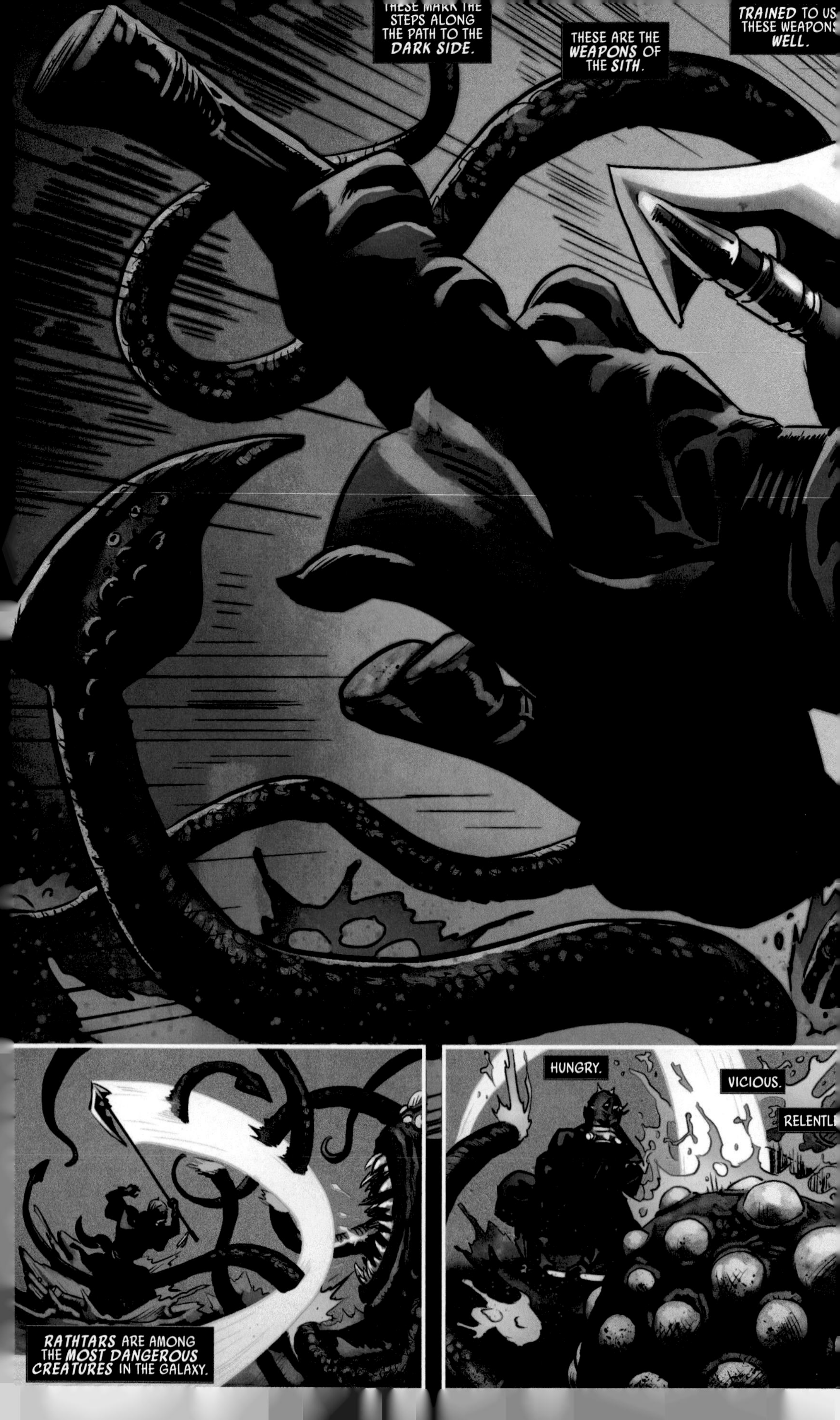
THESE MARK THE STEPS ALONG THE PATH TO THE DARK SIDE.
THESE ARE THE WEAPONS OF THE SITH.
TRAINED TO US THESE WEAPONS WELL.
RATHTARS ARE AMONG THE MOST DANGEROUS CREATURES IN THE GALAXY.
HUNGRY.
VICIOUS.
RELENTL

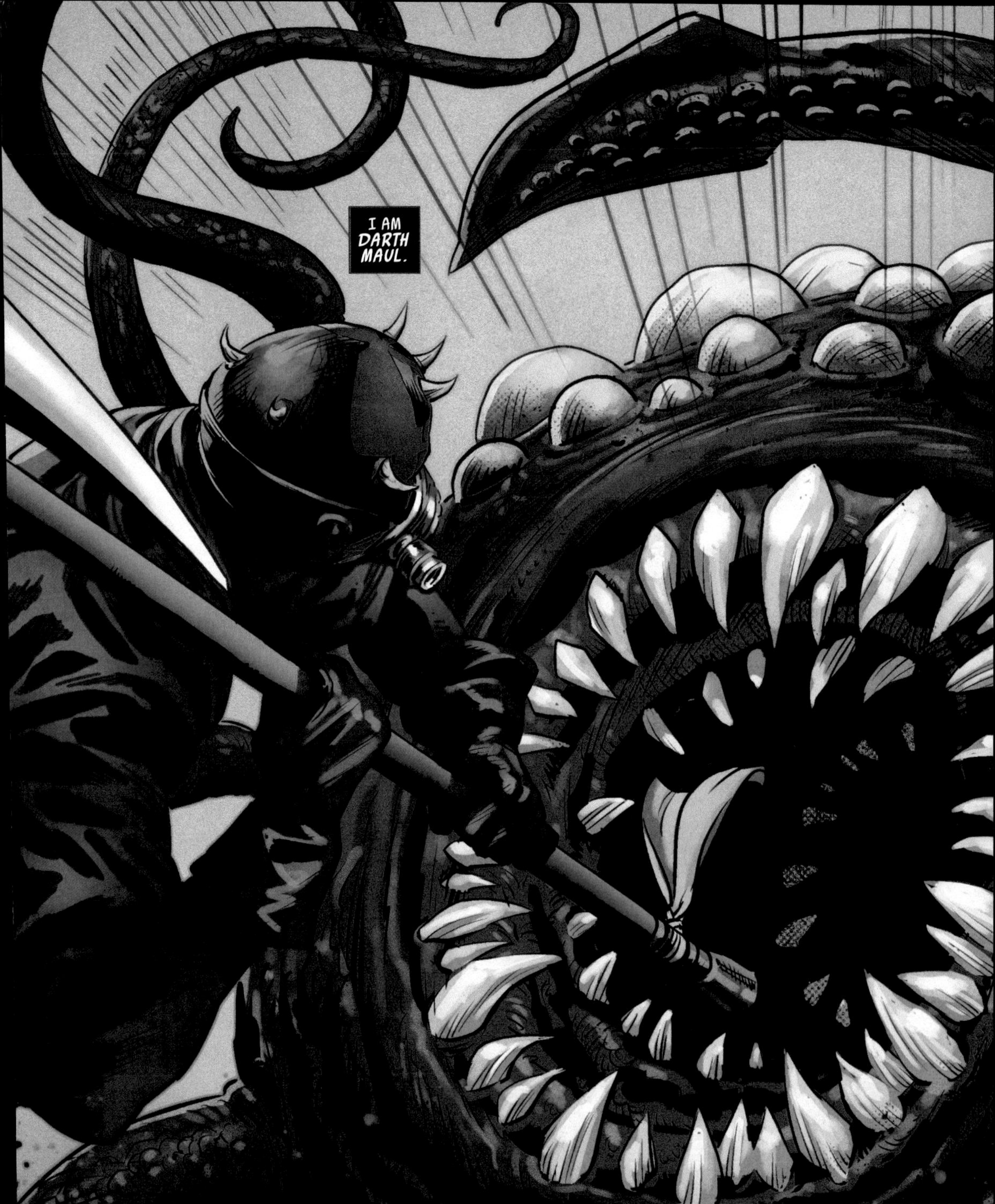
I AM DARTH MAUL.

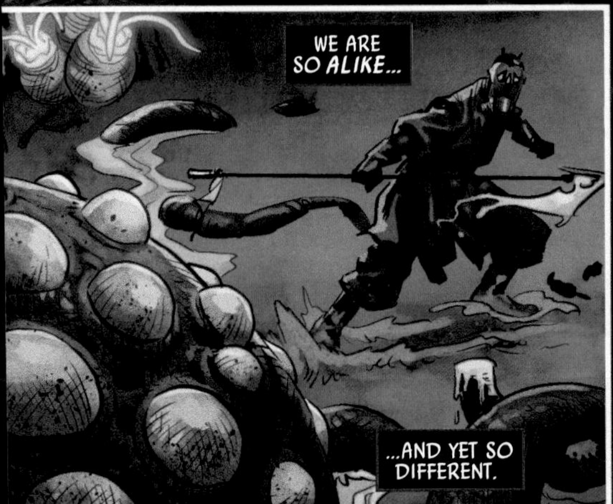
WE ARE SO ALIKE...
...AND YET SO DIFFERENT.

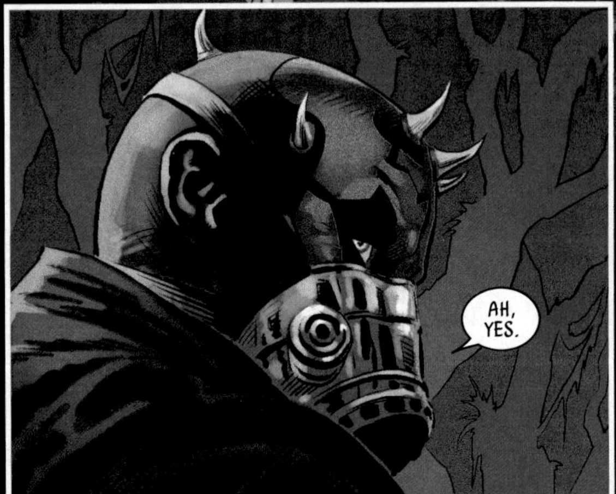
AH, YES.

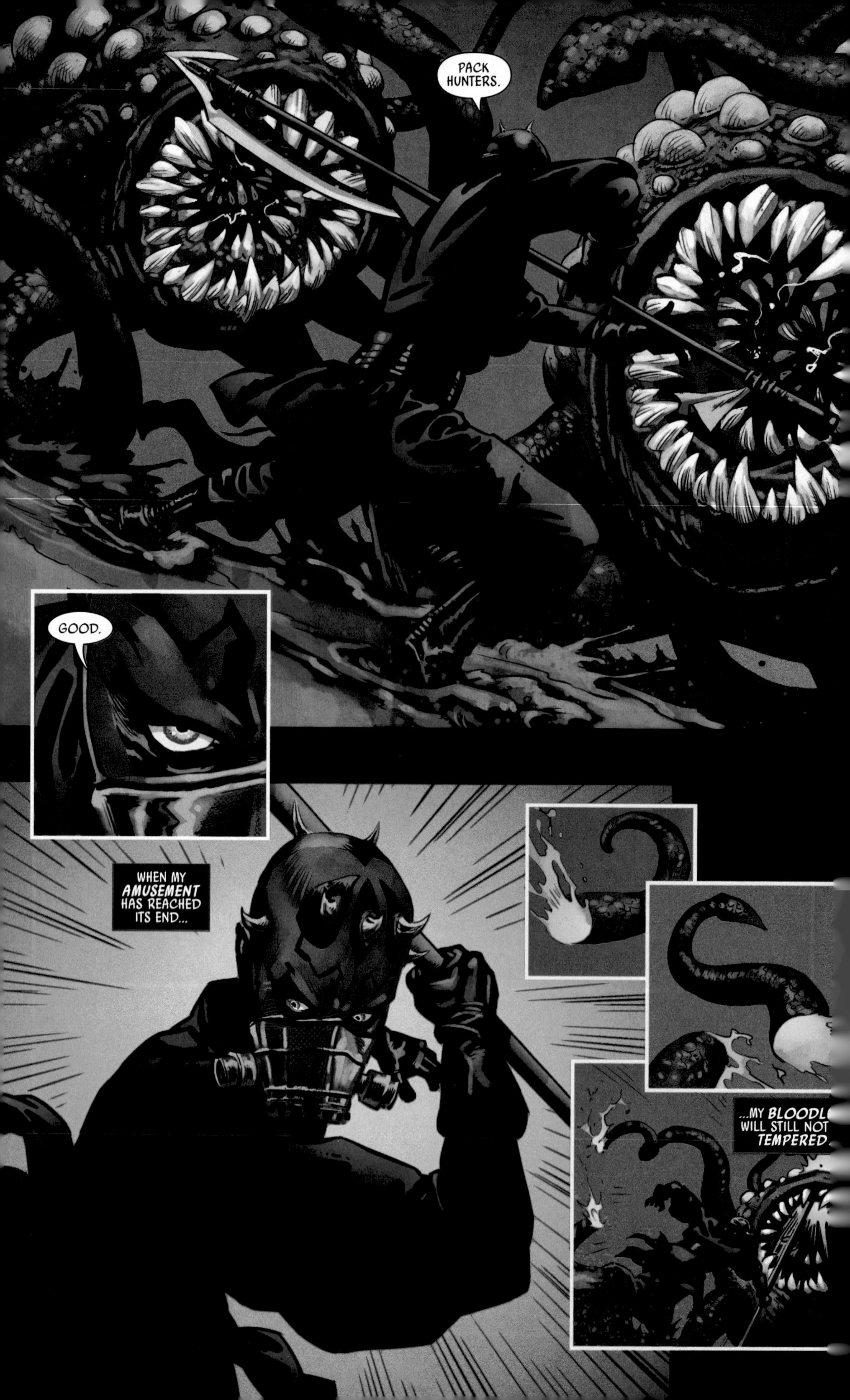
PACK HUNTERS.
GOOD.
WHEN MY AMUSEMENT HAS REACHED ITS END...
...MY BLOODL
WILL STILL NOT
TEMPERED.

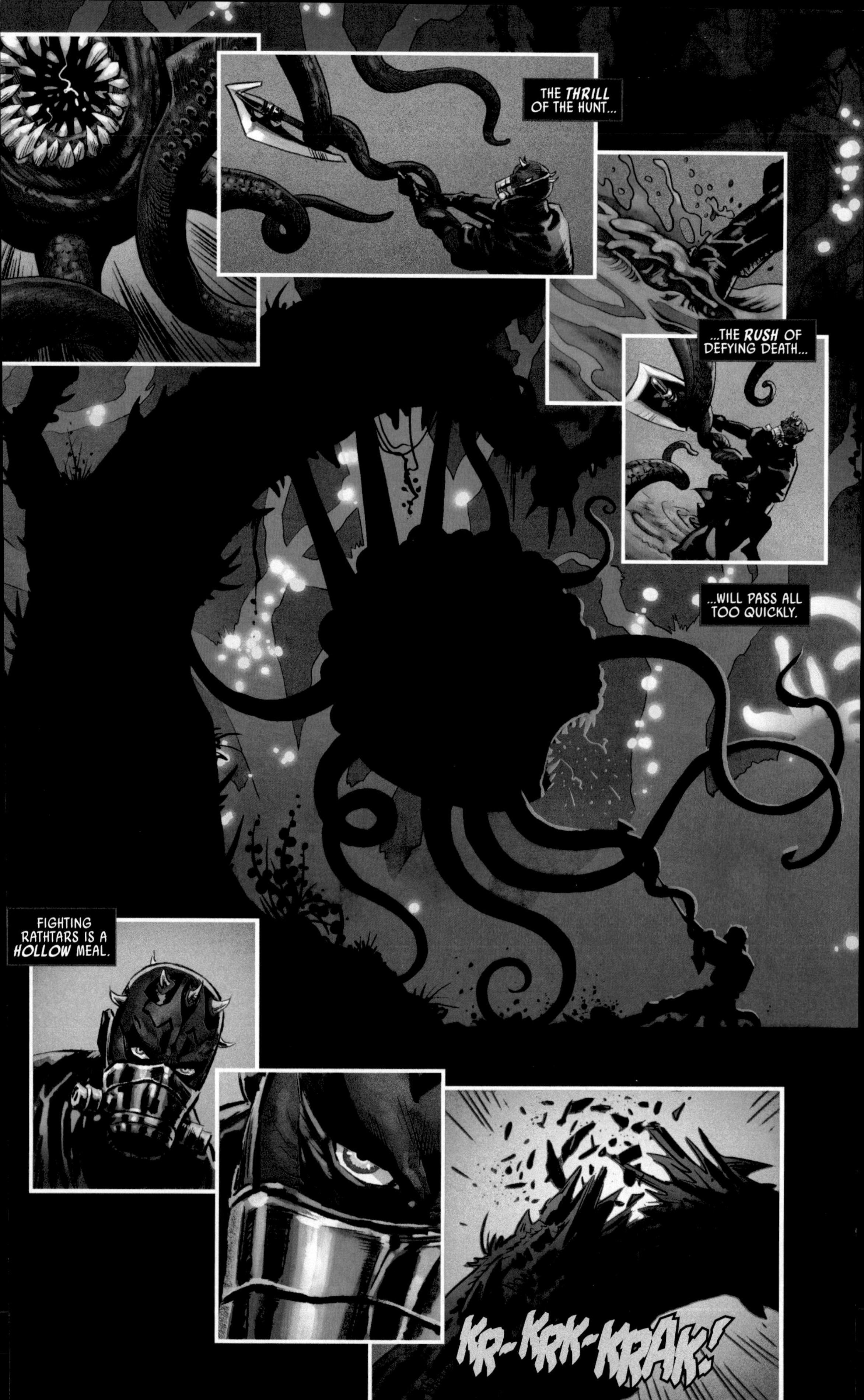
THE THRILL OF THE HUNT...
...THE RUSH OF DEFYING DEATH...
...WILL PASS ALL TOO QUICKLY.
FIGHTING RATHTARS IS A HOLLOW MEAL.
KR-KRK-KRAK!

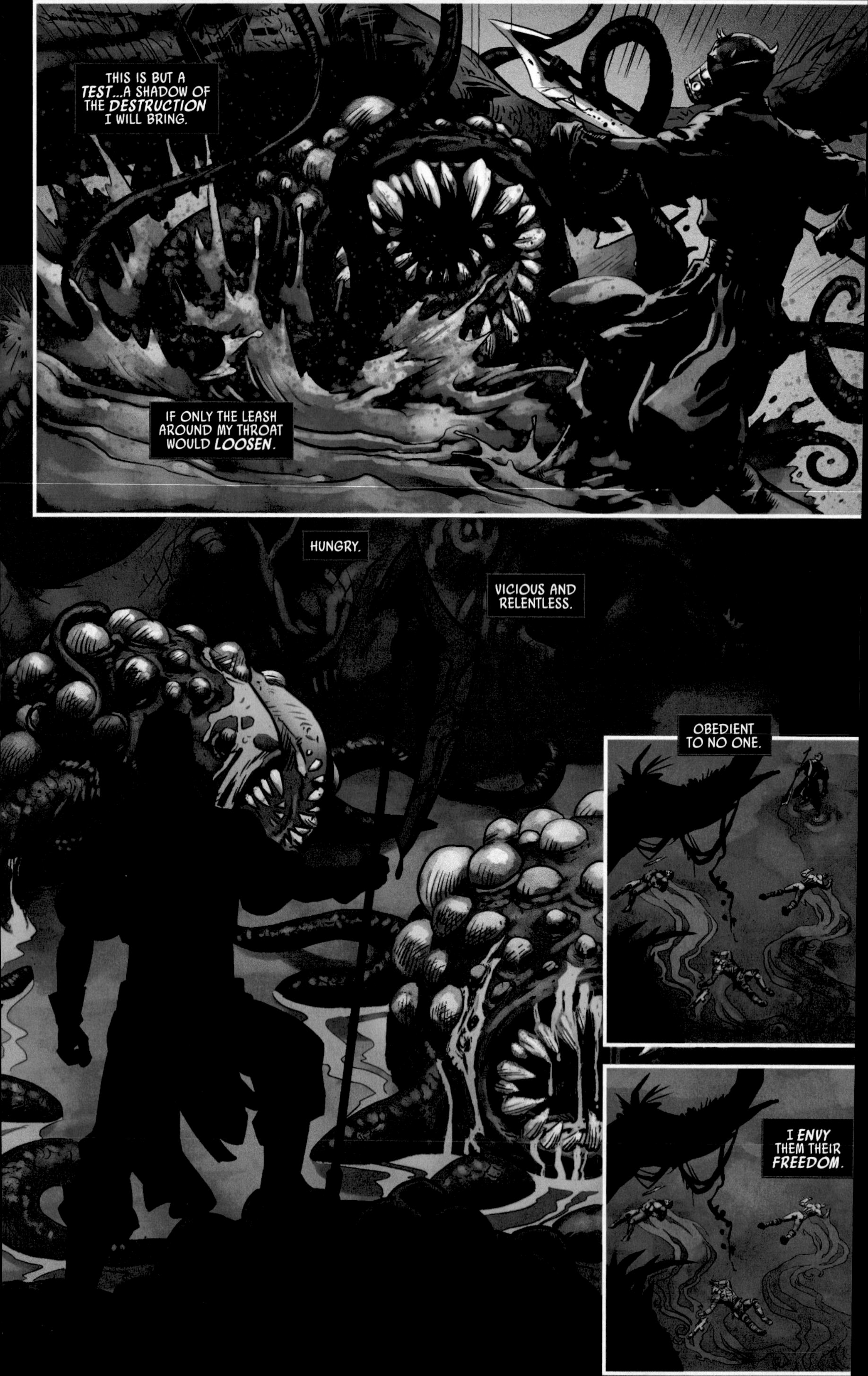
THIS IS BUT A TEST...A SHADOW OF THE DESTRUCTION I WILL BRING.
IF ONLY THE LEASH AROUND MY THROAT WOULD LOOSEN.
HUNGRY.
VICIOUS AND RELENTLESS.
OBEDIENT TO NO ONE.
I ENVY THEM THEIR FREEDOM.

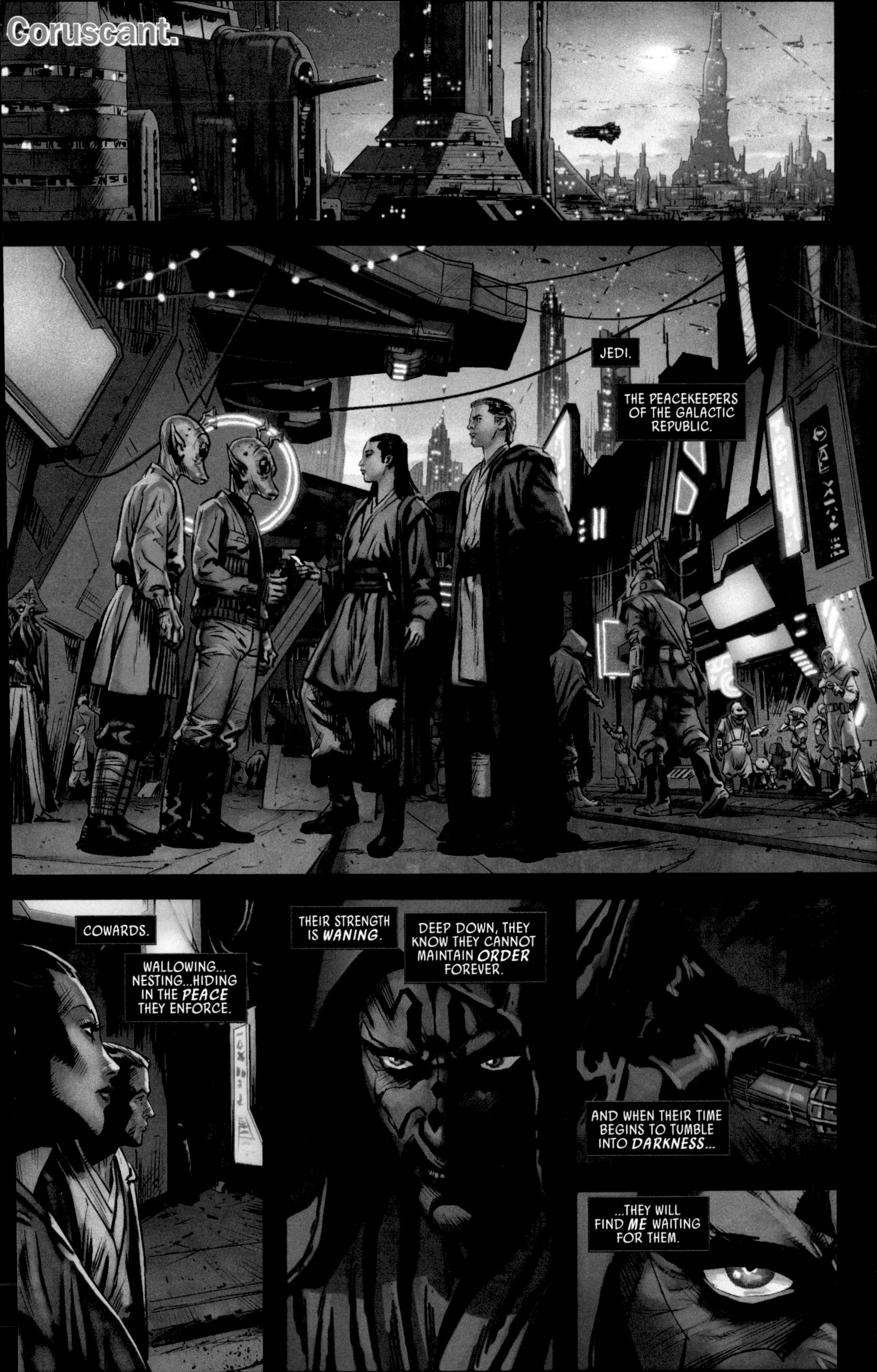
Coruscant.
JEDI.
THE PEACEKEEPERS OF THE GALACTIC REPUBLIC.
COWARDS.
WALLOWING... NESTING...HIDING IN THE *PEACE* THEY ENFORCE.
THEIR STRENGTH IS *WANING*.
DEEP DOWN, THEY KNOW THEY CANNOT MAINTAIN *ORDER* FOREVER.
AND WHEN THEIR TIME BEGINS TO TUMBLE INTO *DARKNESS*...
...THEY WILL FIND *ME* WAITING FOR THEM.

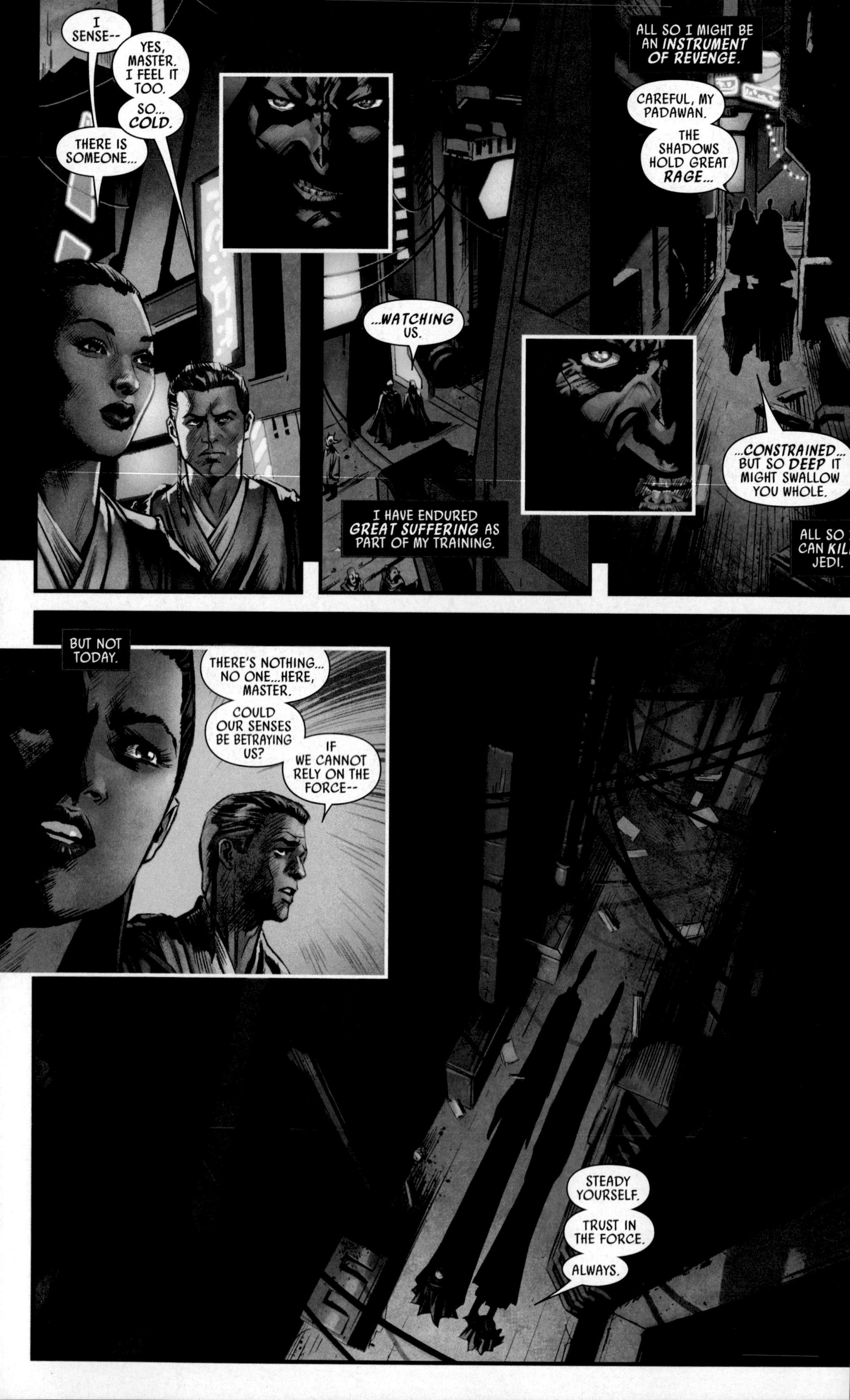
I SENSE--
YES, MASTER. I FEEL IT TOO.
SO... COLD.
THERE IS SOMEONE...
...WATCHING US.
I HAVE ENDURED GREAT SUFFERING AS PART OF MY TRAINING.
ALL SO I MIGHT BE AN INSTRUMENT OF REVENGE.
CAREFUL, MY PADAWAN.
THE SHADOWS HOLD GREAT RAGE...
...CONSTRAINED... BUT SO DEEP IT MIGHT SWALLOW YOU WHOLE.
ALL SO CAN KIL JEDI.
BUT NOT TODAY.
THERE'S NOTHING... NO ONE...HERE, MASTER.
COULD OUR SENSES BE BETRAYING US?
IF WE CANNOT RELY ON THE FORCE--
STEADY YOURSELF.
TRUST IN THE FORCE.
ALWAYS.

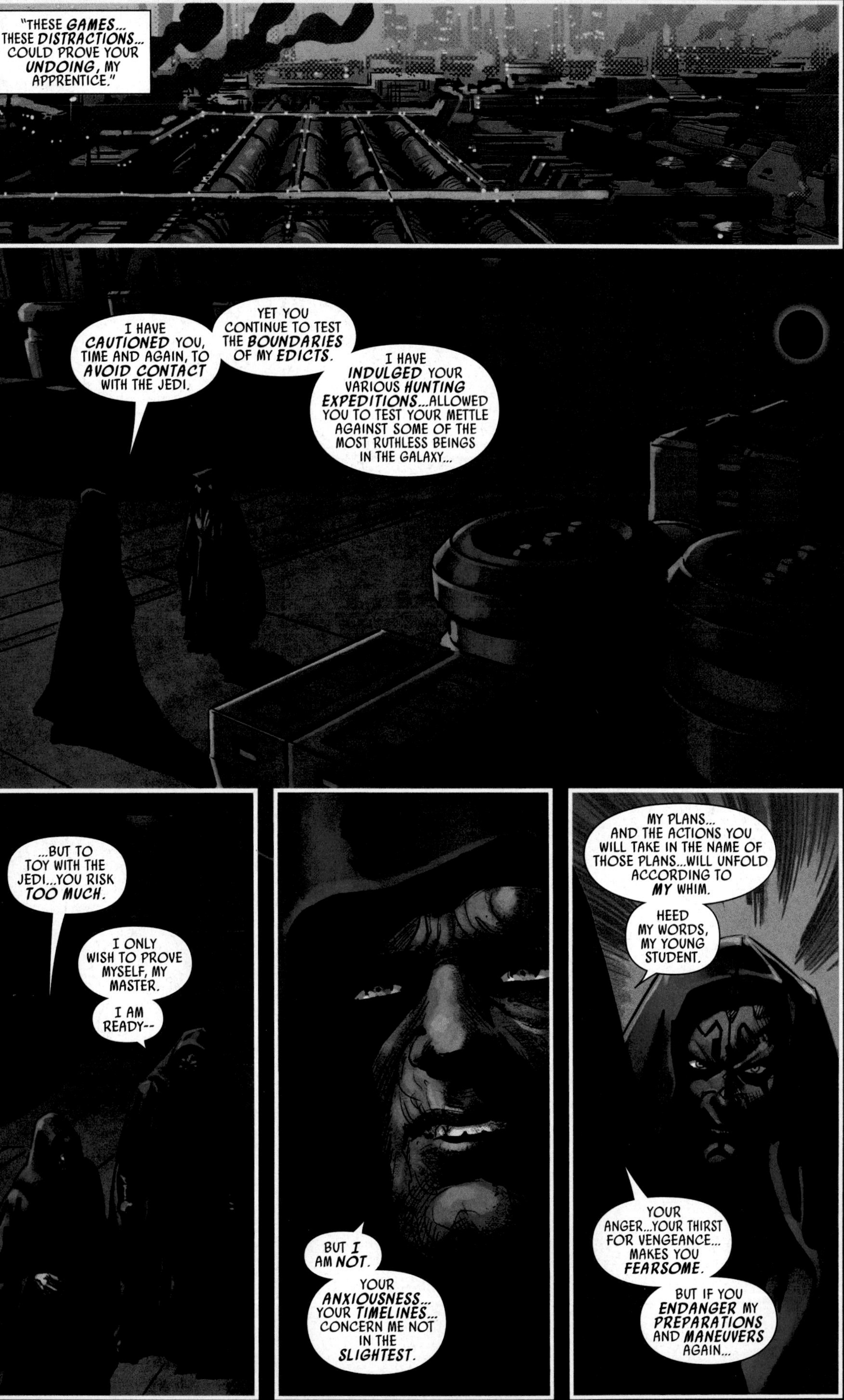
"THESE GAMES... THESE DISTRACTIONS... COULD PROVE YOUR UNDOING, MY APPRENTICE."
I HAVE CAUTIONED YOU, TIME AND AGAIN, TO AVOID CONTACT WITH THE JEDI.
YET YOU CONTINUE TO TEST THE BOUNDARIES OF MY EDICTS.
I HAVE INDULGED YOUR VARIOUS HUNTING EXPEDITIONS...ALLOWED YOU TO TEST YOUR METTLE AGAINST SOME OF THE MOST RUTHLESS BEINGS IN THE GALAXY...
...BUT TO TOY WITH THE JEDI...YOU RISK TOO MUCH.
I ONLY WISH TO PROVE MYSELF, MY MASTER.
I AM READY--
BUT I AM NOT.
YOUR ANXIOUSNESS... YOUR TIMELINES... CONCERN ME NOT IN THE SLIGHTEST.
MY PLANS... AND THE ACTIONS YOU WILL TAKE IN THE NAME OF THOSE PLANS...WILL UNFOLD ACCORDING TO MY WHIM.
HEED MY WORDS, MY YOUNG STUDENT.
YOUR ANGER...YOUR THIRST FOR VENGEANCE... MAKES YOU FEARSOME.
BUT IF YOU ENDANGER MY PREPARATIONS AND MANEUVERS AGAIN...

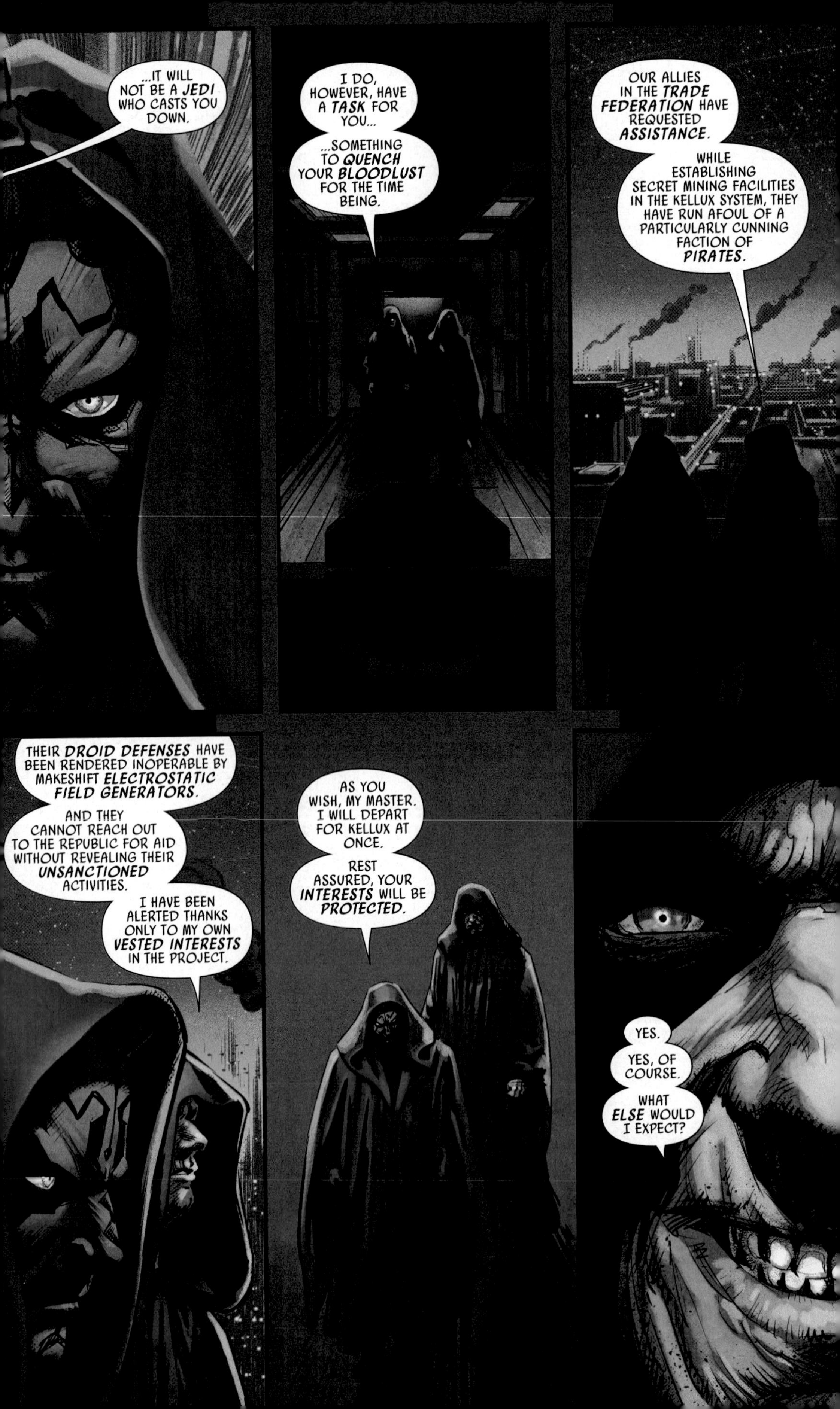
...IT WILL NOT BE A JEDI WHO CASTS YOU DOWN.
I DO, HOWEVER, HAVE A TASK FOR YOU...
...SOMETHING TO QUENCH YOUR BLOODLUST FOR THE TIME BEING.
OUR ALLIES IN THE TRADE FEDERATION HAVE REQUESTED ASSISTANCE.
WHILE ESTABLISHING SECRET MINING FACILITIES IN THE KELLUX SYSTEM, THEY HAVE RUN AFOUL OF A PARTICULARLY CUNNING FACTION OF PIRATES.
THEIR DROID DEFENSES HAVE BEEN RENDERED INOPERABLE BY MAKESHIFT ELECTROSTATIC FIELD GENERATORS.
AND THEY CANNOT REACH OUT TO THE REPUBLIC FOR AID WITHOUT REVEALING THEIR UNSANCTIONED ACTIVITIES.
I HAVE BEEN ALERTED THANKS ONLY TO MY OWN VESTED INTERESTS IN THE PROJECT.
AS YOU WISH, MY MASTER. I WILL DEPART FOR KELLUX AT ONCE.
REST ASSURED, YOUR INTERESTS WILL BE PROTECTED.
YES.
YES, OF COURSE.
WHAT ELSE WOULD I EXPECT?

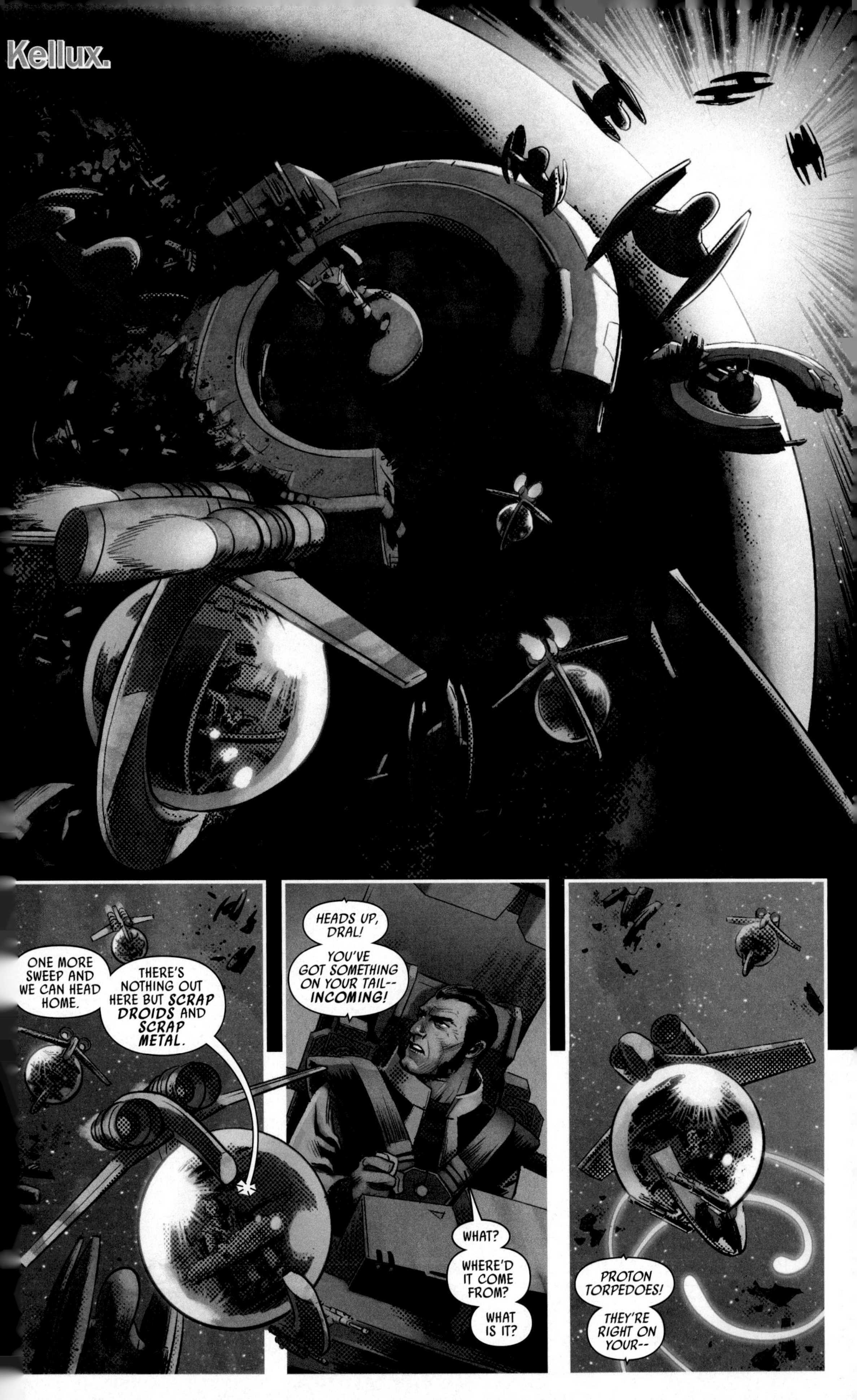
Kellux.
ONE MORE SWEEP AND WE CAN HEAD HOME.
THERE'S NOTHING OUT HERE BUT SCRAP DROIDS AND SCRAP METAL.
HEADS UP, DRAL!
YOU'VE GOT SOMETHING ON YOUR TAIL-- INCOMING!
WHAT?
WHERE'D IT COME FROM?
WHAT IS IT?
PROTON TORPEDOES!
THEY'RE RIGHT ON YOUR--

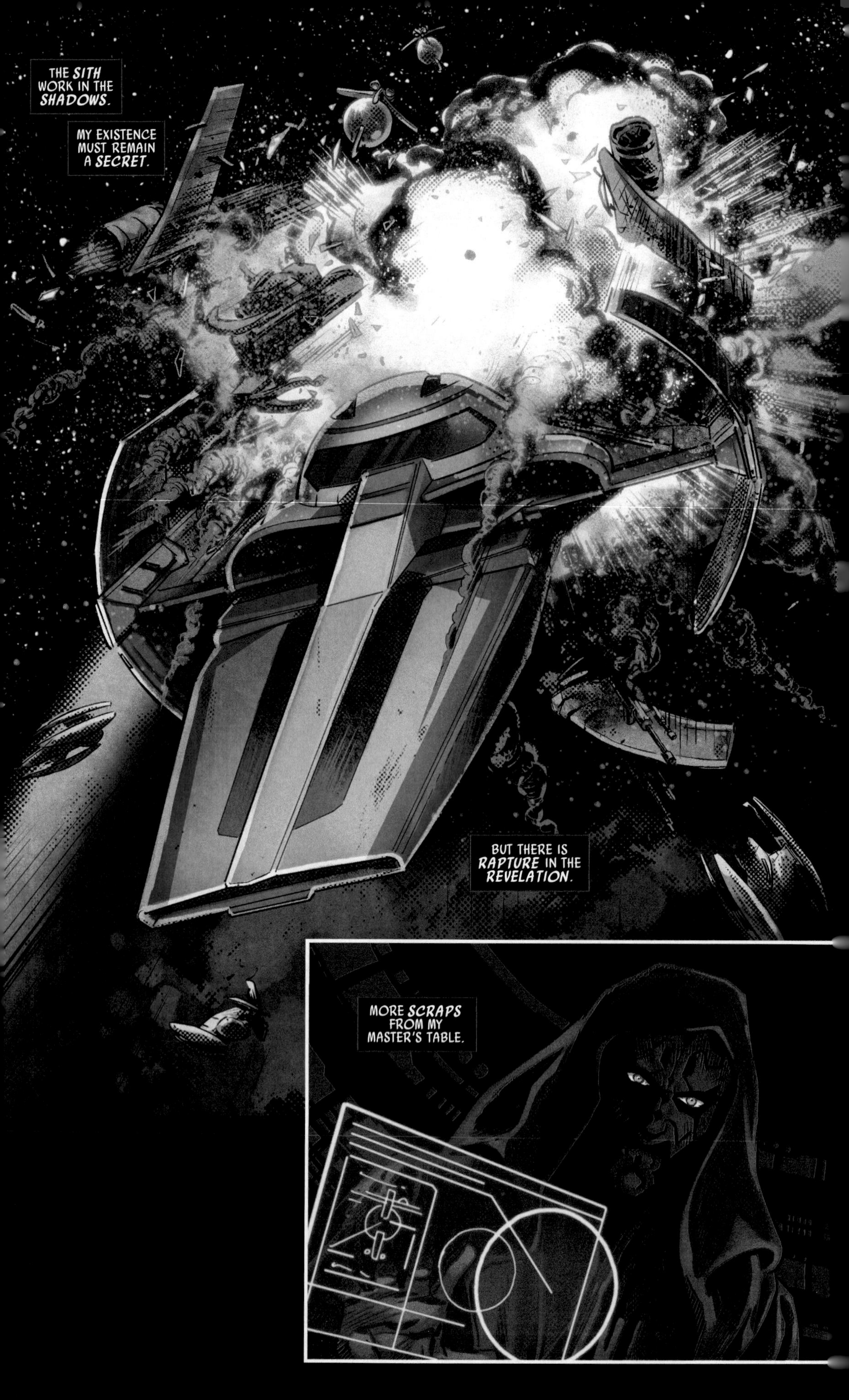
THE SITH WORK IN THE SHADOWS.
MY EXISTENCE MUST REMAIN A SECRET.
BUT THERE IS RAPTURE IN THE REVELATION.
MORE SCRAPS FROM MY MASTER'S TABLE.

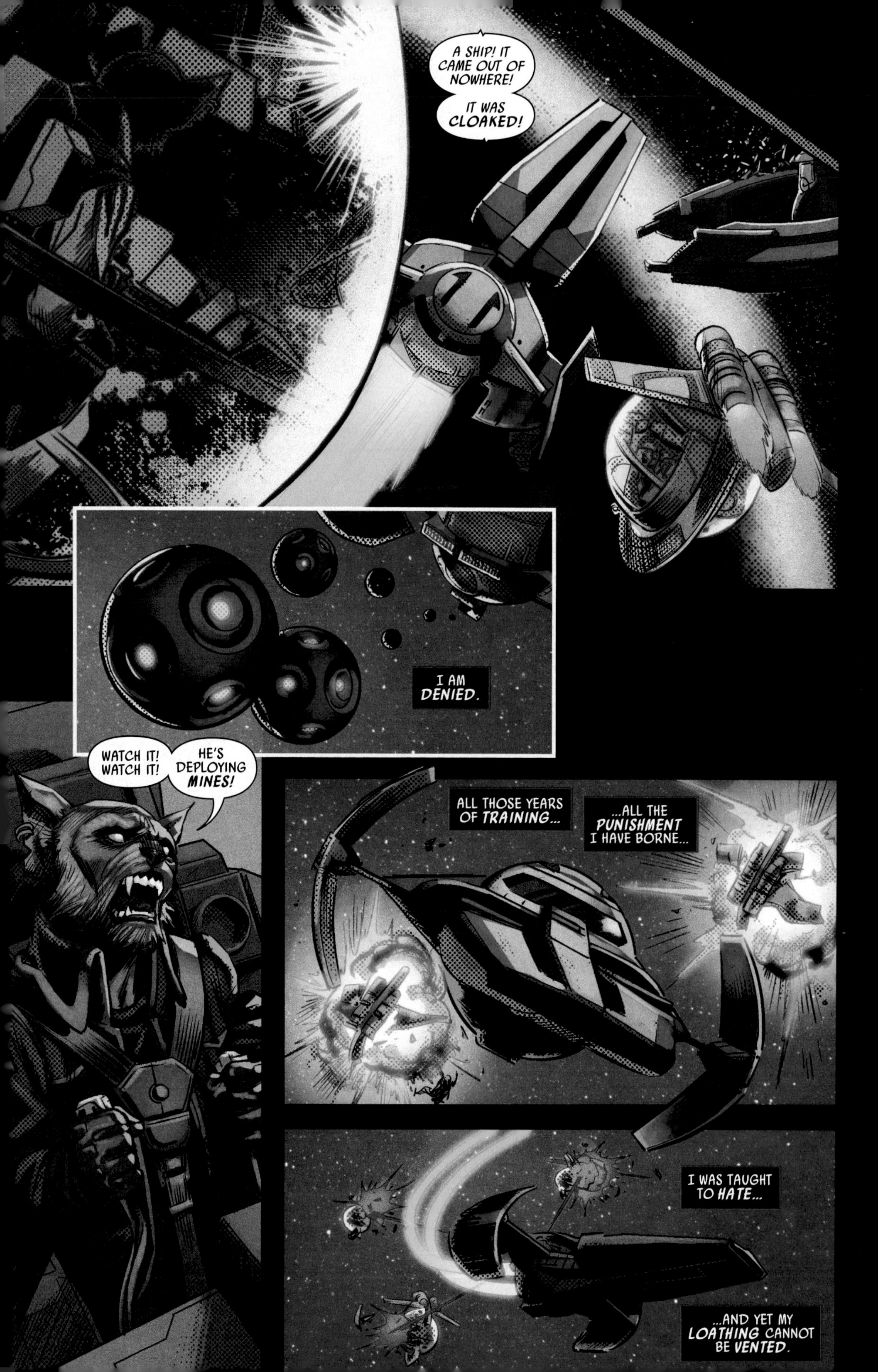
A SHIP! IT CAME OUT OF NOWHERE!
IT WAS CLOAKED!
I AM DENIED.
WATCH IT! WATCH IT!
HE'S DEPLOYING MINES!
ALL THOSE YEARS OF TRAINING...
...ALL THE PUNISHMENT I HAVE BORNE...
I WAS TAUGHT TO HATE...
...AND YET MY LOATHING CANNOT BE VENTED.

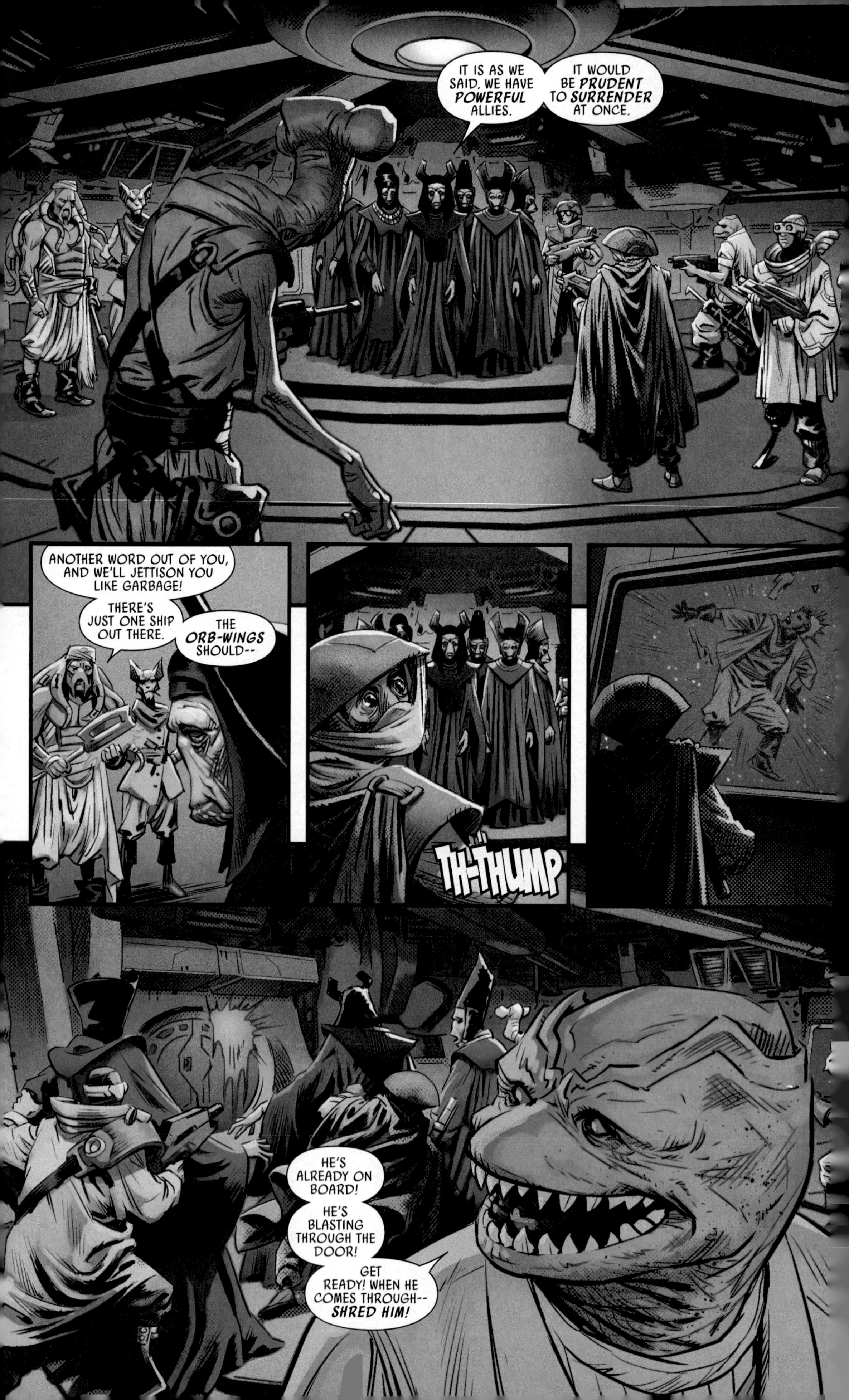
IT IS AS WE SAID. WE HAVE POWERFUL ALLIES.
IT WOULD BE PRUDENT TO SURRENDER AT ONCE.
ANOTHER WORD OUT OF YOU, AND WE'LL JETTISON YOU LIKE GARBAGE!
THERE'S JUST ONE SHIP OUT THERE.
THE ORB-WINGS SHOULD--
TH-THUMP
HE'S ALREADY ON BOARD!
HE'S BLASTING THROUGH THE DOOR!
GET READY! WHEN HE COMES THROUGH-- SHRED HIM!

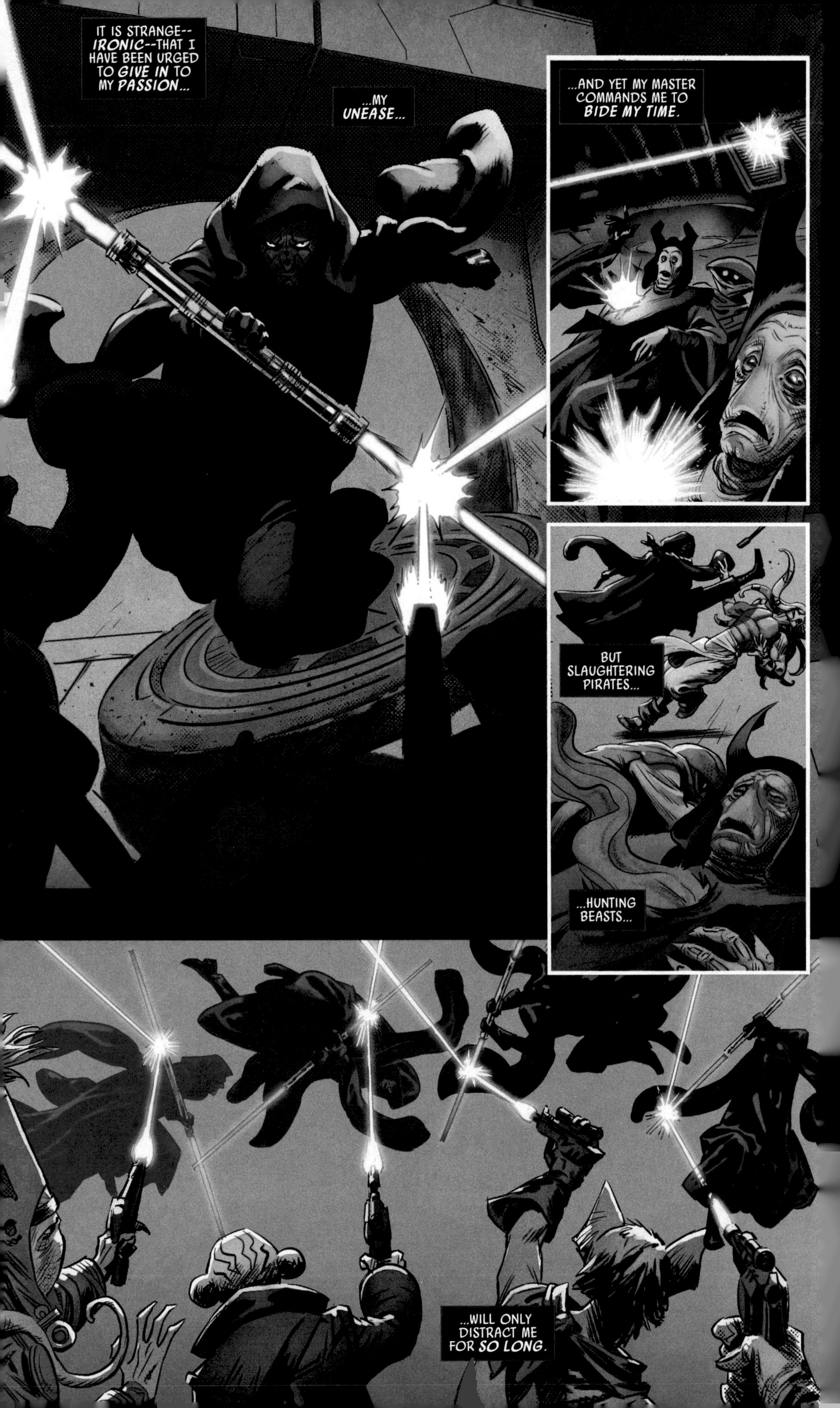
IT IS STRANGE-- IRONIC--THAT I HAVE BEEN URGED TO GIVE IN TO MY PASSION...
...MY UNEASE...
...AND YET MY MASTER COMMANDS ME TO BIDE MY TIME.
BUT SLAUGHTERING PIRATES...
...HUNTING BEASTS...
...WILL ONLY DISTRACT ME FOR SO LONG.

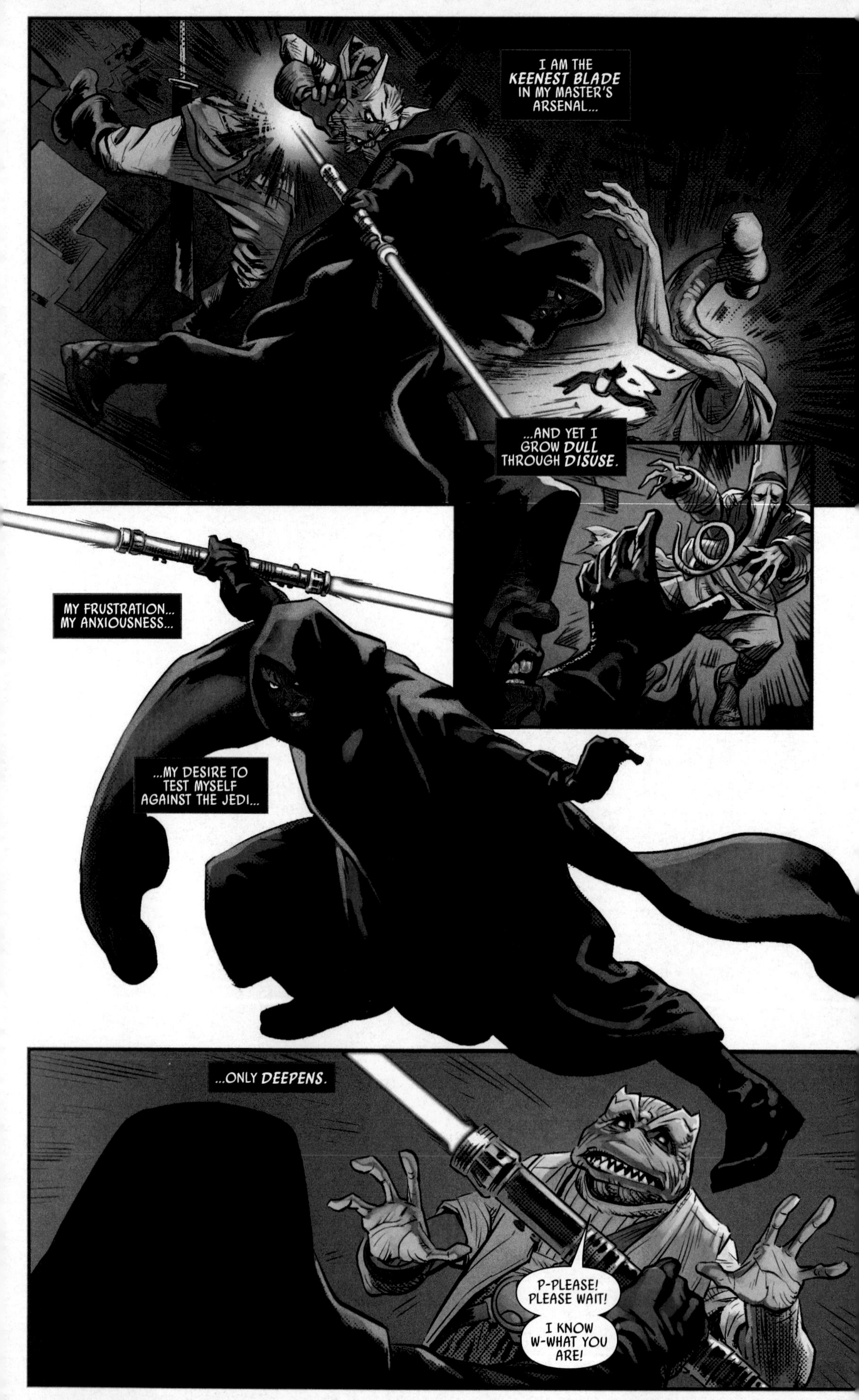
I AM THE KEENEST BLADE IN MY MASTER'S ARSENAL...
...AND YET I GROW DULL THROUGH DISUSE.
MY FRUSTRATION... MY ANXIOUSNESS...
...MY DESIRE TO TEST MYSELF AGAINST THE JEDI...
...ONLY DEEPENS.
P-PLEASE! PLEASE WAIT!
I KNOW W-WHAT YOU ARE!

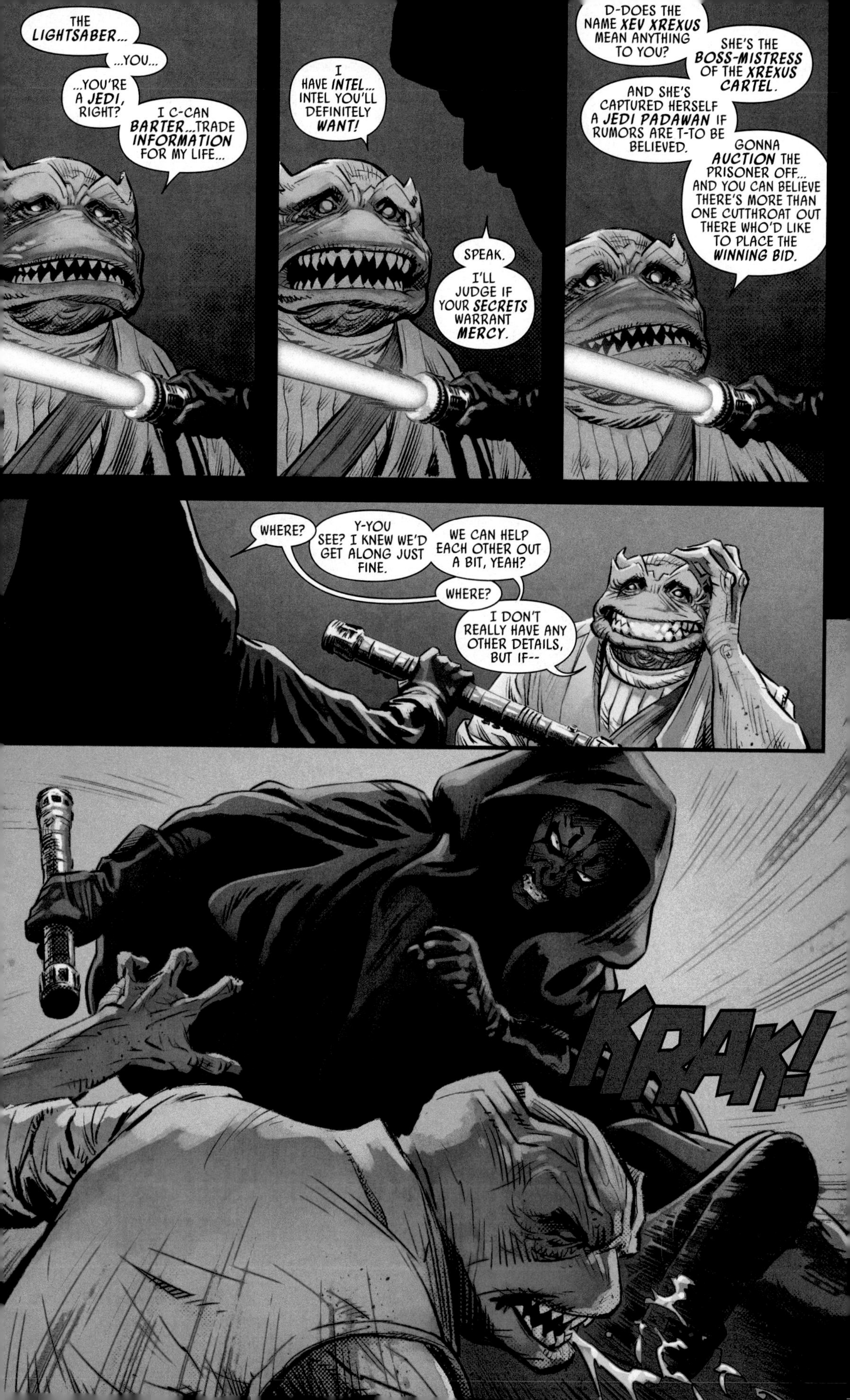
THE LIGHTSABER...
...YOU...
...YOU'RE A JEDI, RIGHT?
I C-CAN BARTER...TRADE INFORMATION FOR MY LIFE...
I HAVE INTEL... INTEL YOU'LL DEFINITELY WANT!
SPEAK. I'LL JUDGE IF YOUR SECRETS WARRANT MERCY.
D-DOES THE NAME XEV XREXUS MEAN ANYTHING TO YOU?
SHE'S THE BOSS-MISTRESS OF THE XREXUS CARTEL.
AND SHE'S CAPTURED HERSELF A JEDI PADAWAN IF RUMORS ARE T-TO BE BELIEVED.
GONNA AUCTION THE PRISONER OFF... AND YOU CAN BELIEVE THERE'S MORE THAN ONE CUTTHROAT OUT THERE WHO'D LIKE TO PLACE THE WINNING BID.
WHERE?
Y-YOU SEE? I KNEW WE'D GET ALONG JUST FINE.
WE CAN HELP EACH OTHER OUT A BIT, YEAH?
WHERE?
I DON'T REALLY HAVE ANY OTHER DETAILS, BUT IF--
KRAK!

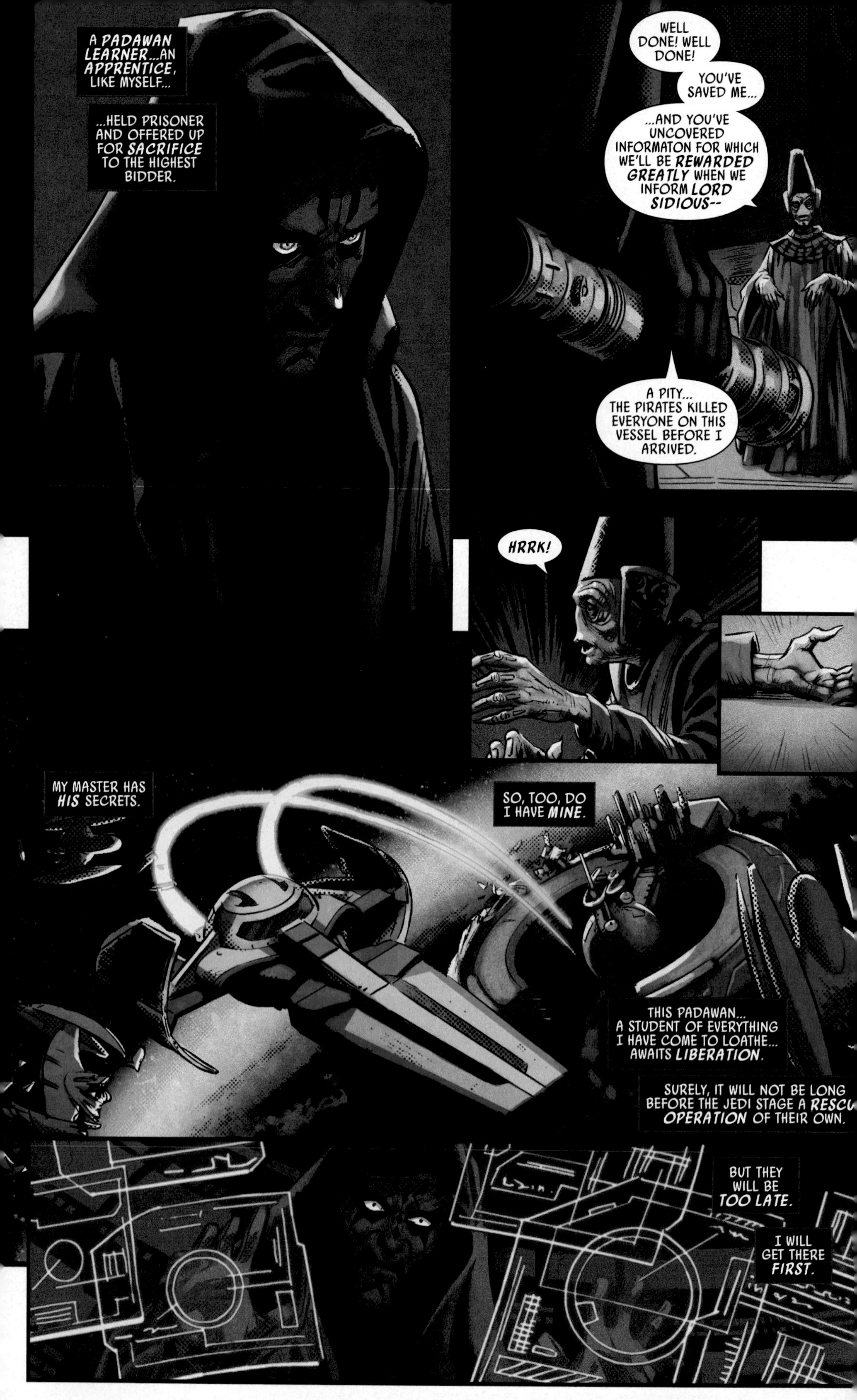
A PADAWAN LEARNER...AN APPRENTICE, LIKE MYSELF...
...HELD PRISONER AND OFFERED UP FOR SACRIFICE TO THE HIGHEST BIDDER.
WELL DONE! WELL DONE!
YOU'VE SAVED ME...
...AND YOU'VE UNCOVERED INFORMATON FOR WHICH WE'LL BE REWARDED GREATLY WHEN WE INFORM LORD SIDIOUS--
A PITY... THE PIRATES KILLED EVERYONE ON THIS VESSEL BEFORE I ARRIVED.
HRRK!
MY MASTER HAS HIS SECRETS.
SO, TOO, DO I HAVE MINE.
THIS PADAWAN... A STUDENT OF EVERYTHING I HAVE COME TO LOATHE... AWAITS LIBERATION.
SURELY, IT WILL NOT BE LONG BEFORE THE JEDI STAGE A RESCU OPERATION OF THEIR OWN.
BUT THEY WILL BE TOO LATE.
I WILL GET THERE FIRST.

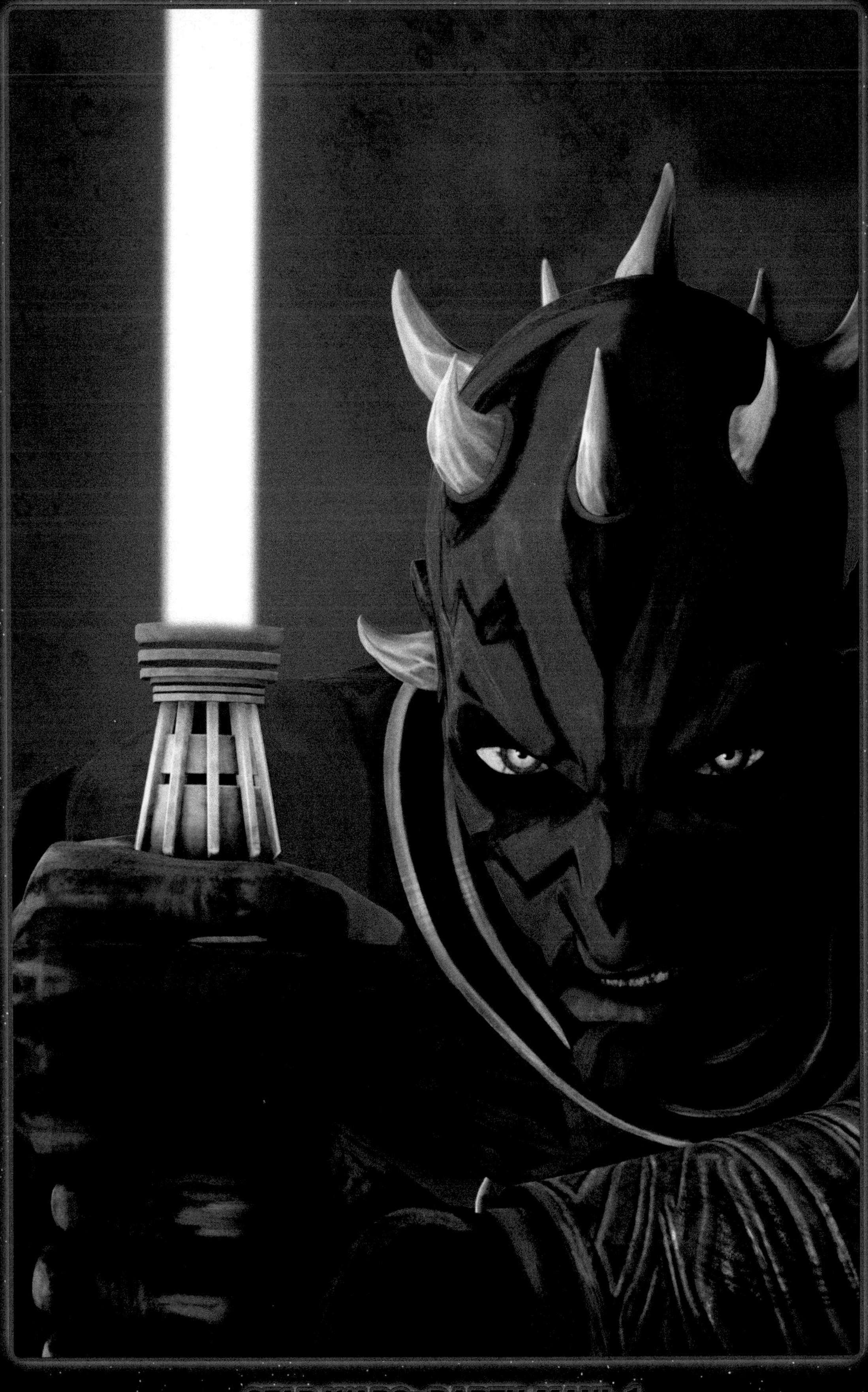

STAR WARS: DARTH MAUL 1
ANIMATION VARIANT

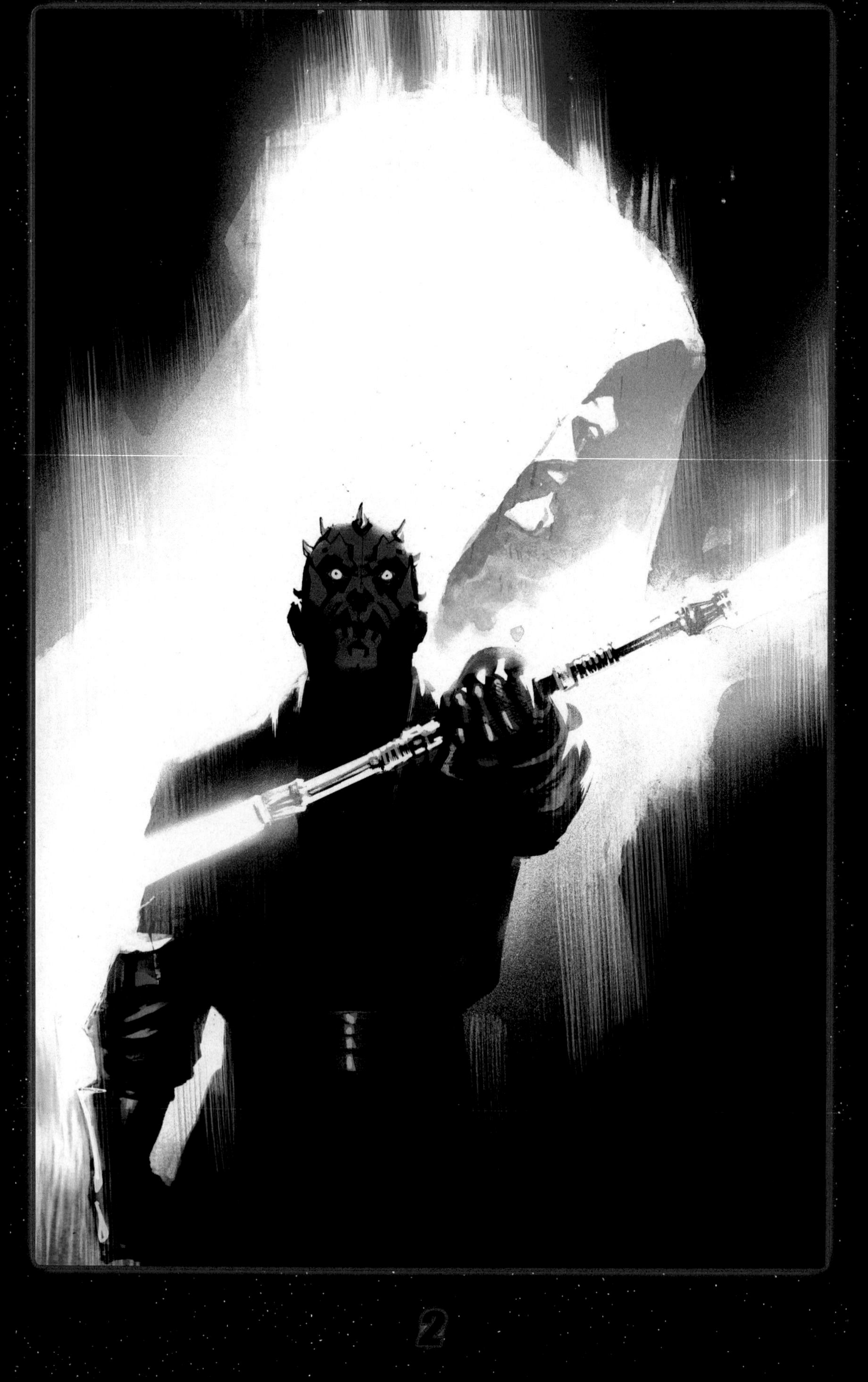

2

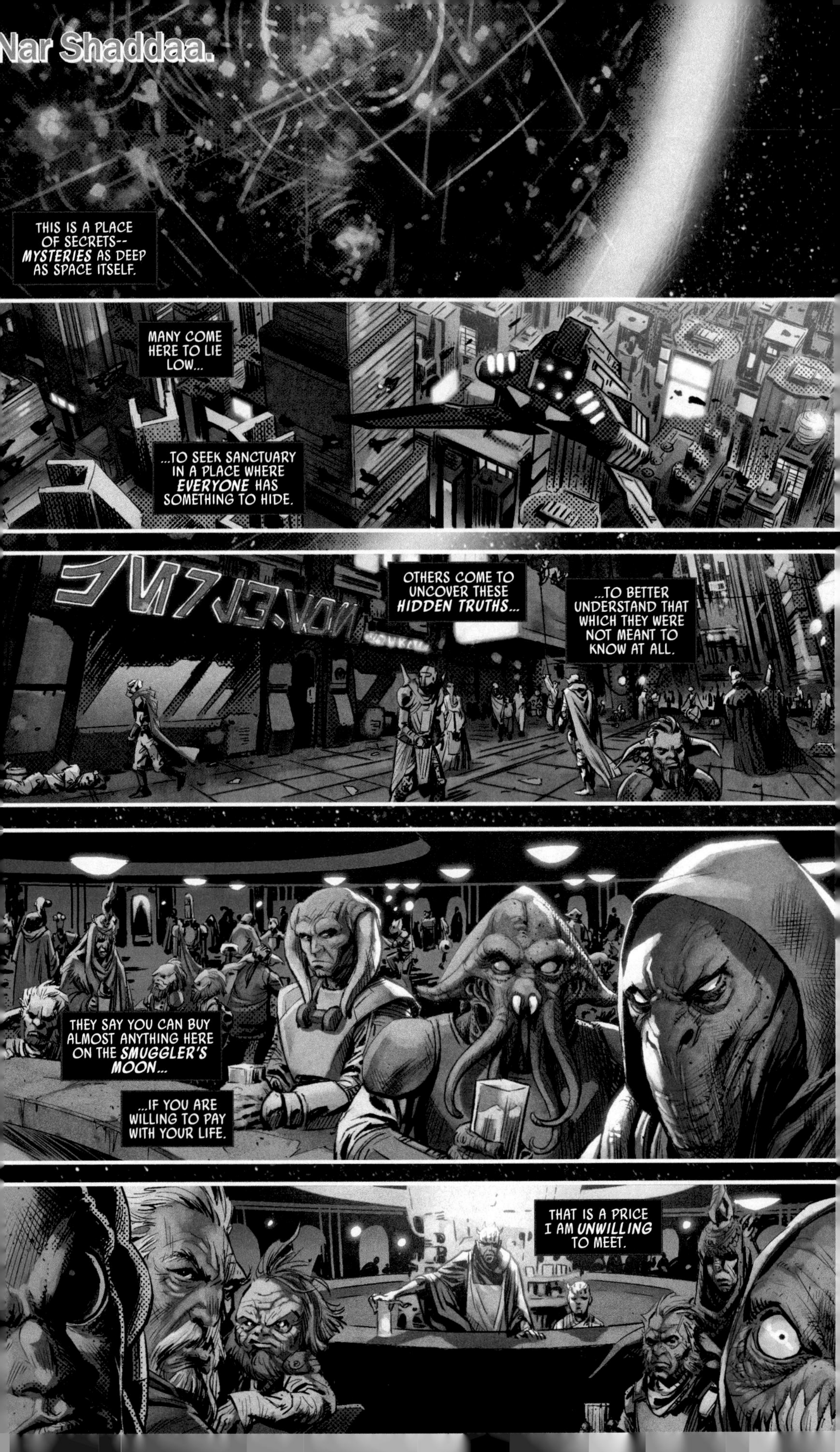
Nar Shaddaa.
THIS IS A PLACE OF SECRETS-- MYSTERIES AS DEEP AS SPACE ITSELF.
MANY COME HERE TO LIE LOW...
...TO SEEK SANCTUARY IN A PLACE WHERE EVERYONE HAS SOMETHING TO HIDE.
OTHERS COME TO UNCOVER THESE HIDDEN TRUTHS...
...TO BETTER UNDERSTAND THAT WHICH THEY WERE NOT MEANT TO KNOW AT ALL.
THEY SAY YOU CAN BUY ALMOST ANYTHING HERE ON THE SMUGGLER'S MOON...
...IF YOU ARE WILLING TO PAY WITH YOUR LIFE.
THAT IS A PRICE I AM UNWILLING TO MEET.

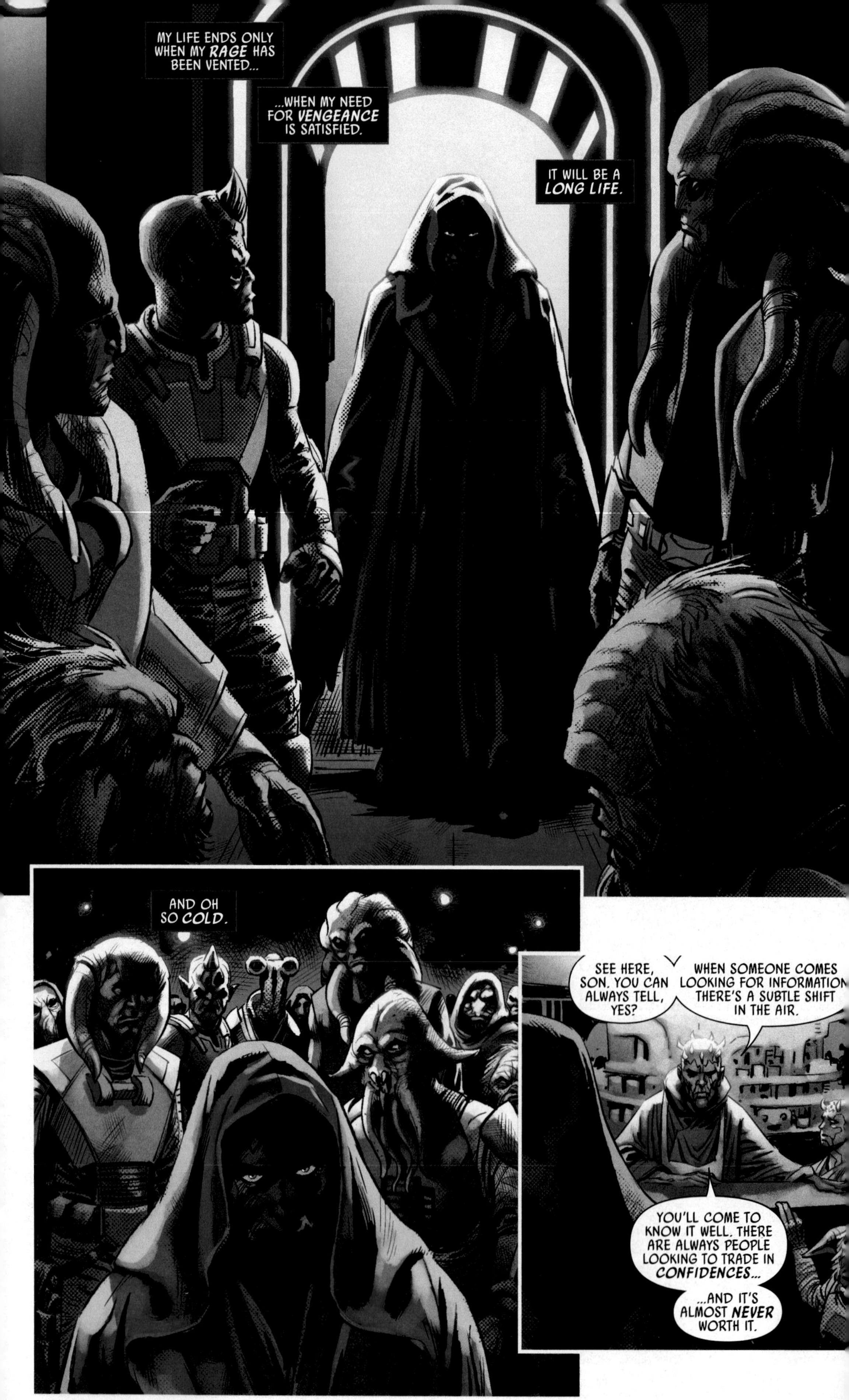
MY LIFE ENDS ONLY WHEN MY RAGE HAS BEEN VENTED...
...WHEN MY NEED FOR VENGEANCE IS SATISFIED.
IT WILL BE A LONG LIFE.
AND OH SO COLD.
SEE HERE, SON. YOU CAN ALWAYS TELL, YES?
WHEN SOMEONE COMES LOOKING FOR INFORMATION THERE'S A SUBTLE SHIFT IN THE AIR.
YOU'LL COME TO KNOW IT WELL. THERE ARE ALWAYS PEOPLE LOOKING TO TRADE IN CONFIDENCES...
...AND IT'S ALMOST NEVER WORTH IT.

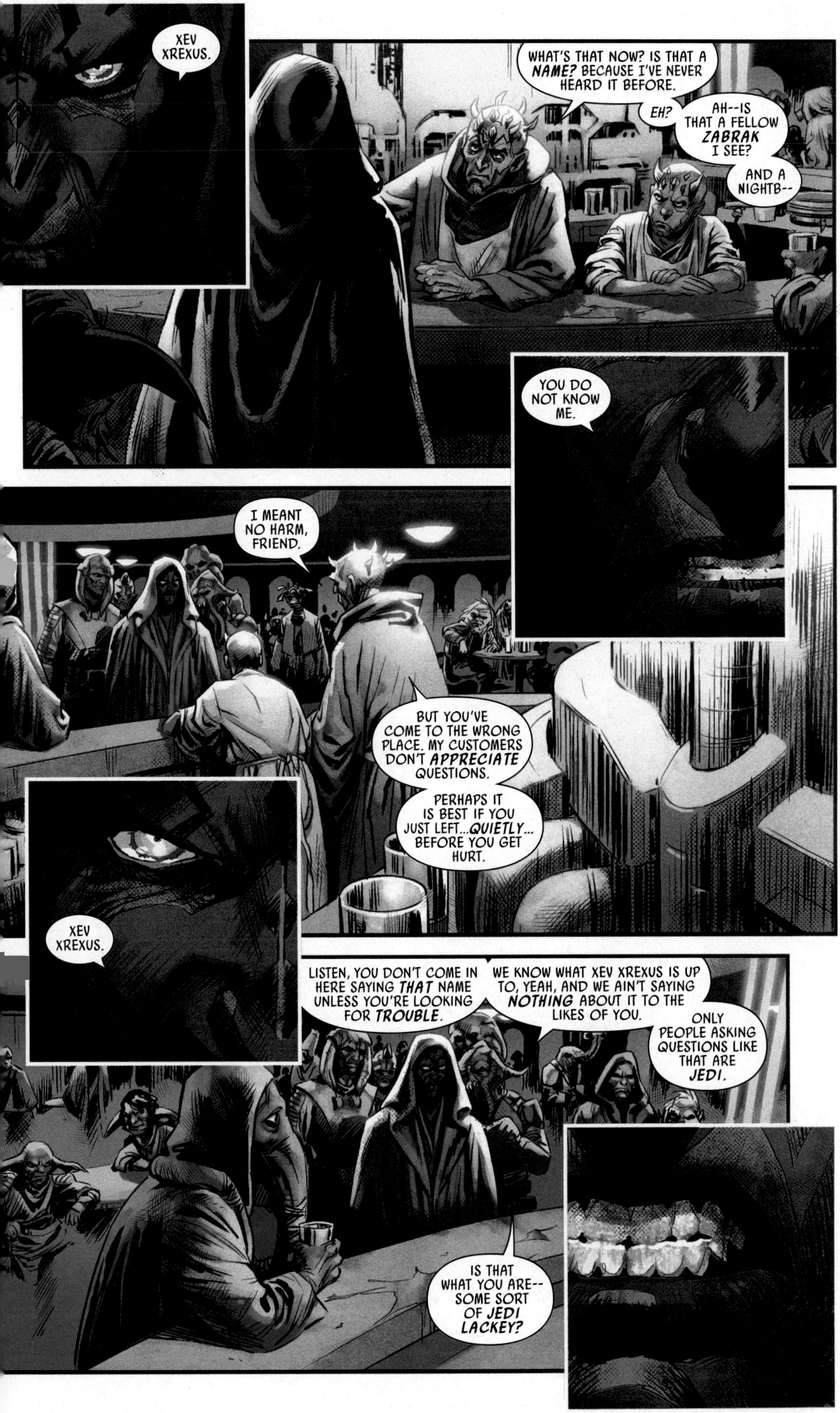
XEV XREXUS.
WHAT'S THAT NOW? IS THAT A NAME? BECAUSE I'VE NEVER HEARD IT BEFORE.
EH?
AH--IS THAT A FELLOW ZABRAK I SEE?
AND A NIGHTB--
YOU DO NOT KNOW ME.
I MEANT NO HARM, FRIEND.
BUT YOU'VE COME TO THE WRONG PLACE. MY CUSTOMERS DON'T APPRECIATE QUESTIONS.
PERHAPS IT IS BEST IF YOU JUST LEFT...QUIETLY... BEFORE YOU GET HURT.
XEV XREXUS.
LISTEN, YOU DON'T COME IN HERE SAYING THAT NAME UNLESS YOU'RE LOOKING FOR TROUBLE.
WE KNOW WHAT XEV XREXUS IS UP TO, YEAH, AND WE AIN'T SAYING NOTHING ABOUT IT TO THE LIKES OF YOU.
ONLY PEOPLE ASKING QUESTIONS LIKE THAT ARE JEDI.
IS THAT WHAT YOU ARE--SOME SORT OF JEDI LACKEY?

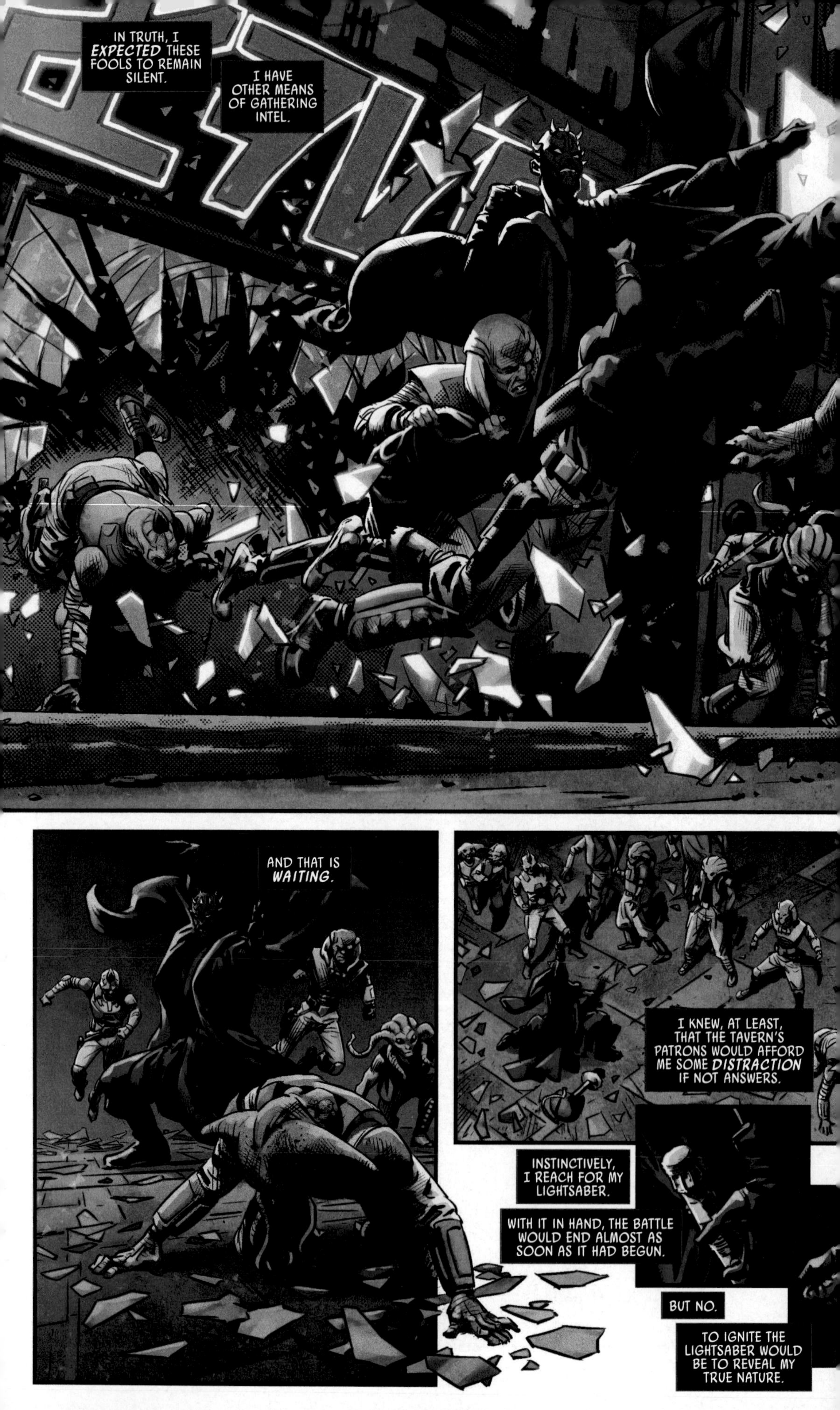
IN TRUTH, I EXPECTED THESE FOOLS TO REMAIN SILENT.
I HAVE OTHER MEANS OF GATHERING INTEL.
AND THAT IS WAITING.
I KNEW, AT LEAST, THAT THE TAVERN'S PATRONS WOULD AFFORD ME SOME DISTRACTION IF NOT ANSWERS.
INSTINCTIVELY, I REACH FOR MY LIGHTSABER.
WITH IT IN HAND, THE BATTLE WOULD END ALMOST AS SOON AS IT HAD BEGUN.
BUT NO.
TO IGNITE THE LIGHTSABER WOULD BE TO REVEAL MY TRUE NATURE.

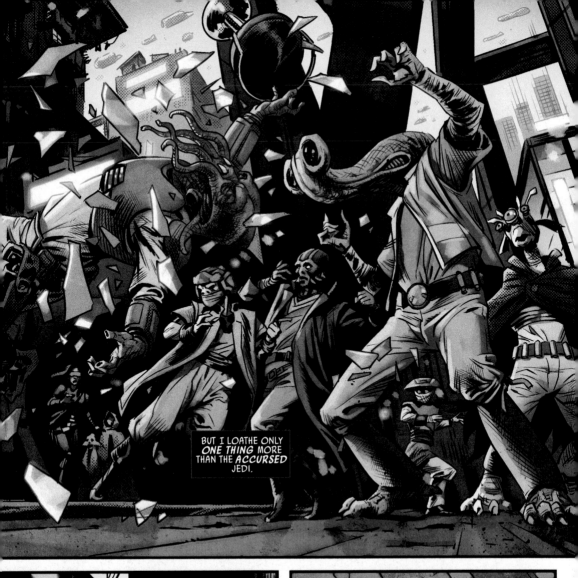

BUT I LOATHE ONLY *ONE THING* MORE THAN THE *ACCURSED* JEDI.

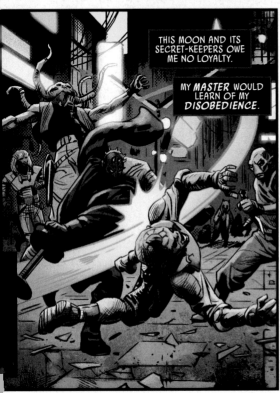

THIS MOON AND ITS SECRET-KEEPERS OWE ME NO LOYALTY.

MY *MASTER* WOULD LEARN OF MY *DISOBEDIENCE*.

THE *PUNISHMENT* WOULD BE *SEVERE*.

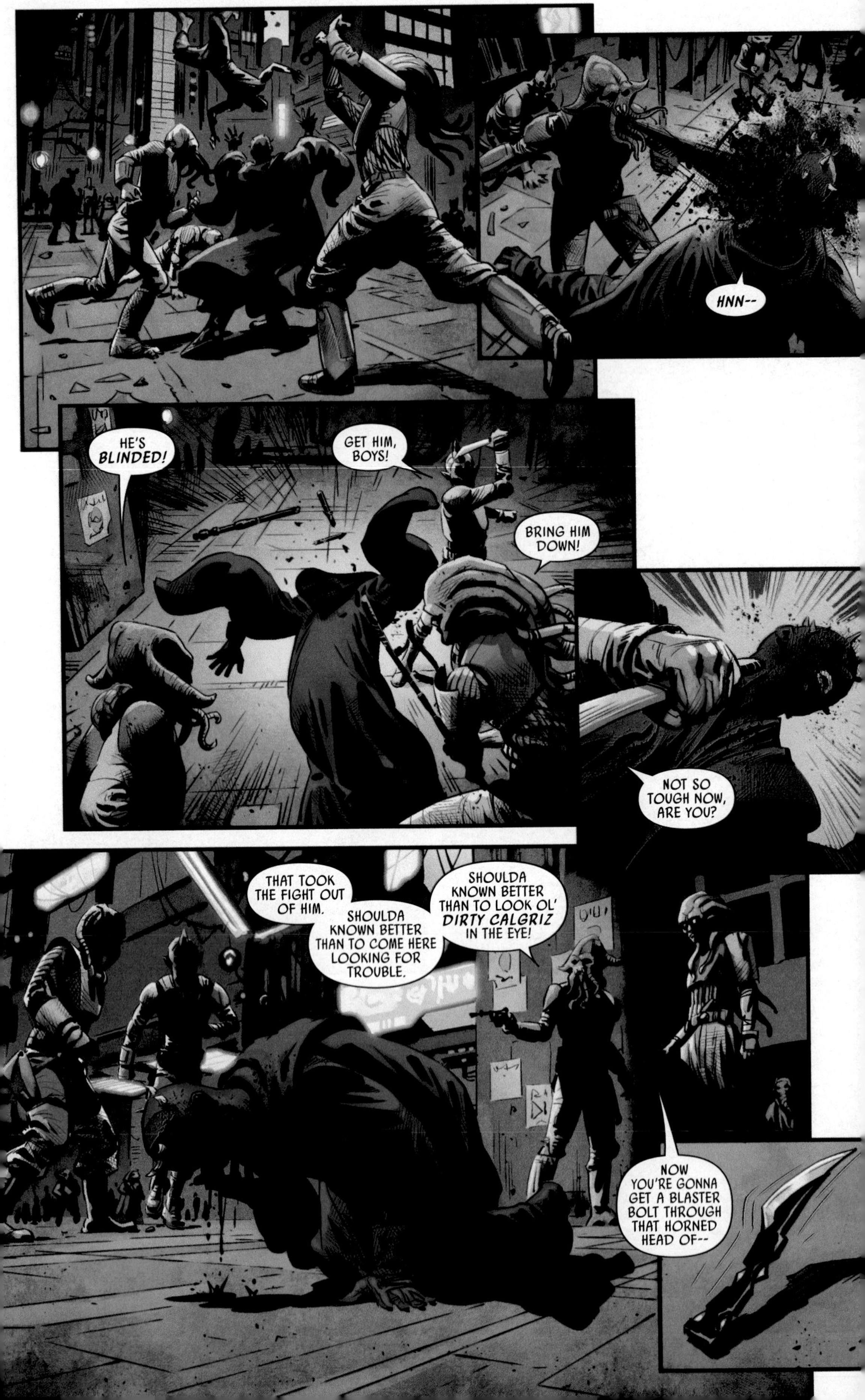
HNN--
HE'S BLINDED!
GET HIM, BOYS!
BRING HIM DOWN!
NOT SO TOUGH NOW, ARE YOU?
THAT TOOK THE FIGHT OUT OF HIM.
SHOULDA KNOWN BETTER THAN TO COME HERE LOOKING FOR TROUBLE.
SHOULDA KNOWN BETTER THAN TO LOOK OL' DIRTY CALGRIZ IN THE EYE!
NOW YOU'RE GONNA GET A BLASTER BOLT THROUGH THAT HORNED HEAD OF--

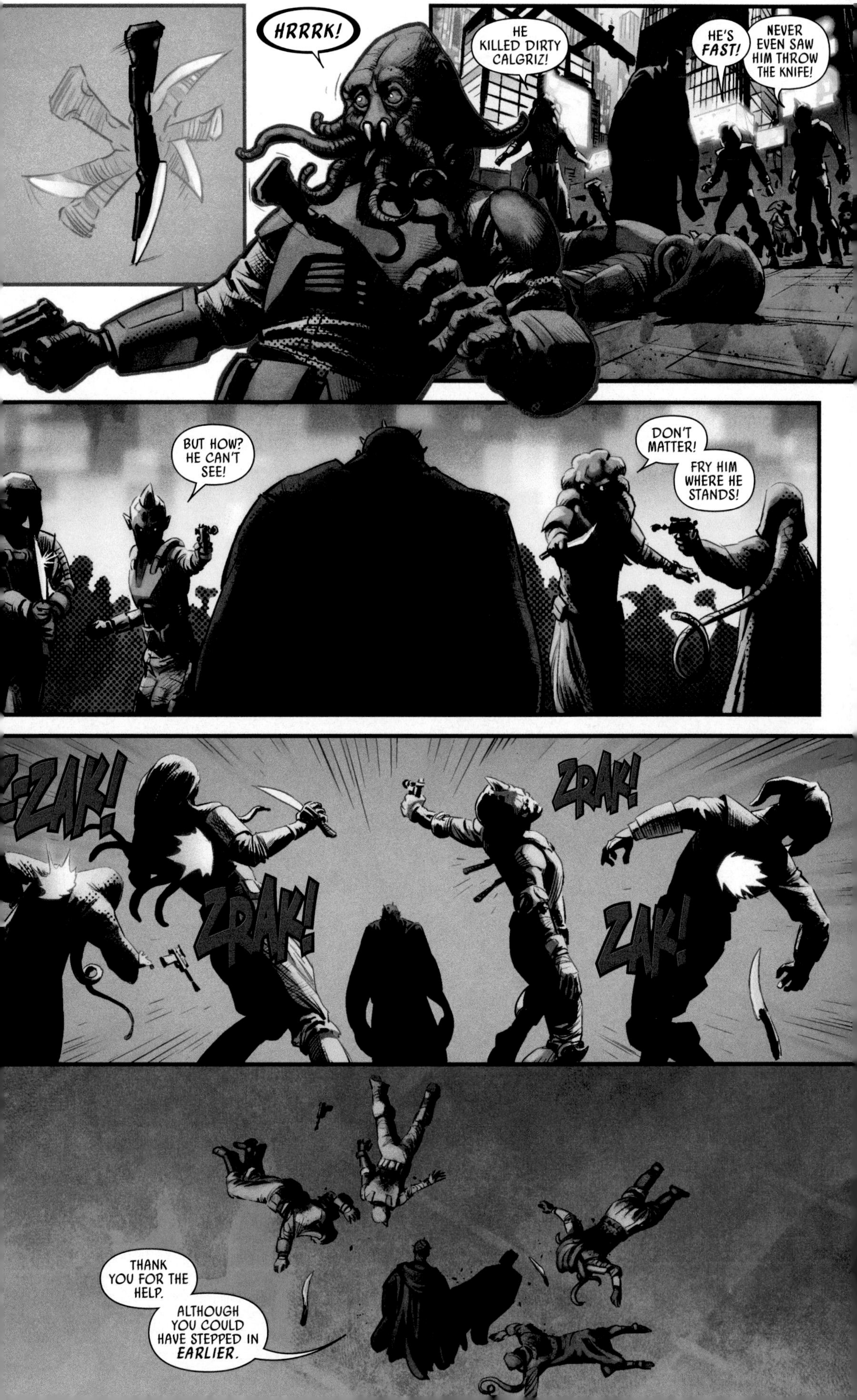
HRRRK!
HE KILLED DIRTY CALGRIZ!
HE'S FAST!
NEVER EVEN SAW HIM THROW THE KNIFE!
BUT HOW? HE CAN'T SEE!
DON'T MATTER!
FRY HIM WHERE HE STANDS!
ZRAK!
ZRAK!
ZAK!
THANK YOU FOR THE HELP.
ALTHOUGH YOU COULD HAVE STEPPED IN EARLIER.

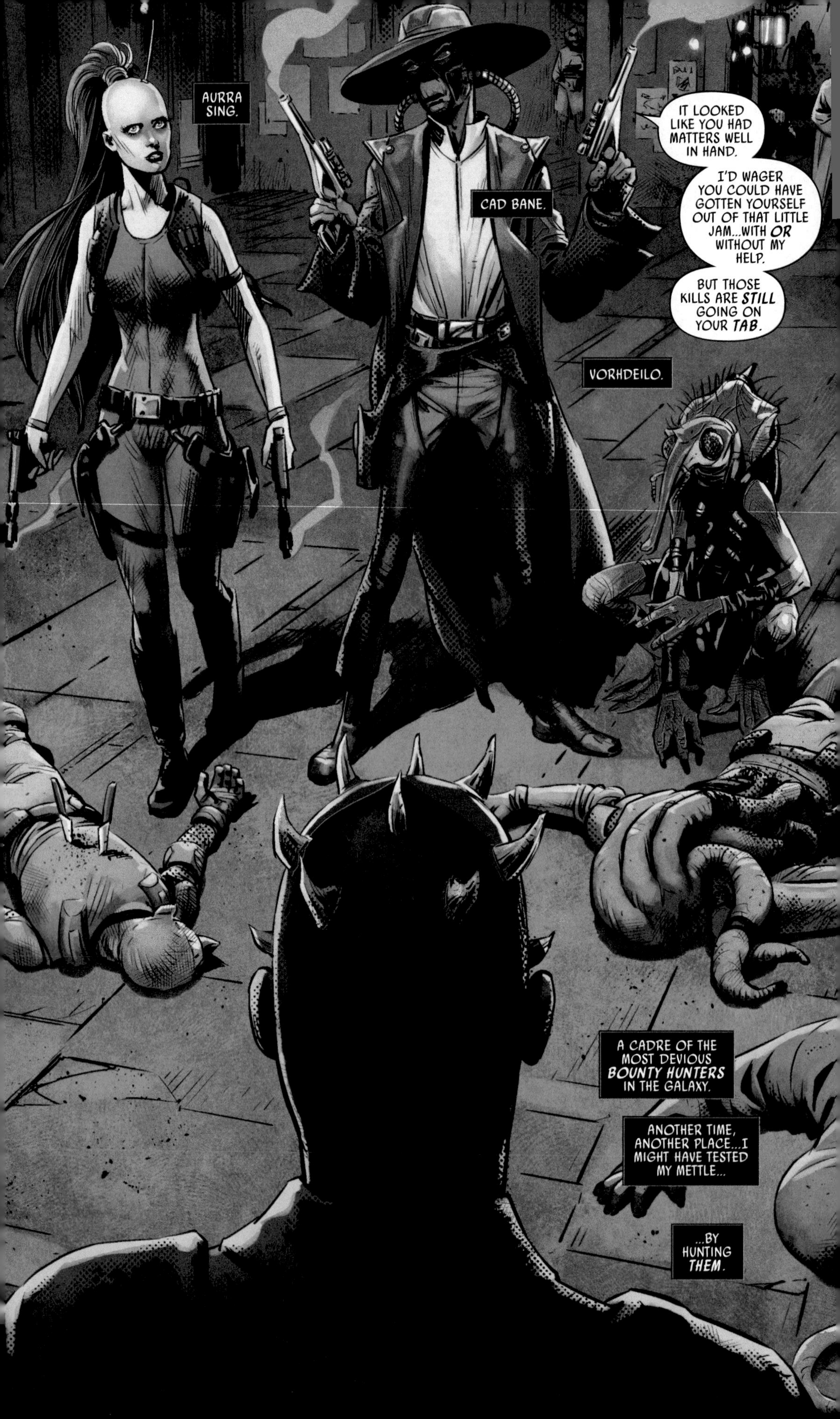
AURRA SING.
CAD BANE.
IT LOOKED LIKE YOU HAD MATTERS WELL IN HAND.
I'D WAGER YOU COULD HAVE GOTTEN YOURSELF OUT OF THAT LITTLE JAM...WITH OR WITHOUT MY HELP.
BUT THOSE KILLS ARE STILL GOING ON YOUR TAB.
VORHDEILO.
A CADRE OF THE MOST DEVIOUS BOUNTY HUNTERS IN THE GALAXY.
ANOTHER TIME, ANOTHER PLACE...I MIGHT HAVE TESTED MY METTLE...
...BY HUNTING THEM.

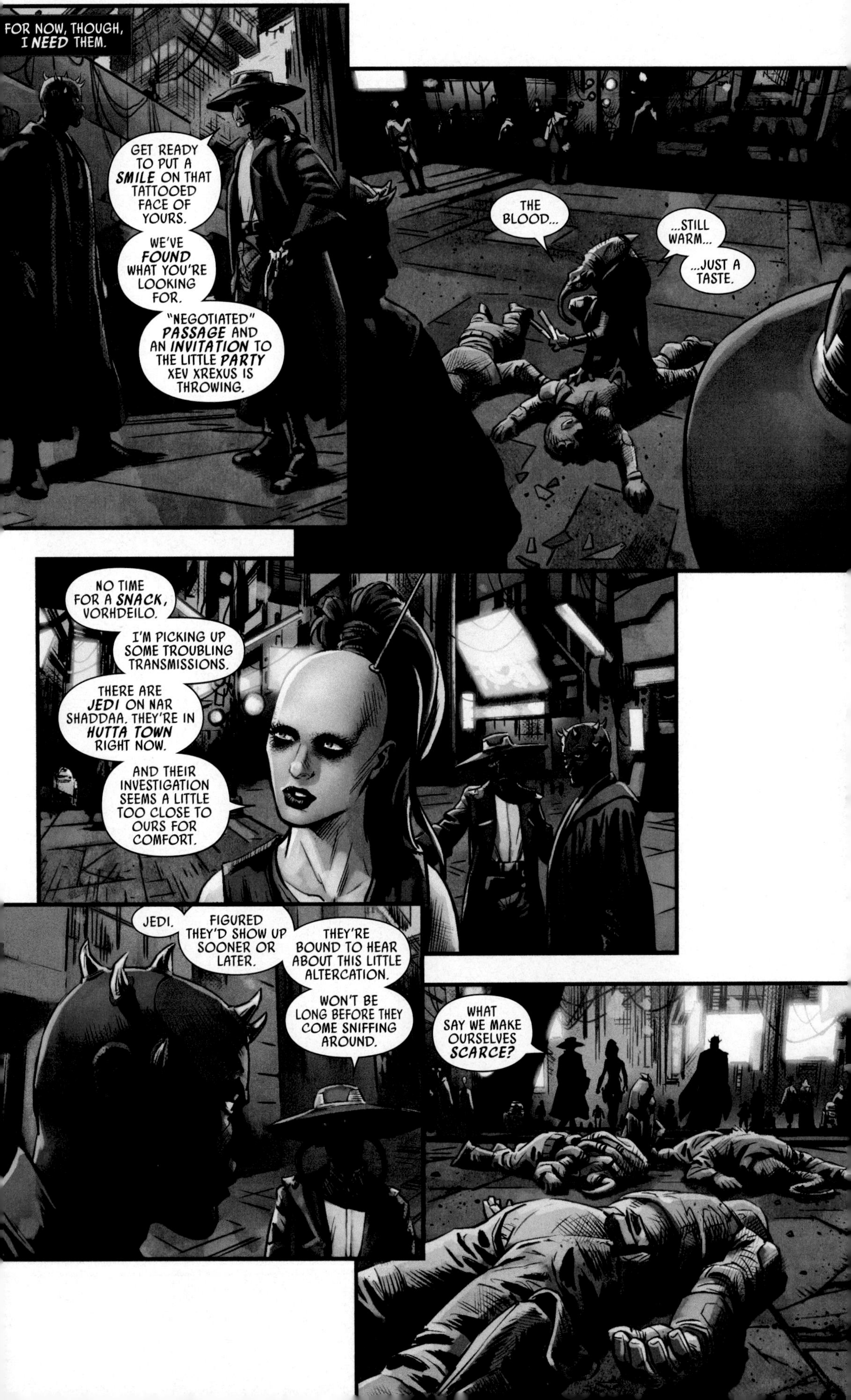
FOR NOW, THOUGH, I NEED THEM.
GET READY TO PUT A SMILE ON THAT TATTOOED FACE OF YOURS.
WE'VE FOUND WHAT YOU'RE LOOKING FOR.
"NEGOTIATED" PASSAGE AND AN INVITATION TO THE LITTLE PARTY XEV XREXUS IS THROWING.
THE BLOOD...
...STILL WARM...
...JUST A TASTE.
NO TIME FOR A SNACK, VORHDEILO.
I'M PICKING UP SOME TROUBLING TRANSMISSIONS.
THERE ARE JEDI ON NAR SHADDAA. THEY'RE IN HUTTA TOWN RIGHT NOW.
AND THEIR INVESTIGATION SEEMS A LITTLE TOO CLOSE TO OURS FOR COMFORT.
JEDI.
FIGURED THEY'D SHOW UP SOONER OR LATER.
THEY'RE BOUND TO HEAR ABOUT THIS LITTLE ALTERCATION.
WON'T BE LONG BEFORE THEY COME SNIFFING AROUND.
WHAT SAY WE MAKE OURSELVES SCARCE?

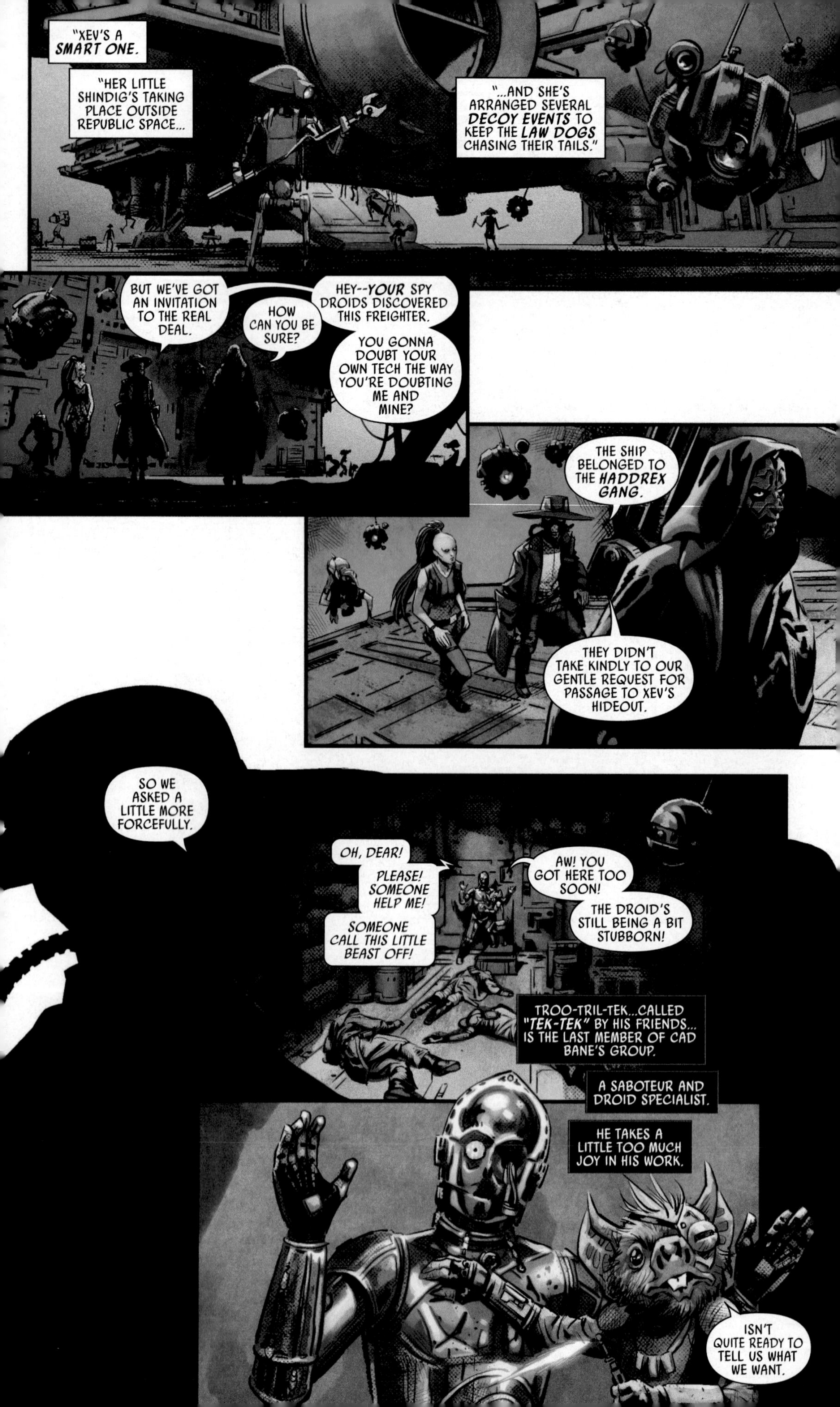
"XEV'S A SMART ONE.
"HER LITTLE SHINDIG'S TAKING PLACE OUTSIDE REPUBLIC SPACE...
"...AND SHE'S ARRANGED SEVERAL DECOY EVENTS TO KEEP THE LAW DOGS CHASING THEIR TAILS."
BUT WE'VE GOT AN INVITATION TO THE REAL DEAL.
HOW CAN YOU BE SURE?
HEY--YOUR SPY DROIDS DISCOVERED THIS FREIGHTER.
YOU GONNA DOUBT YOUR OWN TECH THE WAY YOU'RE DOUBTING ME AND MINE?
THE SHIP BELONGED TO THE HADDREX GANG.
THEY DIDN'T TAKE KINDLY TO OUR GENTLE REQUEST FOR PASSAGE TO XEV'S HIDEOUT.
SO WE ASKED A LITTLE MORE FORCEFULLY.
OH, DEAR!
PLEASE! SOMEONE HELP ME!
SOMEONE CALL THIS LITTLE BEAST OFF!
AW! YOU GOT HERE TOO SOON!
THE DROID'S STILL BEING A BIT STUBBORN!
TROO-TRIL-TEK...CALLED "TEK-TEK" BY HIS FRIENDS... IS THE LAST MEMBER OF CAD BANE'S GROUP.
A SABOTEUR AND DROID SPECIALIST.
HE TAKES A LITTLE TOO MUCH JOY IN HIS WORK.
ISN'T QUITE READY TO TELL US WHAT WE WANT.

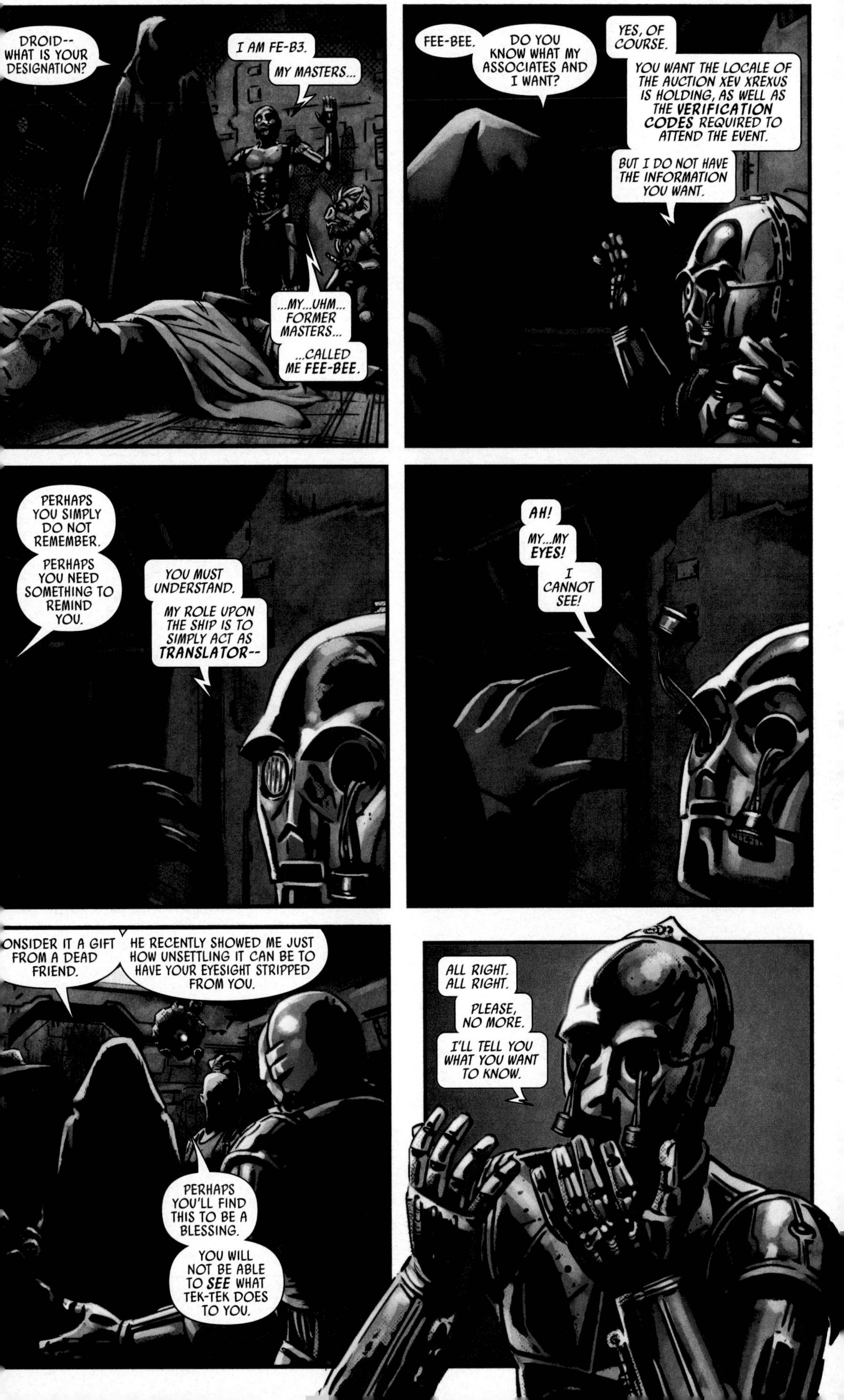
DROID-- WHAT IS YOUR DESIGNATION?
I AM FE-B3.
MY MASTERS...
...MY...UHM... FORMER MASTERS...
...CALLED ME FEE-BEE.
FEE-BEE.
DO YOU KNOW WHAT MY ASSOCIATES AND I WANT?
YES, OF COURSE.
YOU WANT THE LOCALE OF THE AUCTION XEV XREXUS IS HOLDING, AS WELL AS THE VERIFICATION CODES REQUIRED TO ATTEND THE EVENT.
BUT I DO NOT HAVE THE INFORMATION YOU WANT.
PERHAPS YOU SIMPLY DO NOT REMEMBER.
PERHAPS YOU NEED SOMETHING TO REMIND YOU.
YOU MUST UNDERSTAND.
MY ROLE UPON THE SHIP IS TO SIMPLY ACT AS TRANSLATOR--
AH!
MY...MY EYES!
I CANNOT SEE!
ONSIDER IT A GIFT FROM A DEAD FRIEND.
HE RECENTLY SHOWED ME JUST HOW UNSETTLING IT CAN BE TO HAVE YOUR EYESIGHT STRIPPED FROM YOU.
PERHAPS YOU'LL FIND THIS TO BE A BLESSING.
YOU WILL NOT BE ABLE TO SEE WHAT TEK-TEK DOES TO YOU.
ALL RIGHT. ALL RIGHT.
PLEASE, NO MORE.
I'LL TELL YOU WHAT YOU WANT TO KNOW.

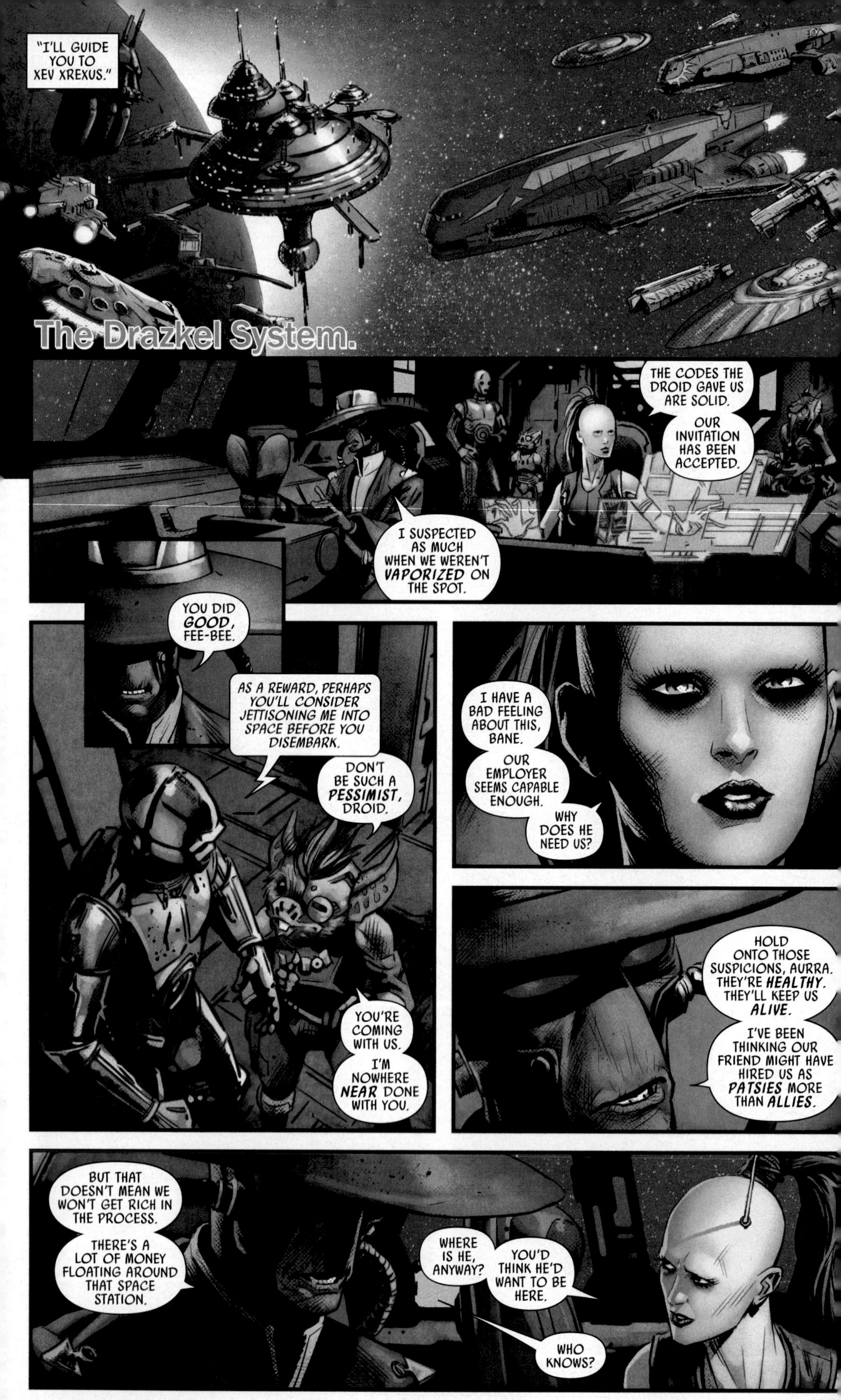
"I'LL GUIDE YOU TO XEV XREXUS."
The Drazkel System.
THE CODES THE DROID GAVE US ARE SOLID.
OUR INVITATION HAS BEEN ACCEPTED.
I SUSPECTED AS MUCH WHEN WE WEREN'T VAPORIZED ON THE SPOT.
YOU DID GOOD, FEE-BEE.
AS A REWARD, PERHAPS YOU'LL CONSIDER JETTISONING ME INTO SPACE BEFORE YOU DISEMBARK.
DON'T BE SUCH A PESSIMIST, DROID.
YOU'RE COMING WITH US.
I'M NOWHERE NEAR DONE WITH YOU.
I HAVE A BAD FEELING ABOUT THIS, BANE.
OUR EMPLOYER SEEMS CAPABLE ENOUGH.
WHY DOES HE NEED US?
HOLD ONTO THOSE SUSPICIONS, AURRA. THEY'RE HEALTHY. THEY'LL KEEP US ALIVE.
I'VE BEEN THINKING OUR FRIEND MIGHT HAVE HIRED US AS PATSIES MORE THAN ALLIES.
BUT THAT DOESN'T MEAN WE WON'T GET RICH IN THE PROCESS.
THERE'S A LOT OF MONEY FLOATING AROUND THAT SPACE STATION.
WHERE IS HE, ANYWAY?
YOU'D THINK HE'D WANT TO BE HERE.
WHO KNOWS?

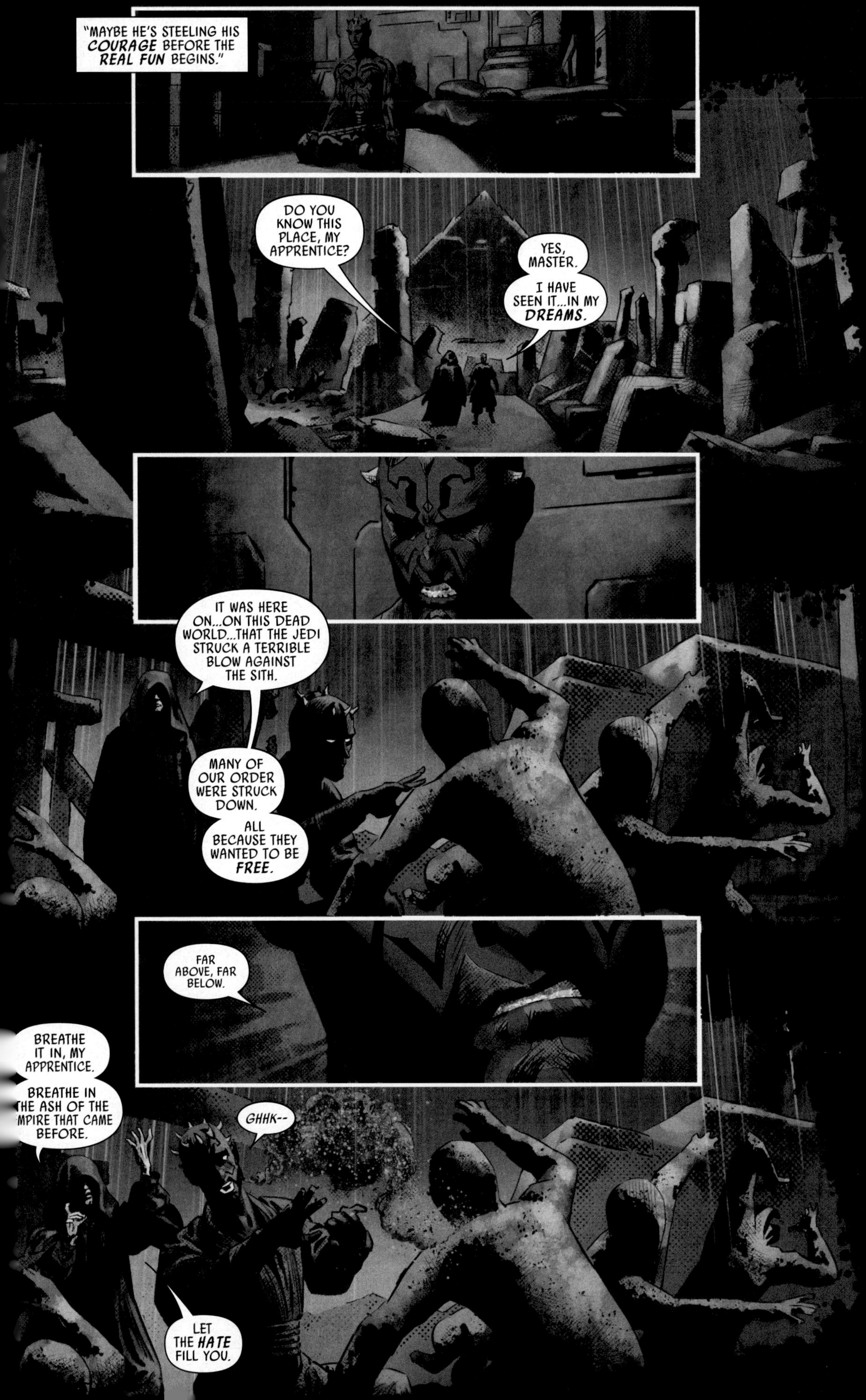
"MAYBE HE'S STEELING HIS COURAGE BEFORE THE REAL FUN BEGINS."
DO YOU KNOW THIS PLACE, MY APPRENTICE?
YES, MASTER.
I HAVE SEEN IT...IN MY DREAMS.
IT WAS HERE ON...ON THIS DEAD WORLD...THAT THE JEDI STRUCK A TERRIBLE BLOW AGAINST THE SITH.
MANY OF OUR ORDER WERE STRUCK DOWN.
ALL BECAUSE THEY WANTED TO BE FREE.
FAR ABOVE, FAR BELOW.
BREATHE IT IN, MY APPRENTICE.
BREATHE IN THE ASH OF THE EMPIRE THAT CAME BEFORE.
GHHK--
LET THE HATE FILL YOU.

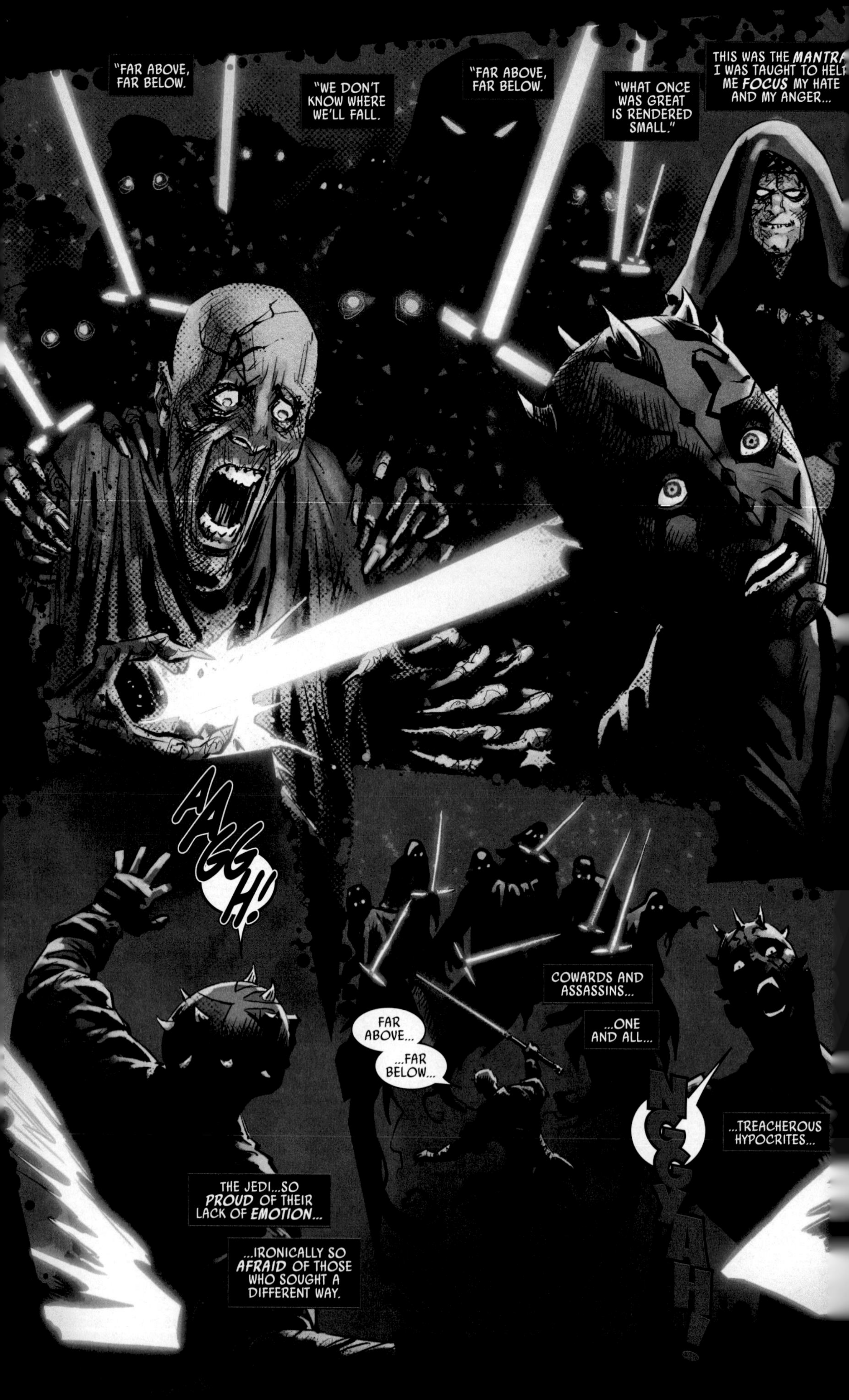
"FAR ABOVE, FAR BELOW.
"WE DON'T KNOW WHERE WE'LL FALL.
"FAR ABOVE, FAR BELOW.
"WHAT ONCE WAS GREAT IS RENDERED SMALL."
THIS WAS THE MANTRA I WAS TAUGHT TO HELP ME FOCUS MY HATE AND MY ANGER...
AAGGH!
THE JEDI...SO PROUD OF THEIR LACK OF EMOTION...
...IRONICALLY SO AFRAID OF THOSE WHO SOUGHT A DIFFERENT WAY.
FAR ABOVE...
...FAR BELOW...
COWARDS AND ASSASSINS...
...ONE AND ALL...
NGGYAH!
...TREACHEROUS HYPOCRITES...

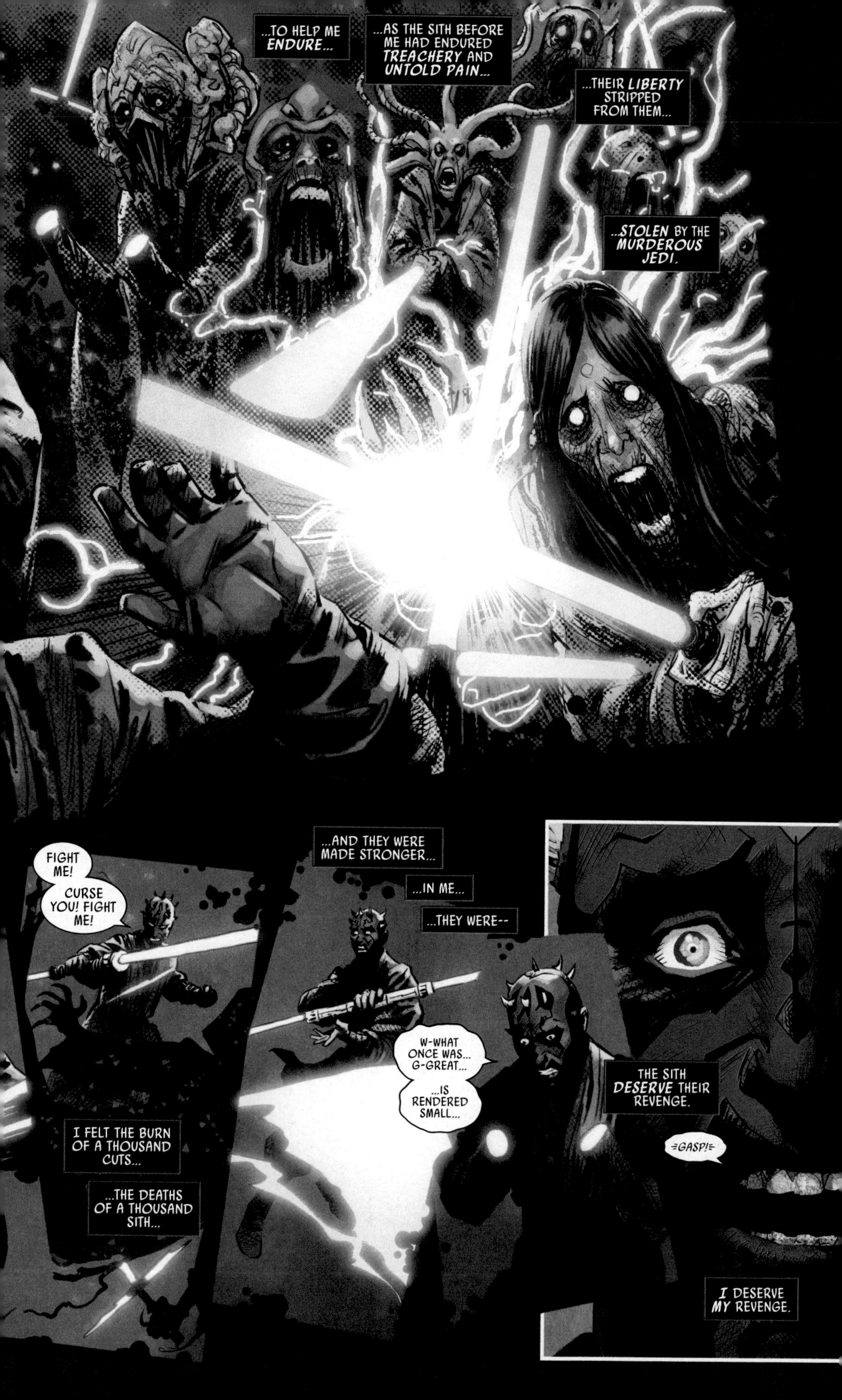
...TO HELP ME ENDURE...
...AS THE SITH BEFORE ME HAD ENDURED TREACHERY AND UNTOLD PAIN...
...THEIR LIBERTY STRIPPED FROM THEM...
...STOLEN BY THE MURDEROUS JEDI.
FIGHT ME!
CURSE YOU! FIGHT ME!
I FELT THE BURN OF A THOUSAND CUTS...
...THE DEATHS OF A THOUSAND SITH...
...AND THEY WERE MADE STRONGER...
...IN ME...
...THEY WERE--
W-WHAT ONCE WAS... G-GREAT...
...IS RENDERED SMALL...
THE SITH DESERVE THEIR REVENGE.
=GASP!=
I DESERVE MY REVENGE.

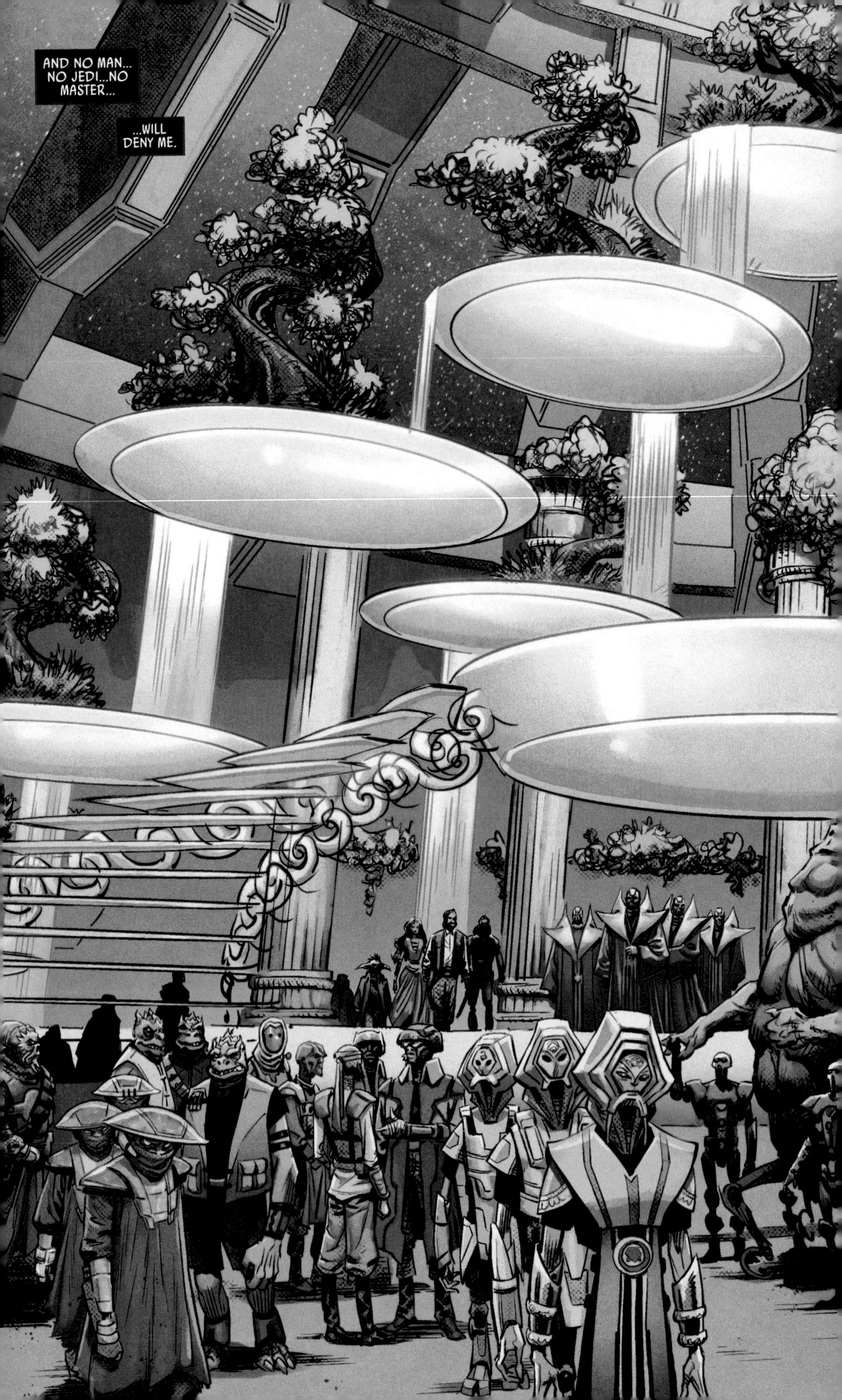
AND NO MAN...
NO JEDI...NO
MASTER...
...WILL
DENY ME.

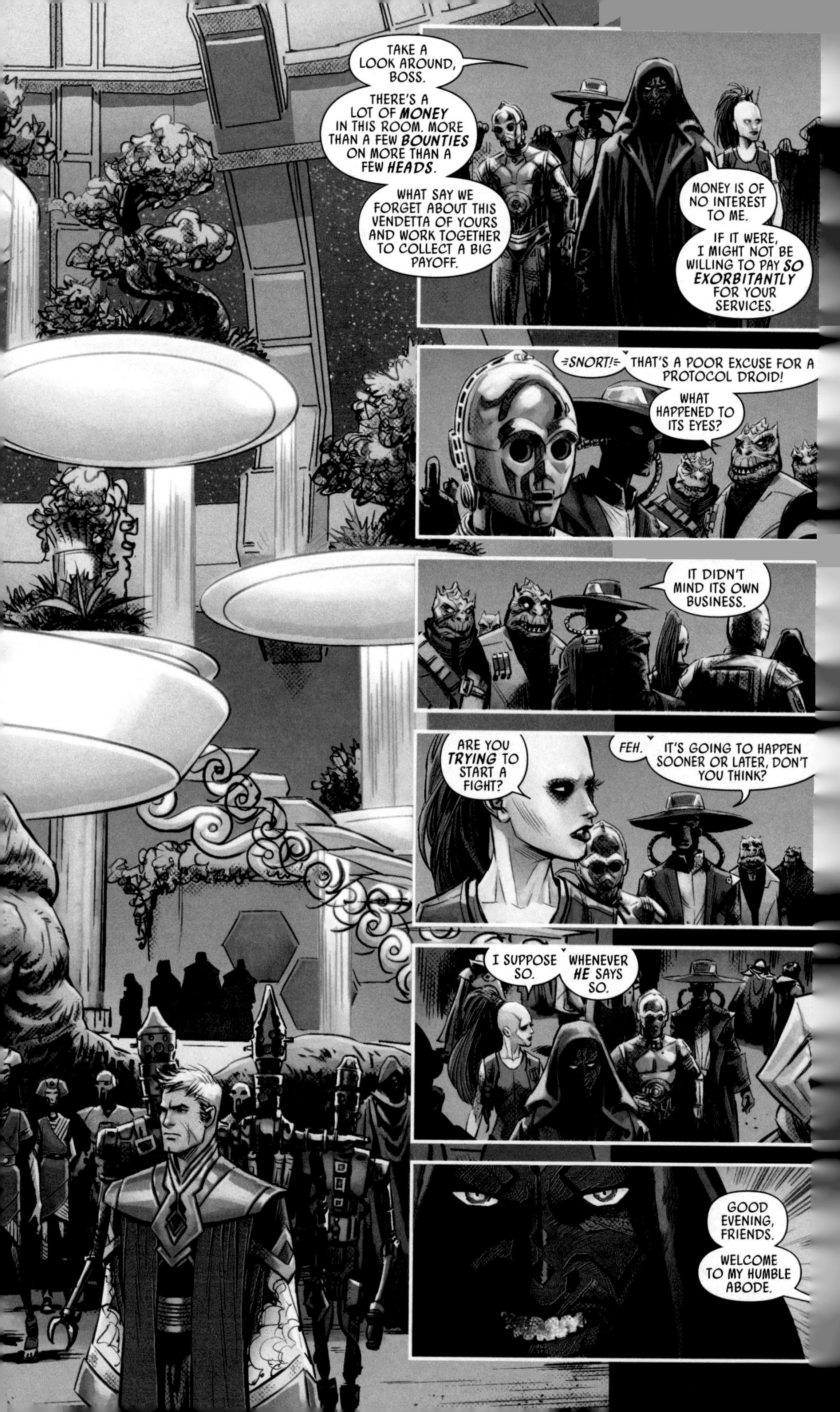

TAKE A LOOK AROUND, BOSS.
THERE'S A LOT OF MONEY IN THIS ROOM. MORE THAN A FEW BOUNTIES ON MORE THAN A FEW HEADS.
WHAT SAY WE FORGET ABOUT THIS VENDETTA OF YOURS AND WORK TOGETHER TO COLLECT A BIG PAYOFF.
MONEY IS OF NO INTEREST TO ME.
IF IT WERE, I MIGHT NOT BE WILLING TO PAY SO EXORBITANTLY FOR YOUR SERVICES.
=SNORT!=
THAT'S A POOR EXCUSE FOR A PROTOCOL DROID!
WHAT HAPPENED TO ITS EYES?
IT DIDN'T MIND ITS OWN BUSINESS.
ARE YOU TRYING TO START A FIGHT?
FEH.
IT'S GOING TO HAPPEN SOONER OR LATER, DON'T YOU THINK?
I SUPPOSE SO.
WHENEVER HE SAYS SO.
GOOD EVENING, FRIENDS.
WELCOME TO MY HUMBLE ABODE.

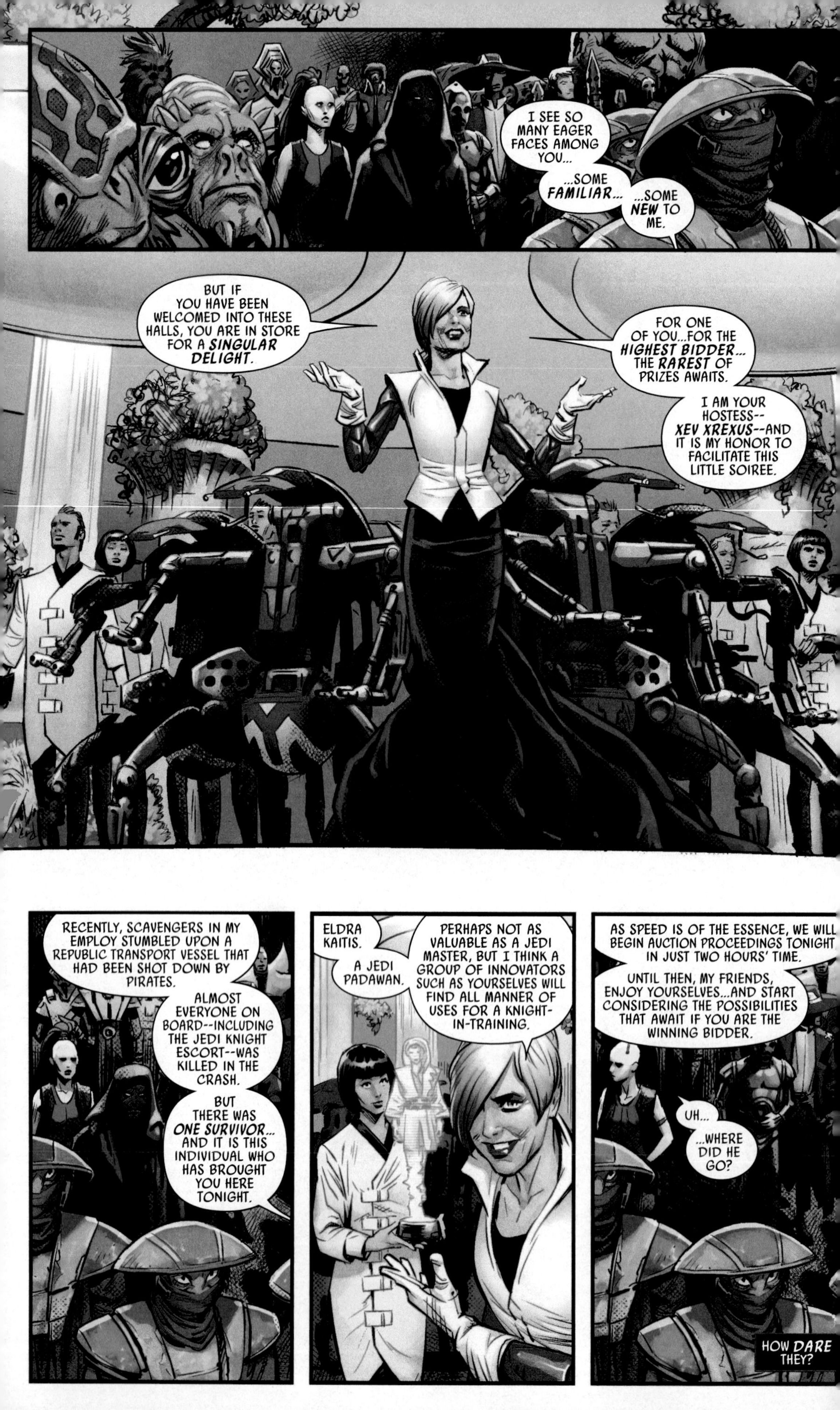

I SEE SO MANY EAGER FACES AMONG YOU...
...SOME FAMILIAR...
...SOME NEW TO ME.
BUT IF YOU HAVE BEEN WELCOMED INTO THESE HALLS, YOU ARE IN STORE FOR A SINGULAR DELIGHT.
FOR ONE OF YOU...FOR THE HIGHEST BIDDER... THE RAREST OF PRIZES AWAITS.
I AM YOUR HOSTESS--XEV XREXUS--AND IT IS MY HONOR TO FACILITATE THIS LITTLE SOIREE.
RECENTLY, SCAVENGERS IN MY EMPLOY STUMBLED UPON A REPUBLIC TRANSPORT VESSEL THAT HAD BEEN SHOT DOWN BY PIRATES.
ALMOST EVERYONE ON BOARD--INCLUDING THE JEDI KNIGHT ESCORT--WAS KILLED IN THE CRASH.
BUT THERE WAS ONE SURVIVOR... AND IT IS THIS INDIVIDUAL WHO HAS BROUGHT YOU HERE TONIGHT.
ELDRA KAITIS.
A JEDI PADAWAN.
PERHAPS NOT AS VALUABLE AS A JEDI MASTER, BUT I THINK A GROUP OF INNOVATORS SUCH AS YOURSELVES WILL FIND ALL MANNER OF USES FOR A KNIGHT-IN-TRAINING.
AS SPEED IS OF THE ESSENCE, WE WILL BEGIN AUCTION PROCEEDINGS TONIGHT IN JUST TWO HOURS' TIME.
UNTIL THEN, MY FRIENDS, ENJOY YOURSELVES...AND START CONSIDERING THE POSSIBILITIES THAT AWAIT IF YOU ARE THE WINNING BIDDER.
UH...
...WHERE DID HE GO?
HOW DARE THEY?

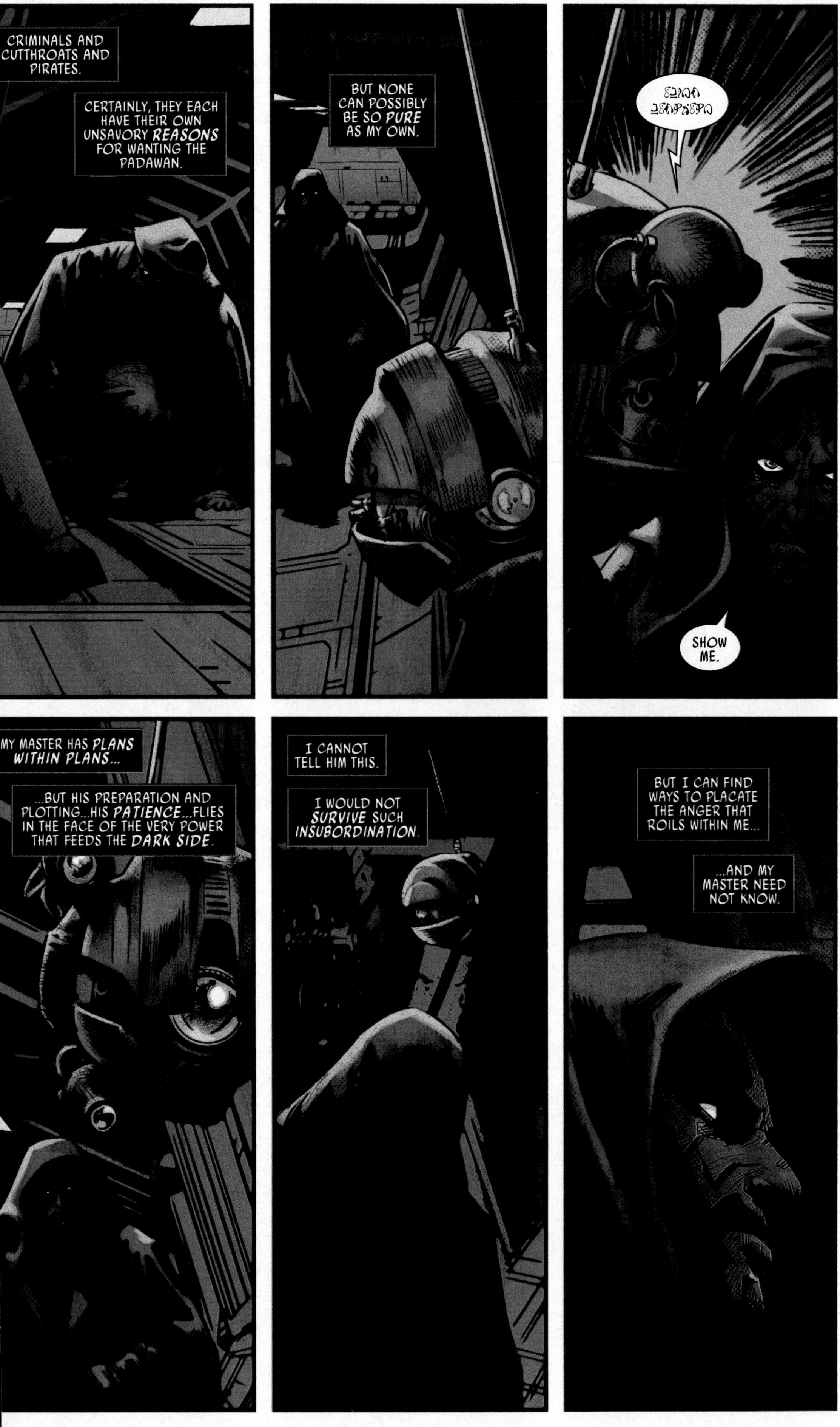
CRIMINALS AND CUTTHROATS AND PIRATES.
CERTAINLY, THEY EACH HAVE THEIR OWN UNSAVORY REASONS FOR WANTING THE PADAWAN.
BUT NONE CAN POSSIBLY BE SO PURE AS MY OWN.
SHOW ME.
MY MASTER HAS PLANS WITHIN PLANS...
...BUT HIS PREPARATION AND PLOTTING...HIS PATIENCE...FLIES IN THE FACE OF THE VERY POWER THAT FEEDS THE DARK SIDE.
I CANNOT TELL HIM THIS.
I WOULD NOT SURVIVE SUCH INSUBORDINATION.
BUT I CAN FIND WAYS TO PLACATE THE ANGER THAT ROILS WITHIN ME...
...AND MY MASTER NEED NOT KNOW.

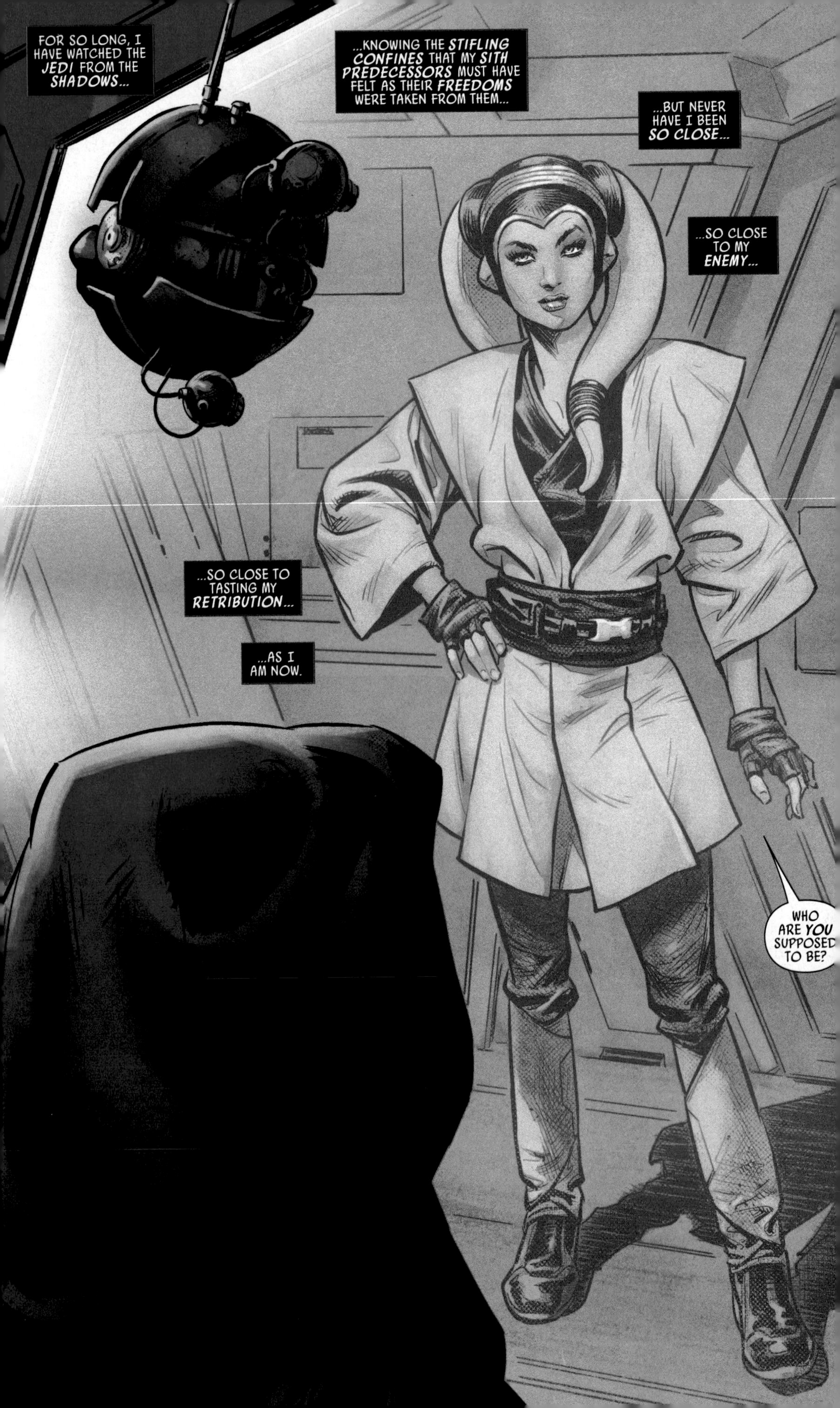

FOR SO LONG, I HAVE WATCHED THE JEDI FROM THE SHADOWS...
...KNOWING THE STIFLING CONFINES THAT MY SITH PREDECESSORS MUST HAVE FELT AS THEIR FREEDOMS WERE TAKEN FROM THEM...
...BUT NEVER HAVE I BEEN SO CLOSE...
...SO CLOSE TO MY ENEMY...
...SO CLOSE TO TASTING MY RETRIBUTION...
...AS I AM NOW.
WHO ARE YOU SUPPOSED TO BE?

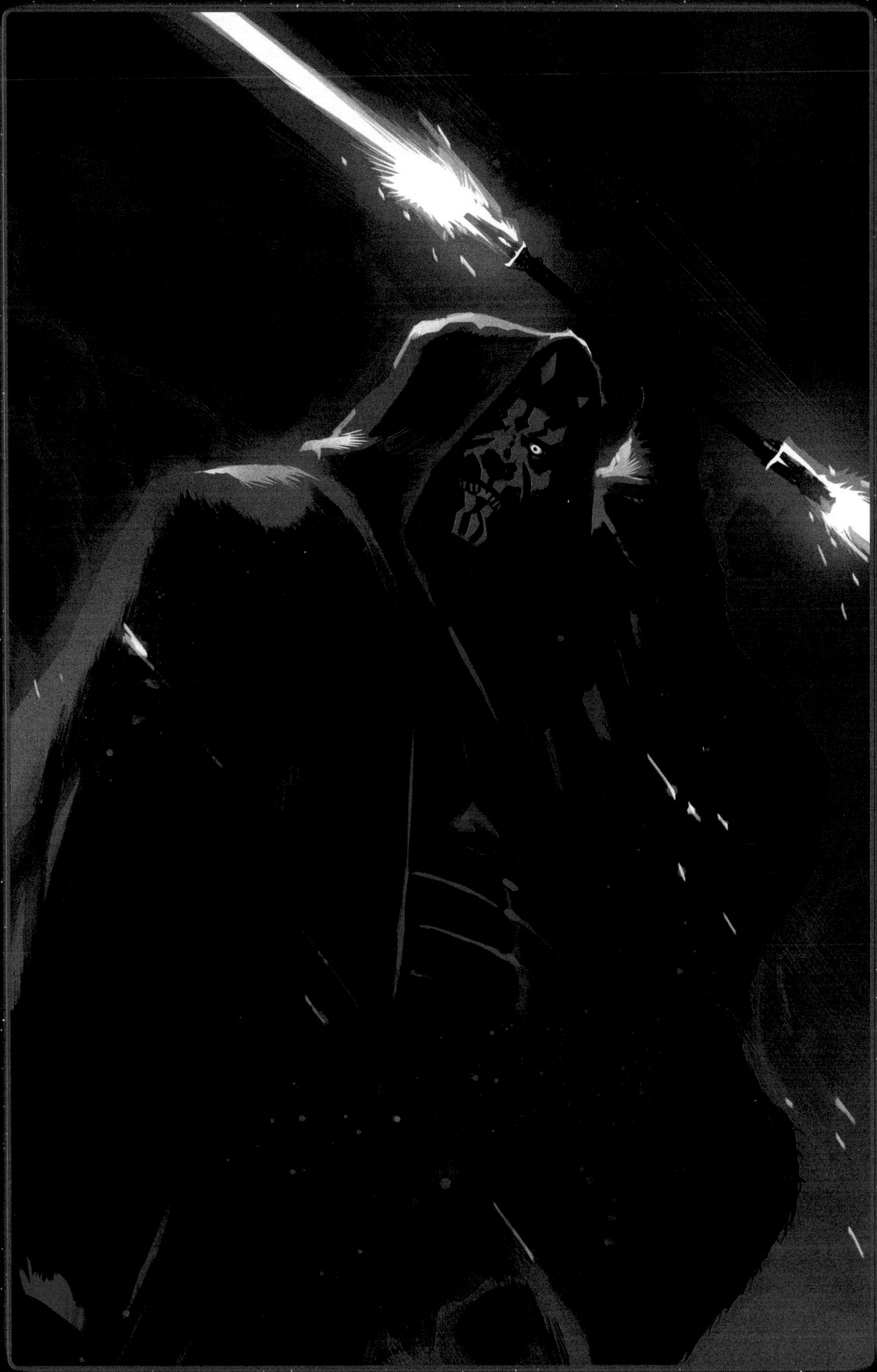

STAR WARS: DARTH MAUL 1
VARIANT BY RAFAEL ALBUQUERQUE

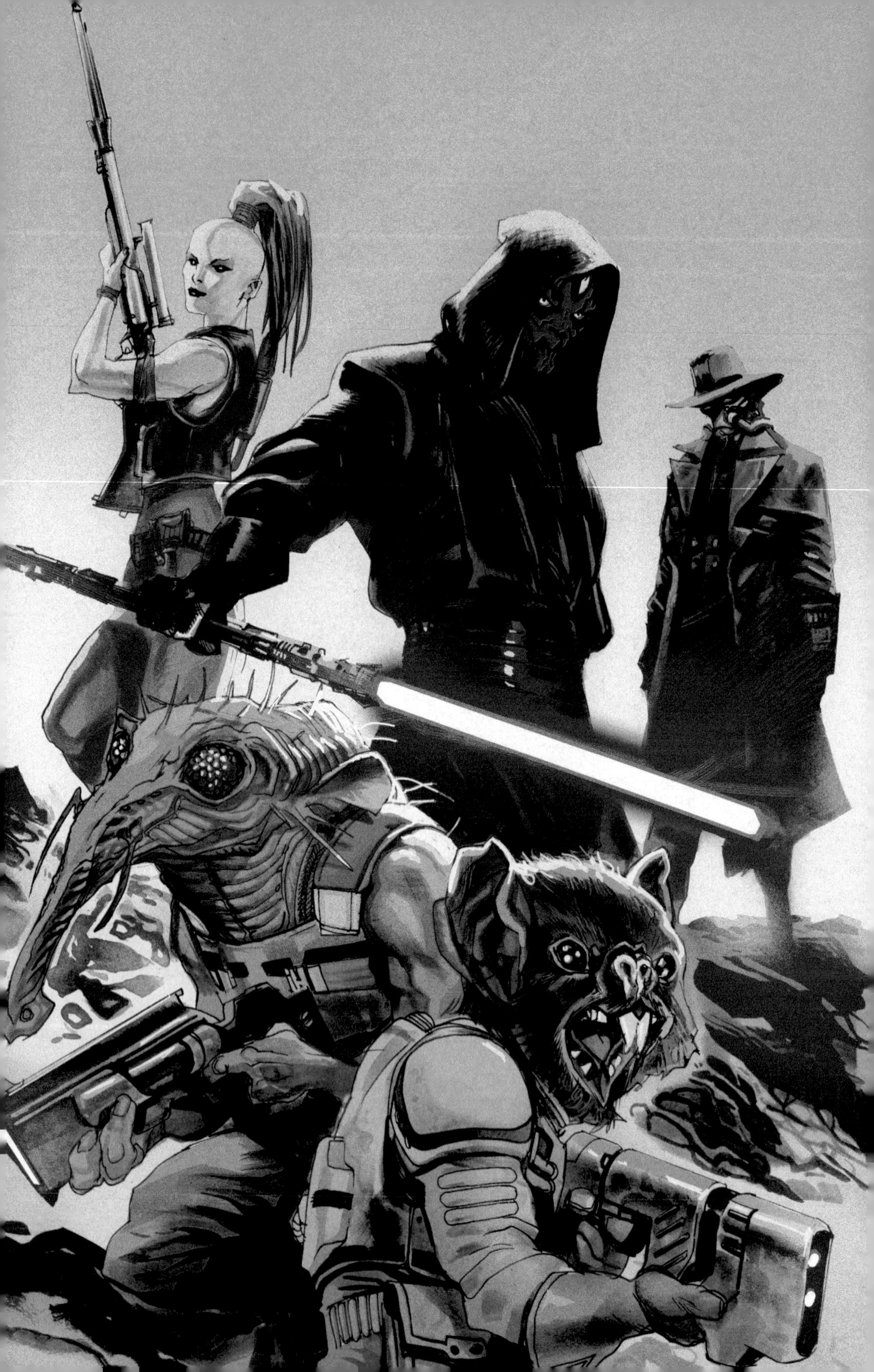

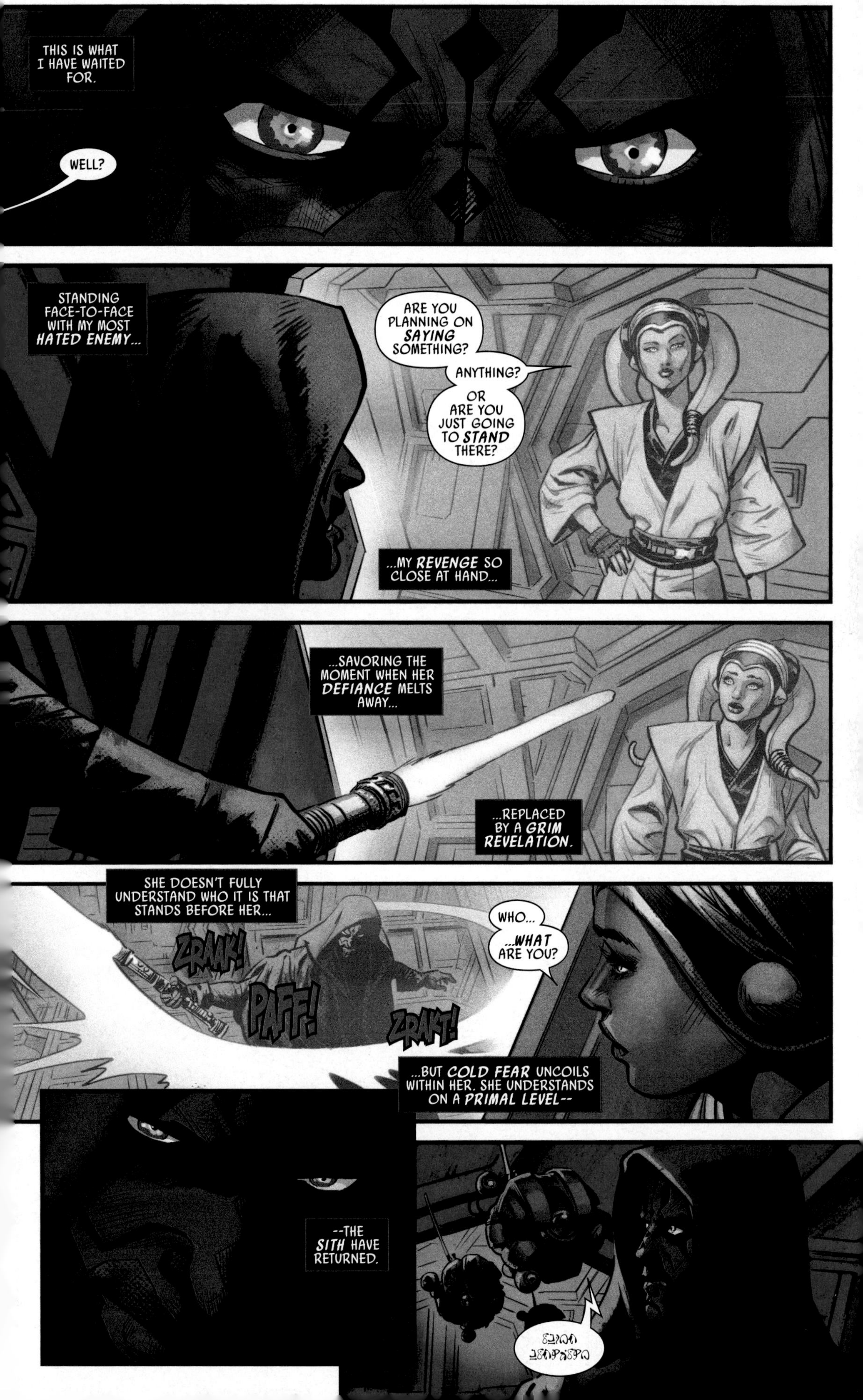
THIS IS WHAT I HAVE WAITED FOR.
WELL?
STANDING FACE-TO-FACE WITH MY MOST HATED ENEMY...
ARE YOU PLANNING ON SAYING SOMETHING?
ANYTHING?
OR ARE YOU JUST GOING TO STAND THERE?
...MY REVENGE SO CLOSE AT HAND...
...SAVORING THE MOMENT WHEN HER DEFIANCE MELTS AWAY...
...REPLACED BY A GRIM REVELATION.
SHE DOESN'T FULLY UNDERSTAND WHO IT IS THAT STANDS BEFORE HER...
ZRAAK!
PAFF!
ZRAKT!
WHO...
...WHAT ARE YOU?
...BUT COLD FEAR UNCOILS WITHIN HER. SHE UNDERSTANDS ON A PRIMAL LEVEL--
--THE SITH HAVE RETURNED.

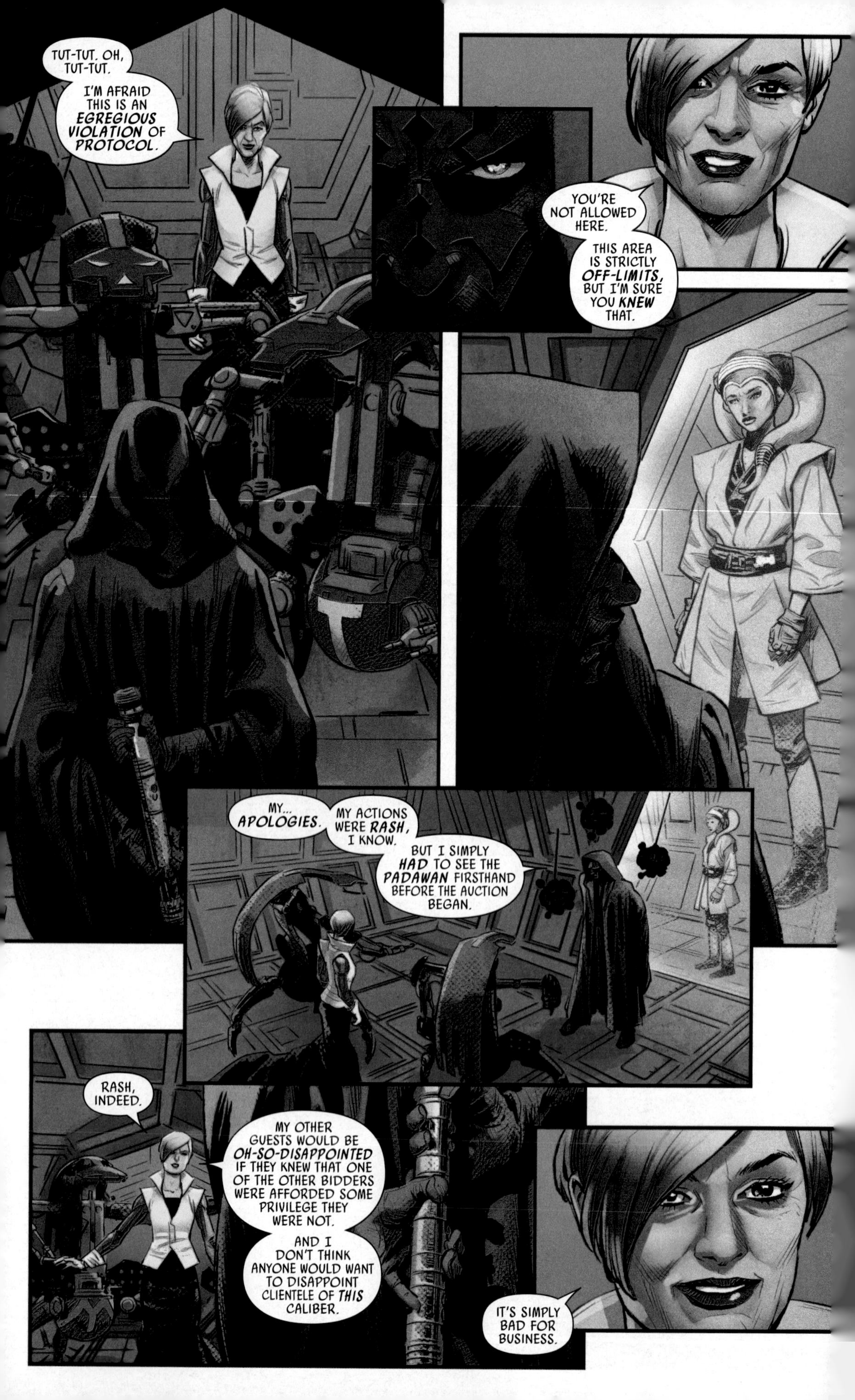

TUT-TUT. OH, TUT-TUT.
I'M AFRAID THIS IS AN EGREGIOUS VIOLATION OF PROTOCOL.
YOU'RE NOT ALLOWED HERE.
THIS AREA IS STRICTLY OFF-LIMITS, BUT I'M SURE YOU KNEW THAT.
MY... APOLOGIES.
MY ACTIONS WERE RASH, I KNOW.
BUT I SIMPLY HAD TO SEE THE PADAWAN FIRSTHAND BEFORE THE AUCTION BEGAN.
RASH, INDEED.
MY OTHER GUESTS WOULD BE OH-SO-DISAPPOINTED IF THEY KNEW THAT ONE OF THE OTHER BIDDERS WERE AFFORDED SOME PRIVILEGE THEY WERE NOT.
AND I DON'T THINK ANYONE WOULD WANT TO DISAPPOINT CLIENTELE OF THIS CALIBER.
IT'S SIMPLY BAD FOR BUSINESS.

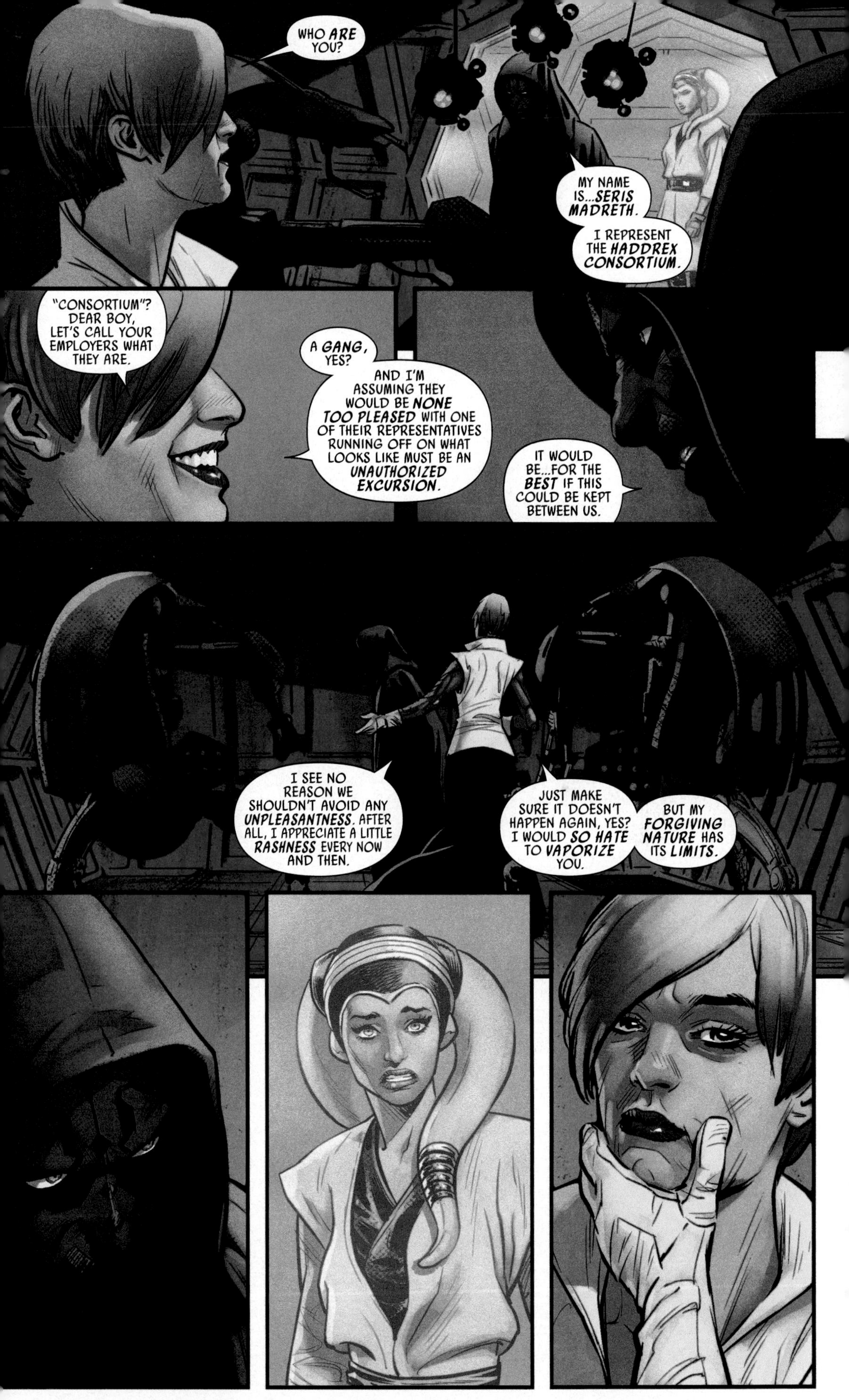
WHO ARE YOU?
MY NAME IS...SERIS MADRETH.
I REPRESENT THE HADDREX CONSORTIUM.
"CONSORTIUM"? DEAR BOY, LET'S CALL YOUR EMPLOYERS WHAT THEY ARE.
A GANG, YES?
AND I'M ASSUMING THEY WOULD BE NONE TOO PLEASED WITH ONE OF THEIR REPRESENTATIVES RUNNING OFF ON WHAT LOOKS LIKE MUST BE AN UNAUTHORIZED EXCURSION.
IT WOULD BE...FOR THE BEST IF THIS COULD BE KEPT BETWEEN US.
I SEE NO REASON WE SHOULDN'T AVOID ANY UNPLEASANTNESS. AFTER ALL, I APPRECIATE A LITTLE RASHNESS EVERY NOW AND THEN.
JUST MAKE SURE IT DOESN'T HAPPEN AGAIN, YES? I WOULD SO HATE TO VAPORIZE YOU.
BUT MY FORGIVING NATURE HAS ITS LIMITS.

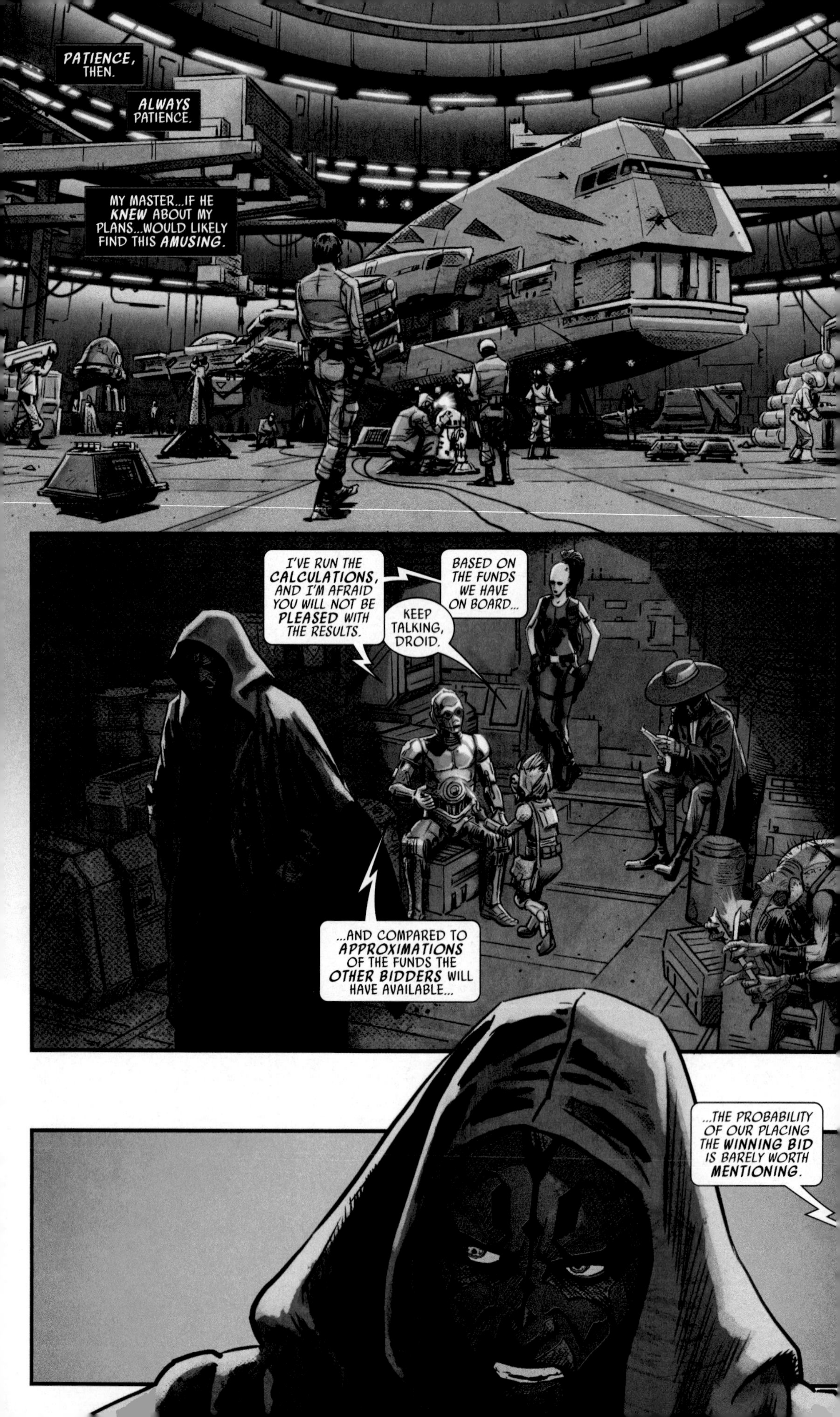

PATIENCE, THEN.
ALWAYS PATIENCE.
MY MASTER...IF HE KNEW ABOUT MY PLANS...WOULD LIKELY FIND THIS AMUSING.
I'VE RUN THE CALCULATIONS, AND I'M AFRAID YOU WILL NOT BE PLEASED WITH THE RESULTS.
BASED ON THE FUNDS WE HAVE ON BOARD...
KEEP TALKING, DROID.
...AND COMPARED TO APPROXIMATIONS OF THE FUNDS THE OTHER BIDDERS WILL HAVE AVAILABLE...
...THE PROBABILITY OF OUR PLACING THE WINNING BID IS BARELY WORTH MENTIONING.

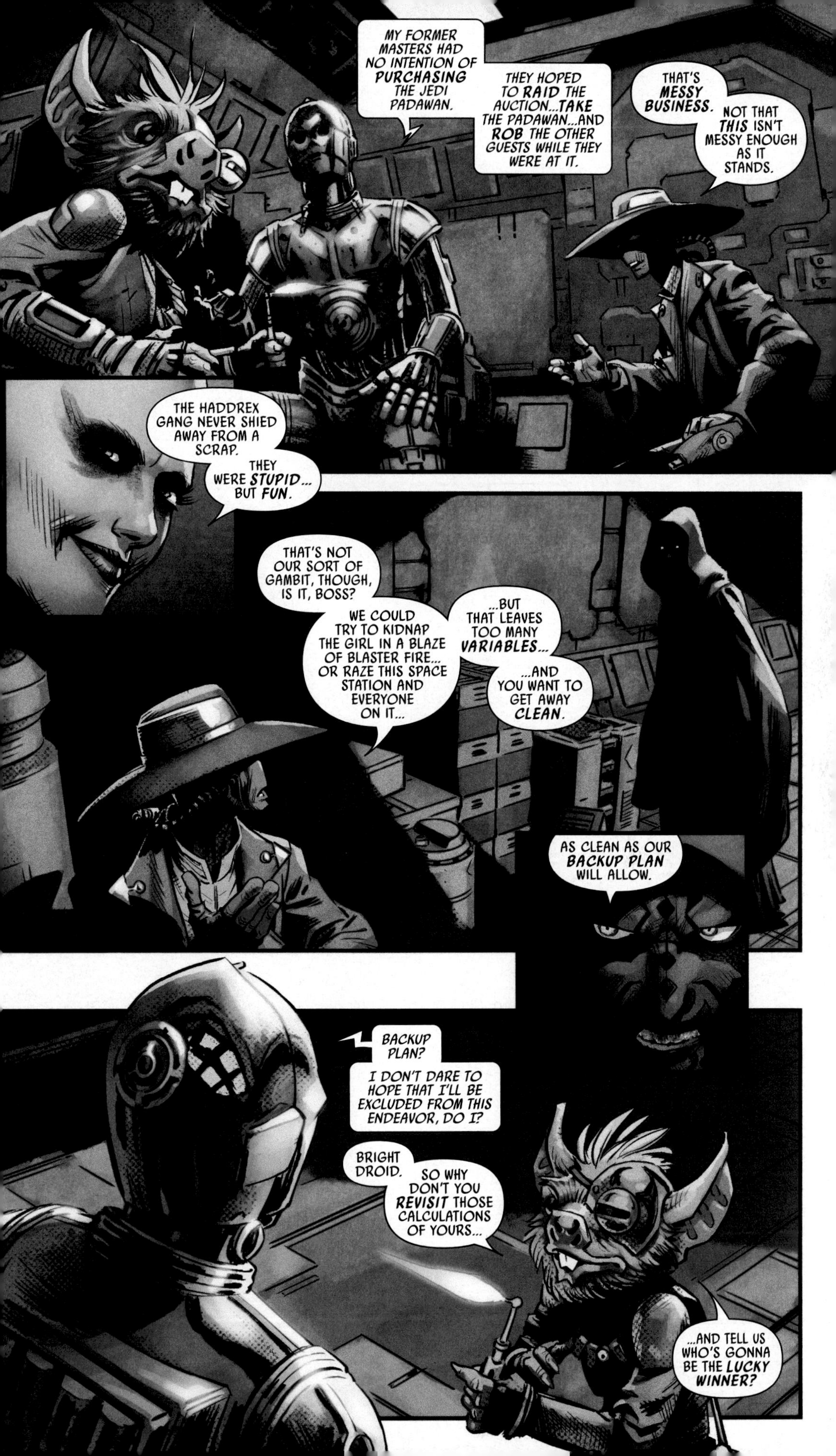
MY FORMER MASTERS HAD NO INTENTION OF **PURCHASING** THE JEDI PADAWAN.
THEY HOPED TO **RAID** THE AUCTION...**TAKE** THE PADAWAN...AND **ROB** THE OTHER GUESTS WHILE THEY WERE AT IT.
THAT'S **MESSY BUSINESS.**
NOT THAT **THIS** ISN'T MESSY ENOUGH AS IT STANDS.
THE HADDREX GANG NEVER SHIED AWAY FROM A SCRAP.
THEY WERE **STUPID**... BUT **FUN**.
THAT'S NOT OUR SORT OF GAMBIT, THOUGH, IS IT, BOSS?
WE COULD TRY TO KIDNAP THE GIRL IN A BLAZE OF BLASTER FIRE... OR RAZE THIS SPACE STATION AND EVERYONE ON IT...
...BUT THAT LEAVES TOO MANY **VARIABLES**...
...AND YOU WANT TO GET AWAY **CLEAN**.
AS CLEAN AS OUR **BACKUP PLAN** WILL ALLOW.
BACKUP PLAN?
I DON'T DARE TO HOPE THAT I'LL BE EXCLUDED FROM THIS ENDEAVOR, DO I?
BRIGHT DROID.
SO WHY DON'T YOU **REVISIT** THOSE CALCULATIONS OF YOURS...
...AND TELL US WHO'S GONNA BE THE **LUCKY WINNER?**

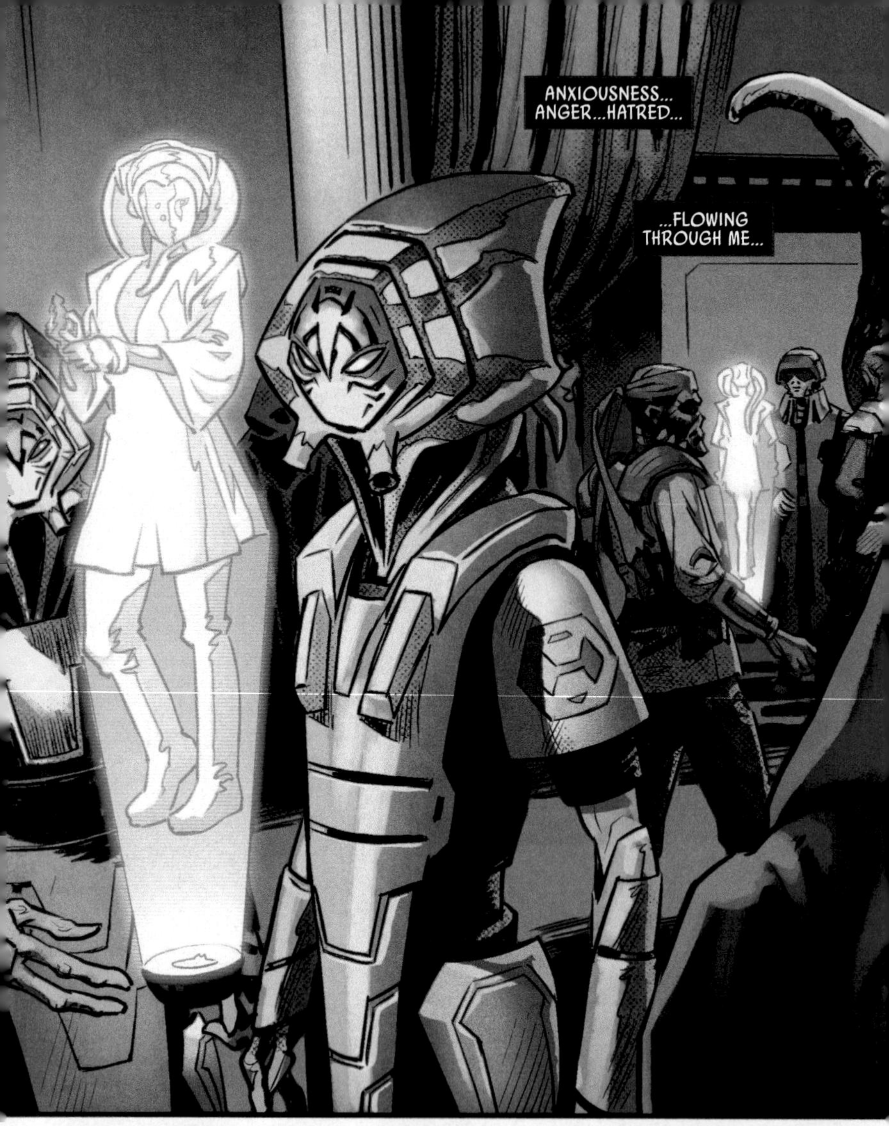
ANXIOUSNESS...
ANGER...HATRED...
...FLOWING THROUGH ME...

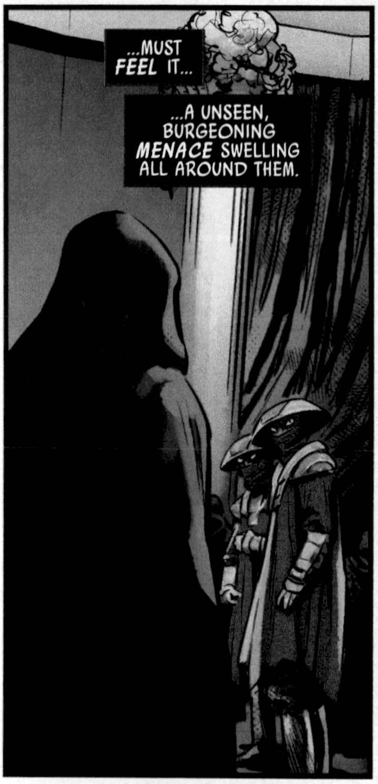
...MUST *FEEL* IT...
...A UNSEEN, BURGEONING *MENACE* SWELLING ALL AROUND THEM.

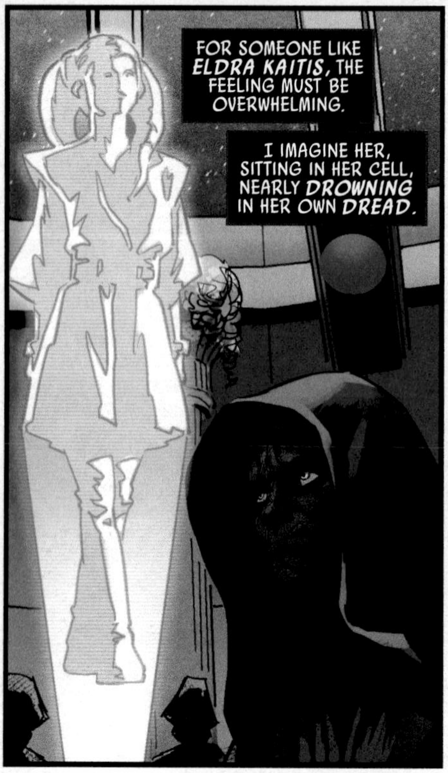
FOR SOMEONE LIKE *ELDRA KAITIS*, THE FEELING MUST BE OVERWHELMING.
I IMAGINE HER, SITTING IN HER CELL, NEARLY *DROWNING* IN HER OWN *DREAD*.

...STRONG ENOUGH THAT THOSE AROUND ME--EVEN THOSE WHO DO NOT KNOW THE FORCE...

IN *DENYING* ME MY NATURE, HE *BETRAYS* ME.

AND SO I BETRAY HIM--MY DREADED MASTER--BY BEING HERE AT ALL.

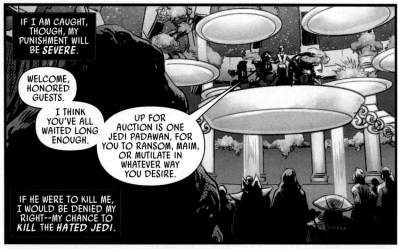

IF I AM CAUGHT, THOUGH, MY PUNISHMENT WILL BE *SEVERE*.

WELCOME, HONORED GUESTS.

I THINK YOU'VE ALL WAITED LONG ENOUGH.

UP FOR AUCTION IS ONE JEDI PADAWAN, FOR YOU TO RANSOM, MAIM, OR MUTILATE IN WHATEVER WAY YOU DESIRE.

IF HE WERE TO KILL ME, I WOULD BE DENIED MY RIGHT--MY CHANCE TO *KILL* THE *HATED JEDI*.

I MUST GIVE MY OWN PLANS *TIME* TO UNFOLD.

LET'S START THE BIDDING AT 500,000 UNMARKED CREDITS, SHALL WE?

IN THIS WAY, I AM MORE LIKE MY MASTER THAN I REALIZED.

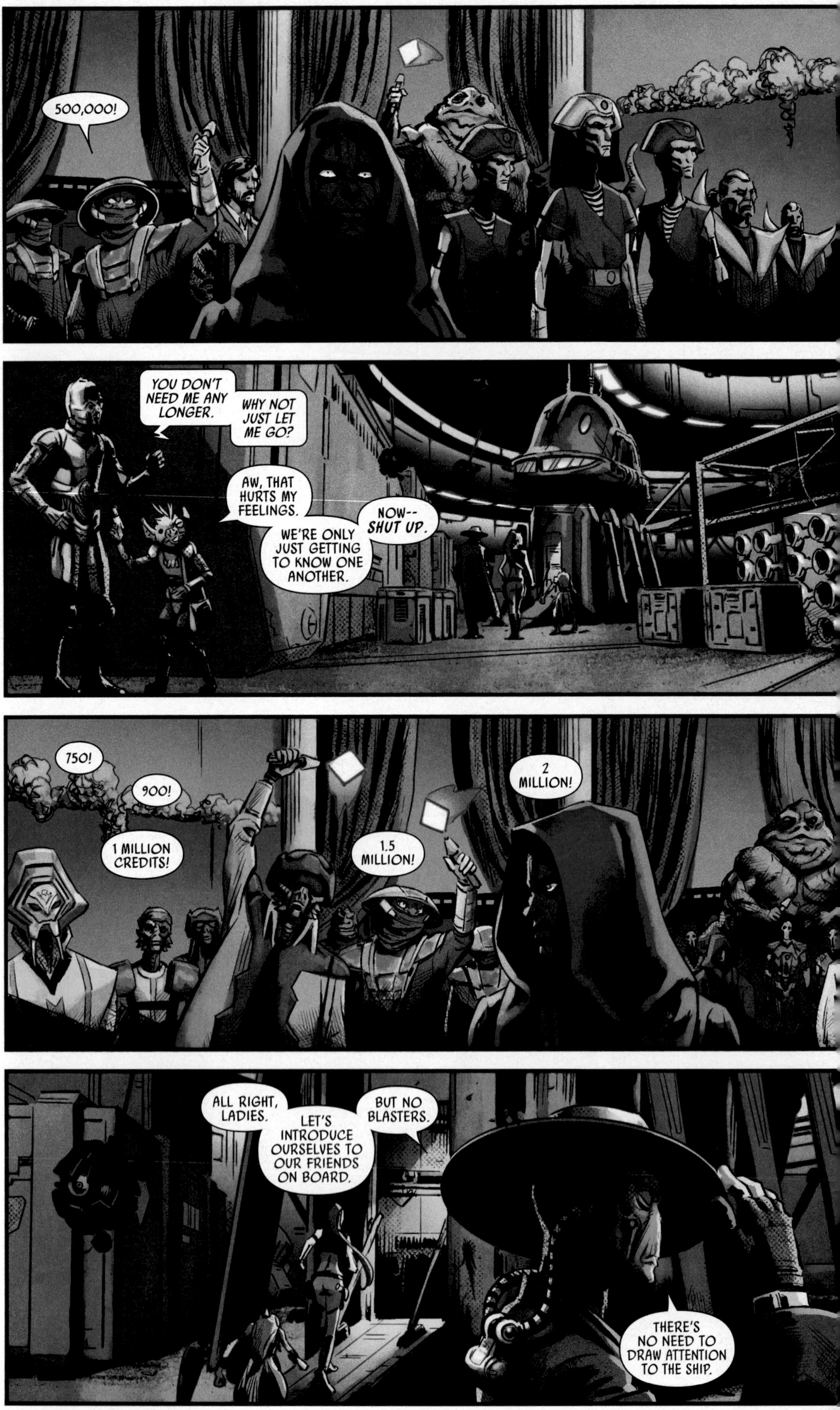
500,000!
YOU DON'T NEED ME ANY LONGER.
WHY NOT JUST LET ME GO?
AW, THAT HURTS MY FEELINGS.
WE'RE ONLY JUST GETTING TO KNOW ONE ANOTHER.
NOW-- SHUT UP.
750!
900!
1 MILLION CREDITS!
1.5 MILLION!
2 MILLION!
ALL RIGHT, LADIES.
LET'S INTRODUCE OURSELVES TO OUR FRIENDS ON BOARD.
BUT NO BLASTERS.
THERE'S NO NEED TO DRAW ATTENTION TO THE SHIP.

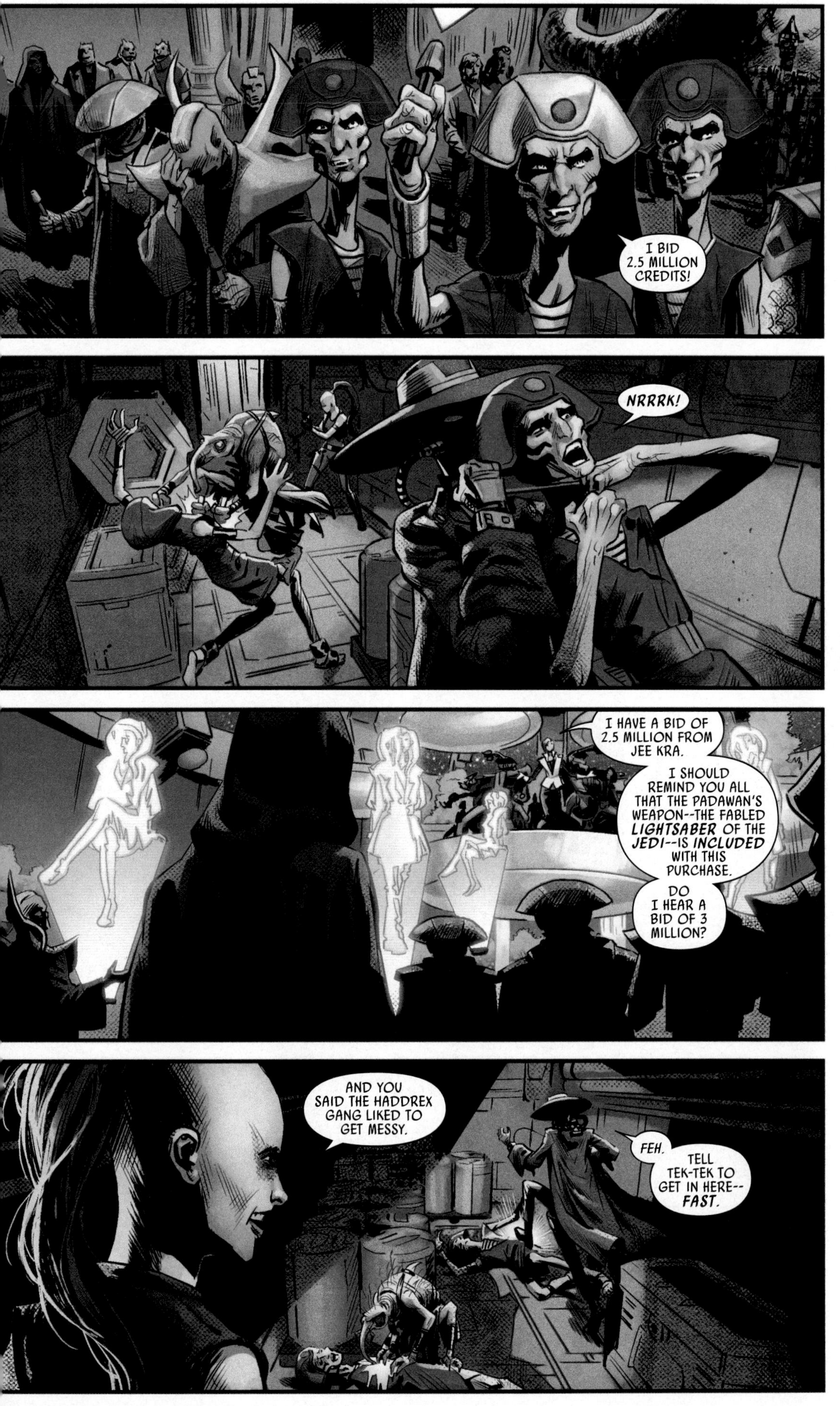

I BID 2.5 MILLION CREDITS!
NRRRK!
I HAVE A BID OF 2.5 MILLION FROM JEE KRA.
I SHOULD REMIND YOU ALL THAT THE PADAWAN'S WEAPON--THE FABLED LIGHTSABER OF THE JEDI--IS INCLUDED WITH THIS PURCHASE.
DO I HEAR A BID OF 3 MILLION?
AND YOU SAID THE HADDREX GANG LIKED TO GET MESSY.
FEH.
TELL TEK-TEK TO GET IN HERE--FAST.

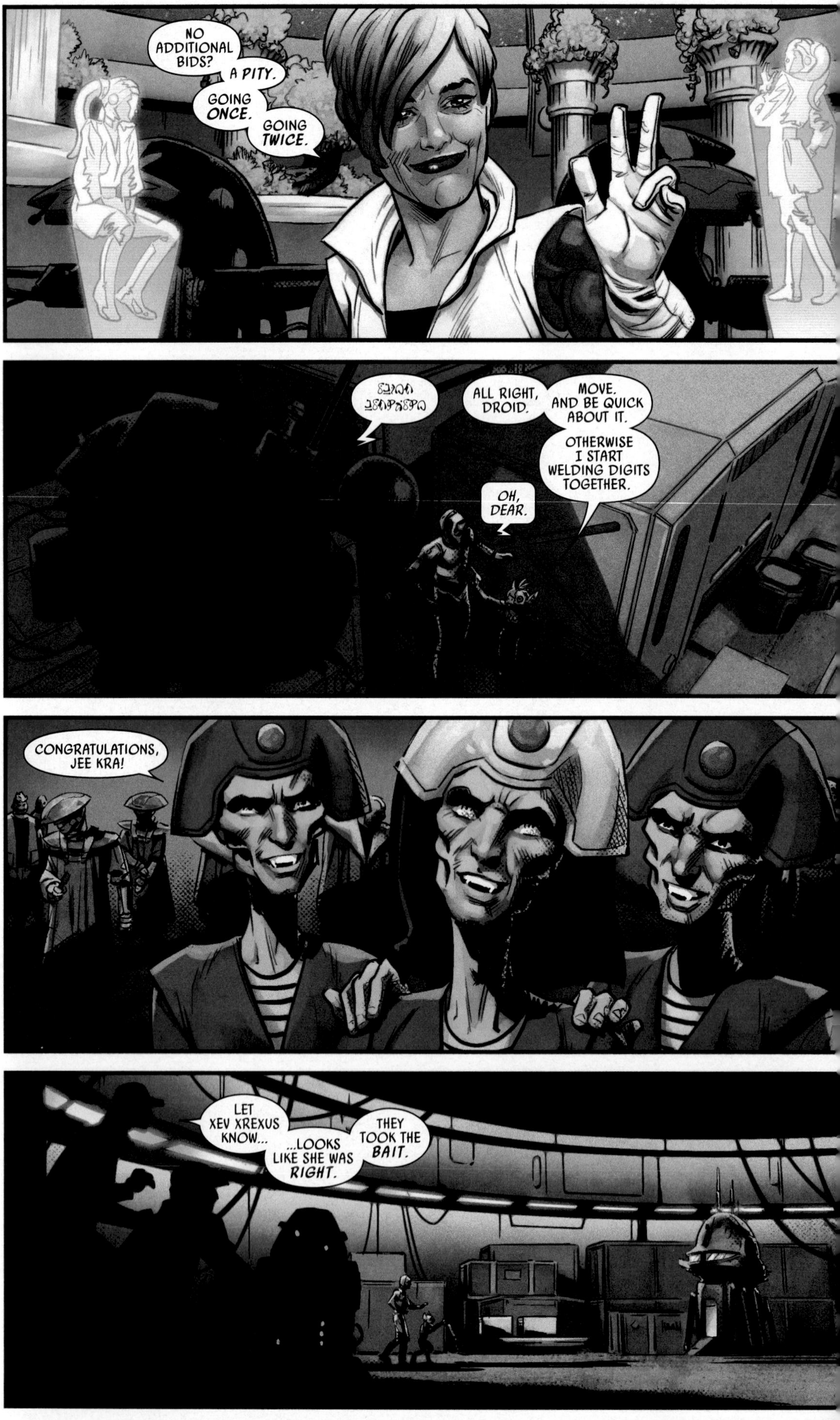
NO ADDITIONAL BIDS?
A PITY.
GOING ONCE.
GOING TWICE.
ALL RIGHT, DROID.
MOVE. AND BE QUICK ABOUT IT.
OTHERWISE I START WELDING DIGITS TOGETHER.
OH, DEAR.
CONGRATULATIONS, JEE KRA!
LET XEV XREXUS KNOW...
...LOOKS LIKE SHE WAS RIGHT.
THEY TOOK THE BAIT.

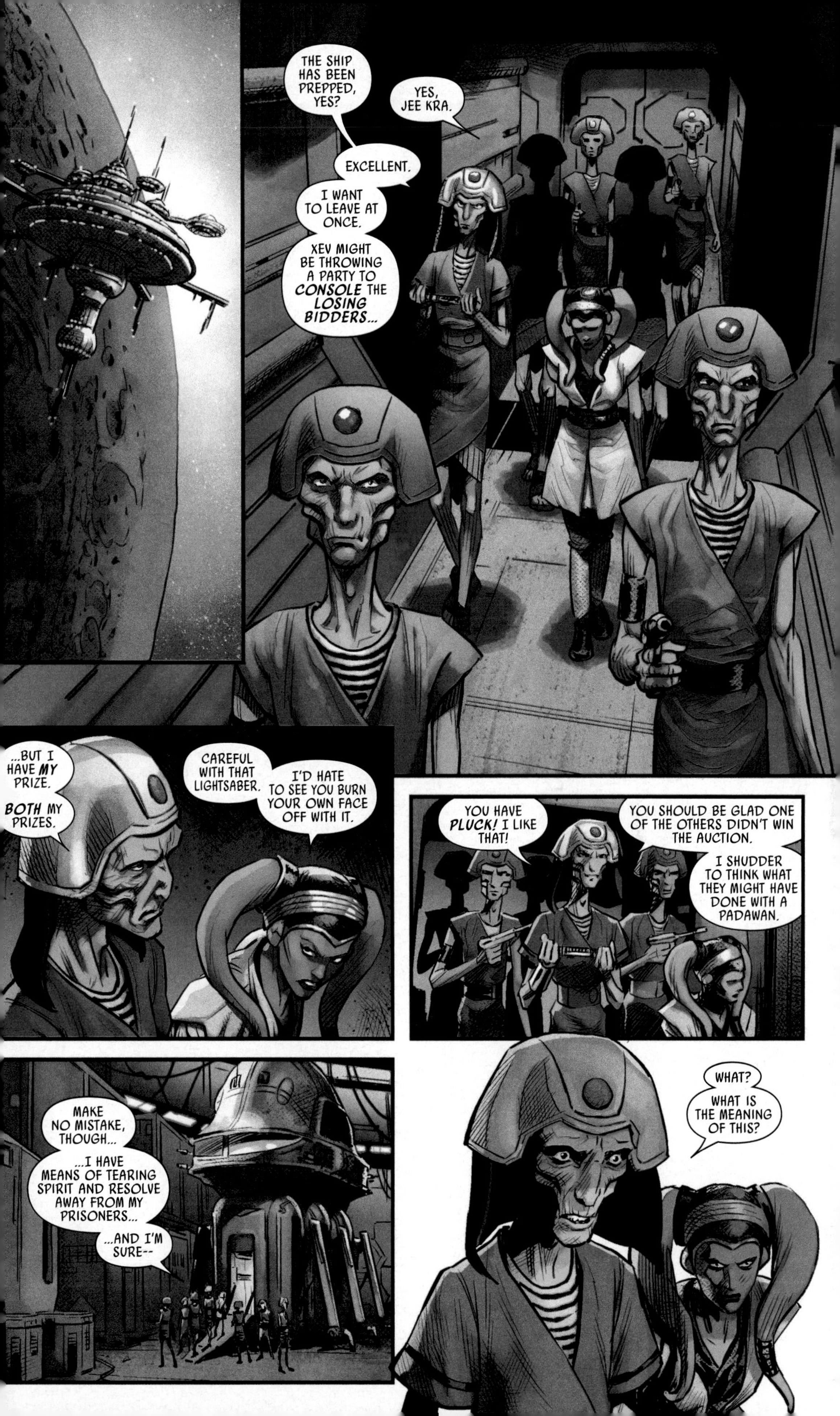
THE SHIP HAS BEEN PREPPED, YES?
YES, JEE KRA.
EXCELLENT.
I WANT TO LEAVE AT ONCE.
XEV MIGHT BE THROWING A PARTY TO CONSOLE THE LOSING BIDDERS...
...BUT I HAVE MY PRIZE.
BOTH MY PRIZES.
CAREFUL WITH THAT LIGHTSABER.
I'D HATE TO SEE YOU BURN YOUR OWN FACE OFF WITH IT.
YOU HAVE PLUCK! I LIKE THAT!
YOU SHOULD BE GLAD ONE OF THE OTHERS DIDN'T WIN THE AUCTION.
I SHUDDER TO THINK WHAT THEY MIGHT HAVE DONE WITH A PADAWAN.
MAKE NO MISTAKE, THOUGH...
...I HAVE MEANS OF TEARING SPIRIT AND RESOLVE AWAY FROM MY PRISONERS...
...AND I'M SURE--
WHAT?
WHAT IS THE MEANING OF THIS?

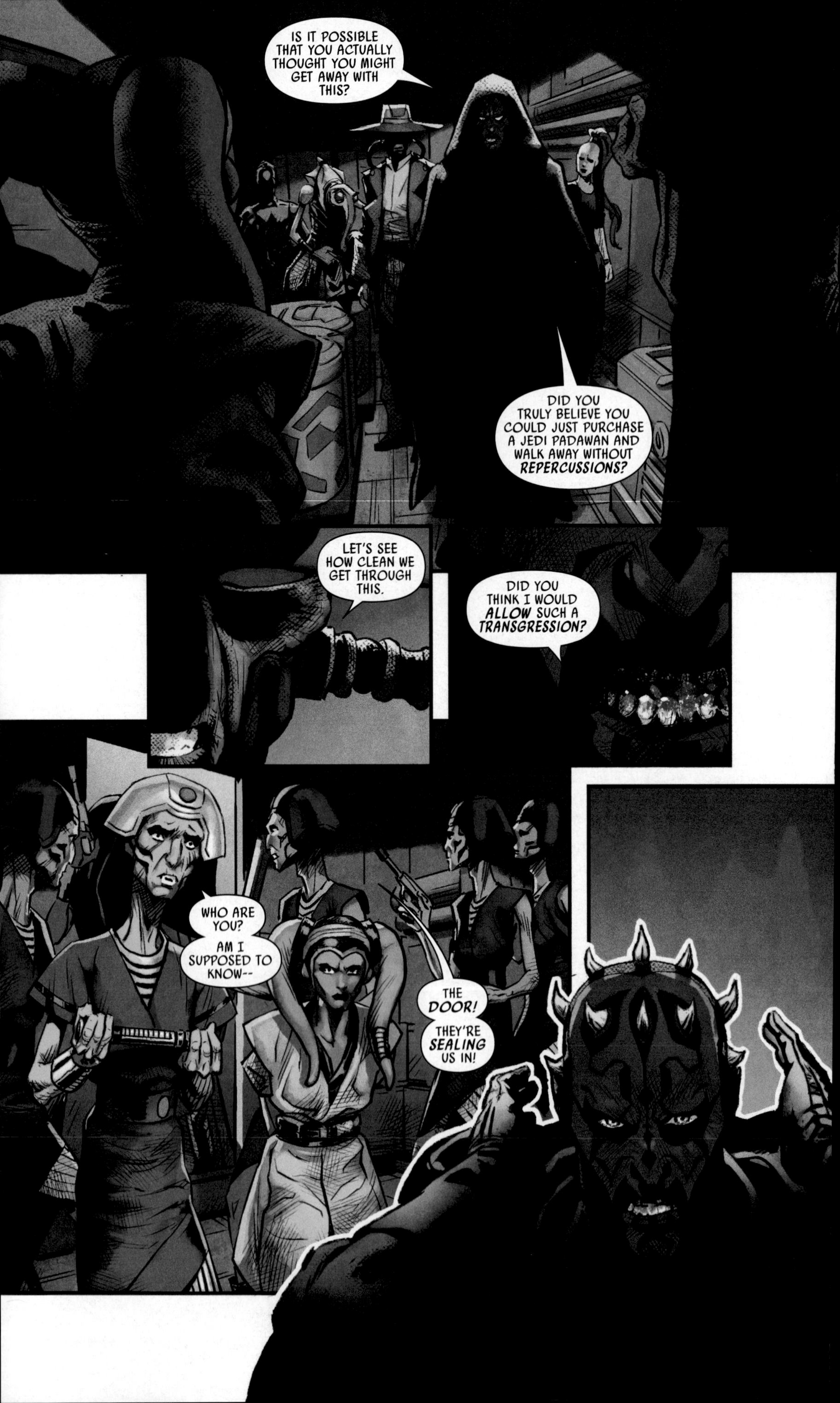
IS IT POSSIBLE THAT YOU ACTUALLY THOUGHT YOU MIGHT GET AWAY WITH THIS?
DID YOU TRULY BELIEVE YOU COULD JUST PURCHASE A JEDI PADAWAN AND WALK AWAY WITHOUT REPERCUSSIONS?
LET'S SEE HOW CLEAN WE GET THROUGH THIS.
DID YOU THINK I WOULD ALLOW SUCH A TRANSGRESSION?
WHO ARE YOU?
AM I SUPPOSED TO KNOW--
THE DOOR!
THEY'RE SEALING US IN!

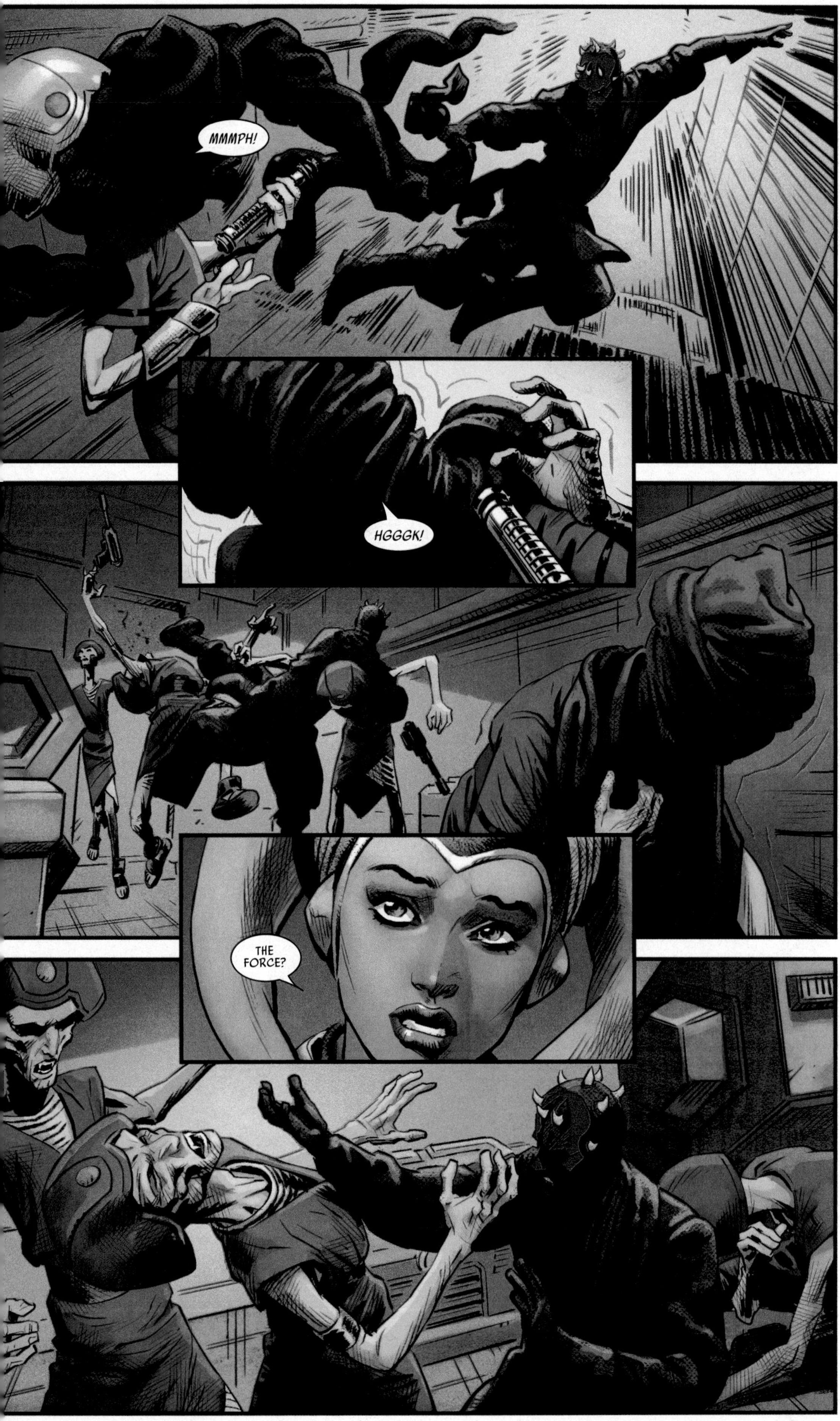
MMMPH!
HGGGK!
THE FORCE?

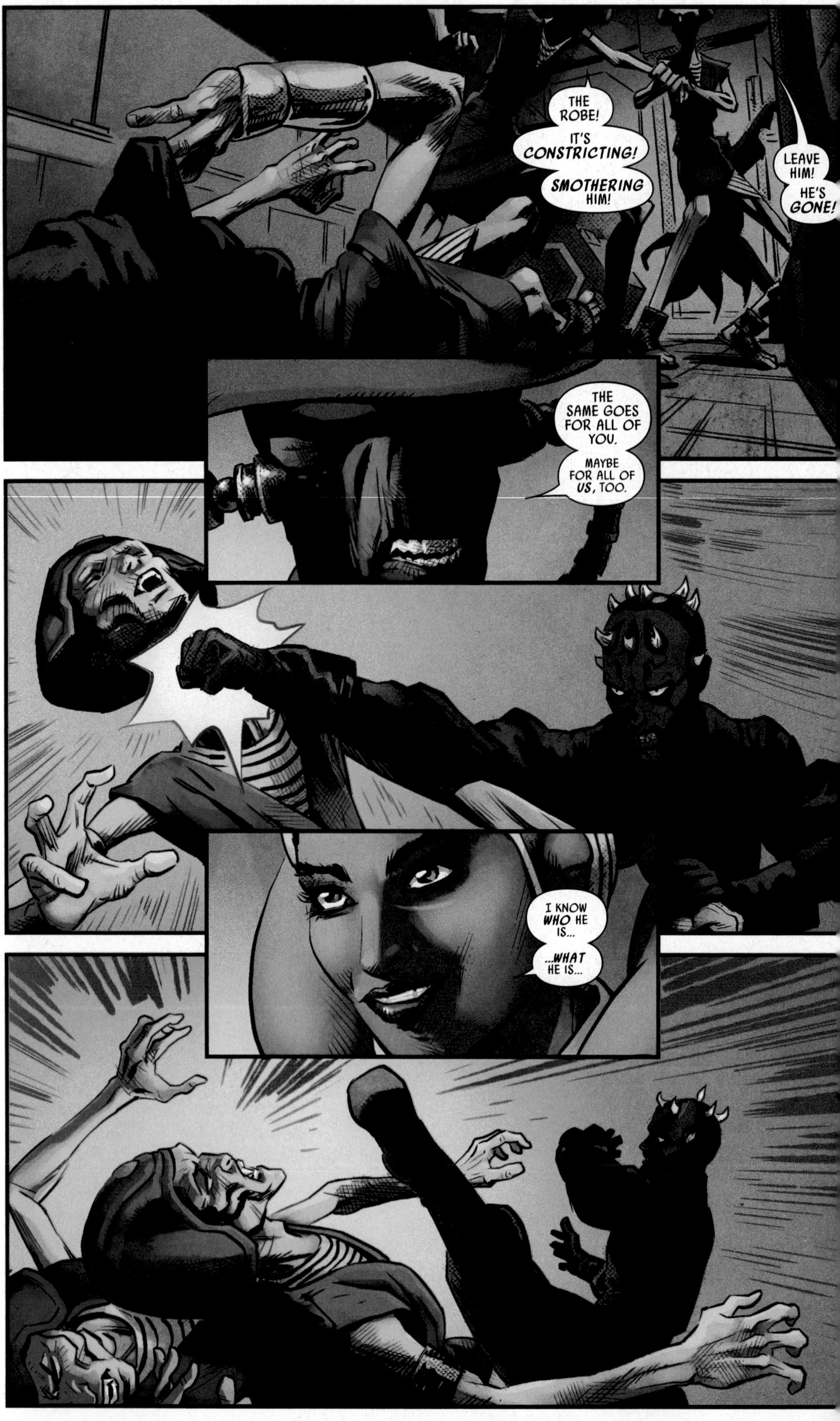
THE ROBE!
IT'S CONSTRICTING!
SMOTHERING HIM!
LEAVE HIM!
HE'S GONE!
THE SAME GOES FOR ALL OF YOU.
MAYBE FOR ALL OF US, TOO.
I KNOW WHO HE IS...
...WHAT HE IS...

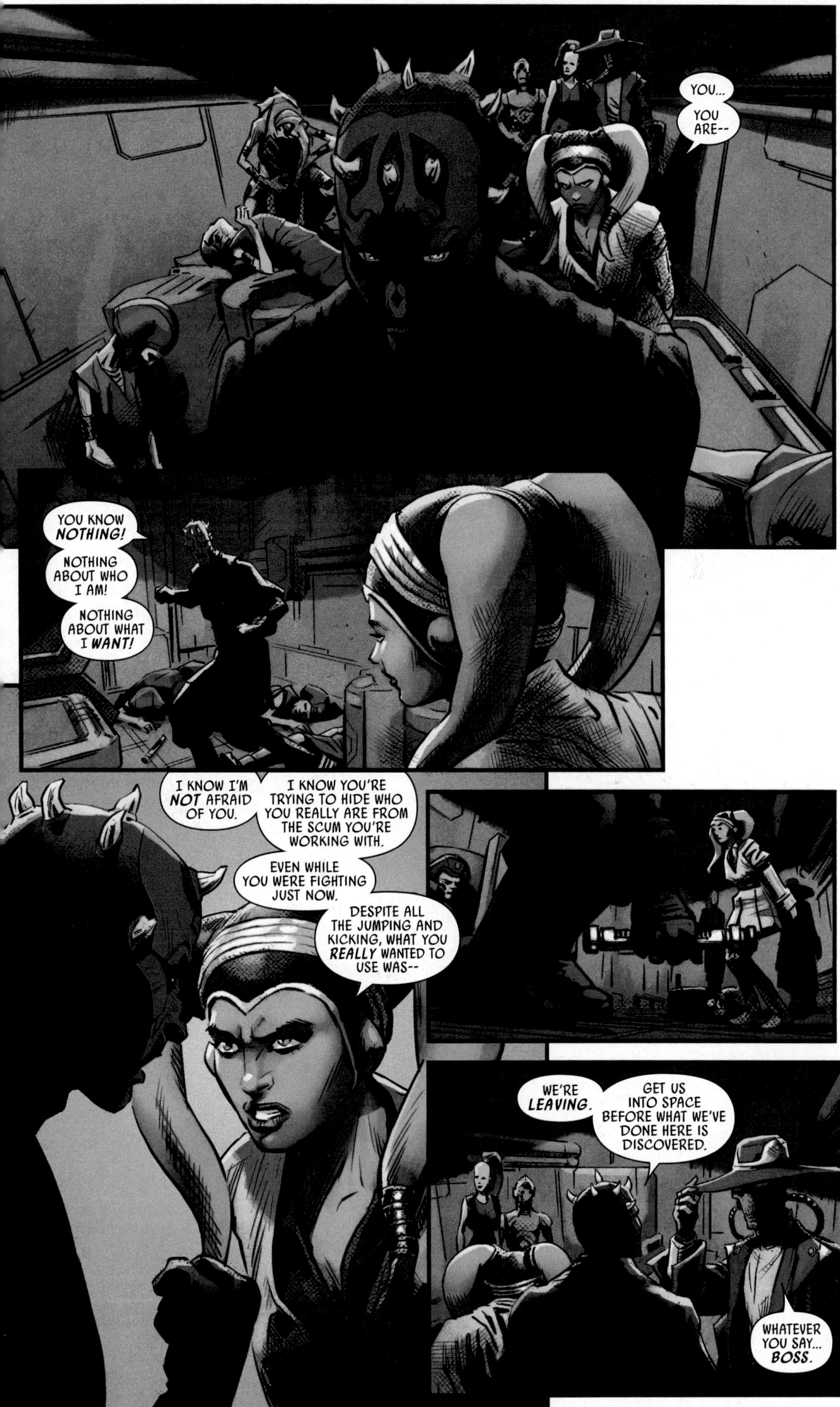
YOU...
YOU ARE--
YOU KNOW *NOTHING!*
NOTHING ABOUT WHO I AM!
NOTHING ABOUT WHAT I *WANT!*
I KNOW I'M *NOT* AFRAID OF YOU.
I KNOW YOU'RE TRYING TO HIDE WHO YOU REALLY ARE FROM THE SCUM YOU'RE WORKING WITH.
EVEN WHILE YOU WERE FIGHTING JUST NOW.
DESPITE ALL THE JUMPING AND KICKING, WHAT YOU *REALLY* WANTED TO USE WAS--
WE'RE *LEAVING.*
GET US INTO SPACE BEFORE WHAT WE'VE DONE HERE IS DISCOVERED.
WHATEVER YOU SAY... *BOSS.*

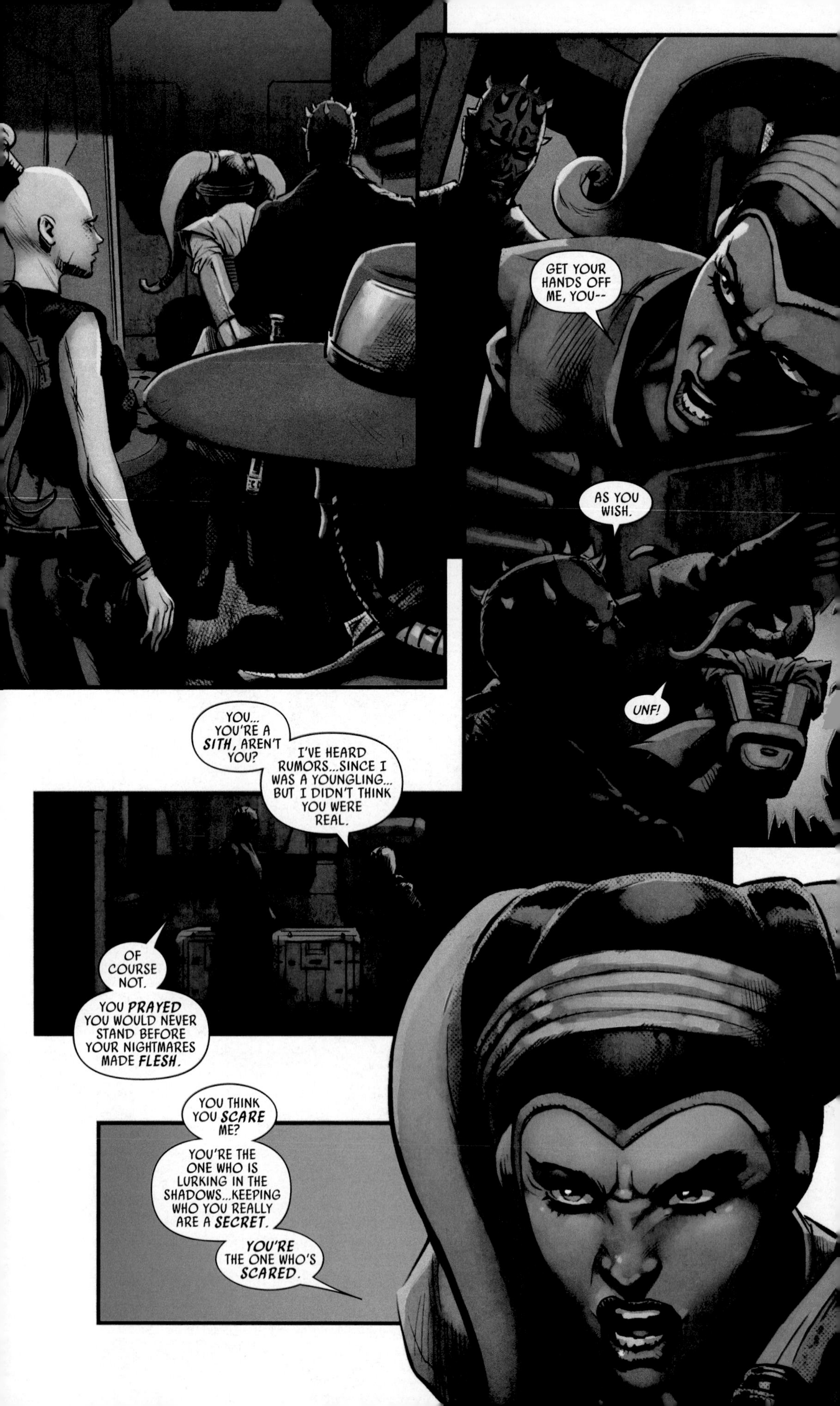
GET YOUR HANDS OFF ME, YOU--
AS YOU WISH.
UNF!
YOU... YOU'RE A SITH, AREN'T YOU?
I'VE HEARD RUMORS...SINCE I WAS A YOUNGLING... BUT I DIDN'T THINK YOU WERE REAL.
OF COURSE NOT.
YOU PRAYED YOU WOULD NEVER STAND BEFORE YOUR NIGHTMARES MADE FLESH.
YOU THINK YOU SCARE ME?
YOU'RE THE ONE WHO IS LURKING IN THE SHADOWS...KEEPING WHO YOU REALLY ARE A SECRET.
YOU'RE THE ONE WHO'S SCARED.

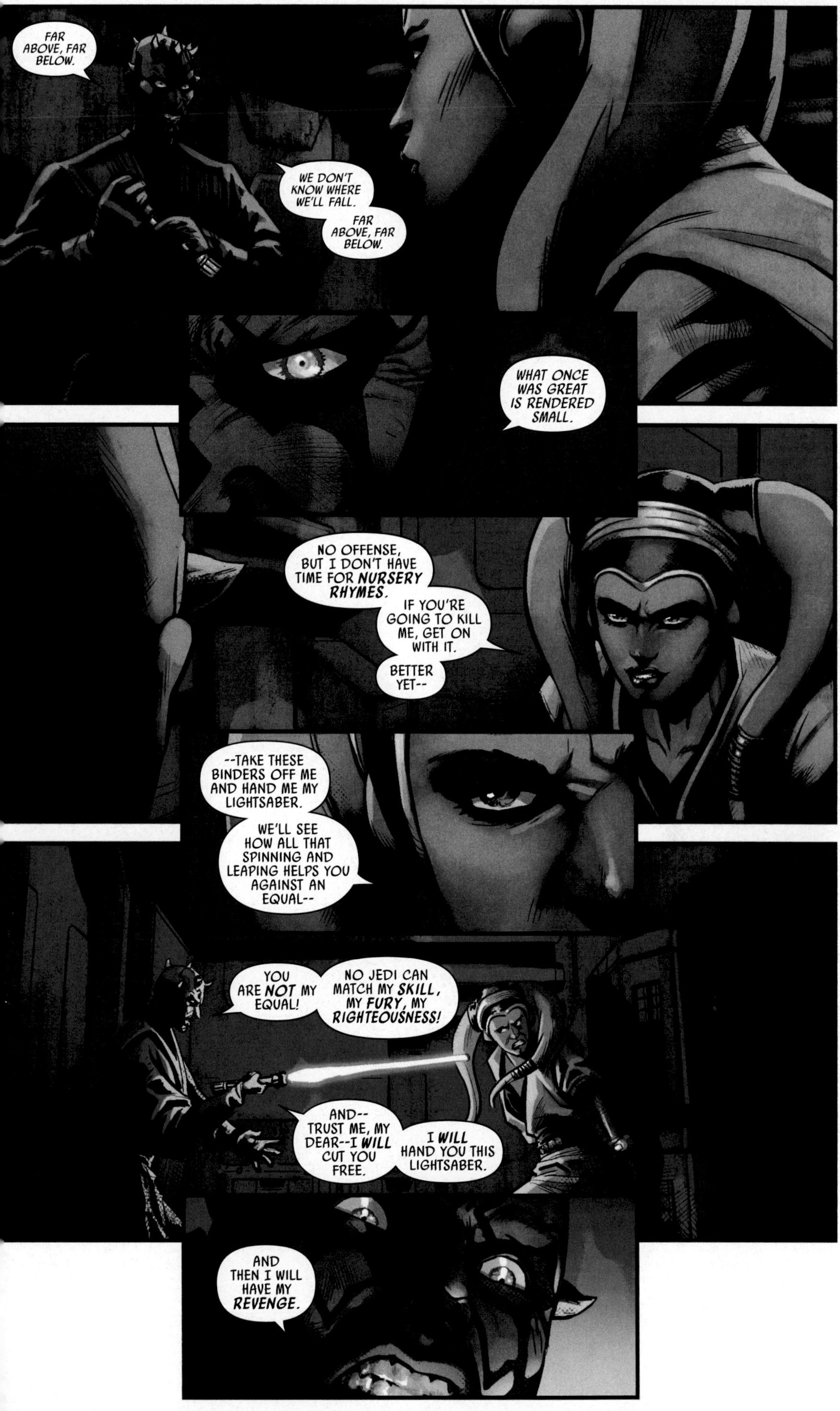
FAR ABOVE, FAR BELOW.
WE DON'T KNOW WHERE WE'LL FALL.
FAR ABOVE, FAR BELOW.
WHAT ONCE WAS GREAT IS RENDERED SMALL.
NO OFFENSE, BUT I DON'T HAVE TIME FOR NURSERY RHYMES.
IF YOU'RE GOING TO KILL ME, GET ON WITH IT.
BETTER YET--
--TAKE THESE BINDERS OFF ME AND HAND ME MY LIGHTSABER.
WE'LL SEE HOW ALL THAT SPINNING AND LEAPING HELPS YOU AGAINST AN EQUAL--
YOU ARE NOT MY EQUAL!
NO JEDI CAN MATCH MY SKILL, MY FURY, MY RIGHTEOUSNESS!
AND--TRUST ME, MY DEAR--I WILL CUT YOU FREE.
I WILL HAND YOU THIS LIGHTSABER.
AND THEN I WILL HAVE MY REVENGE.

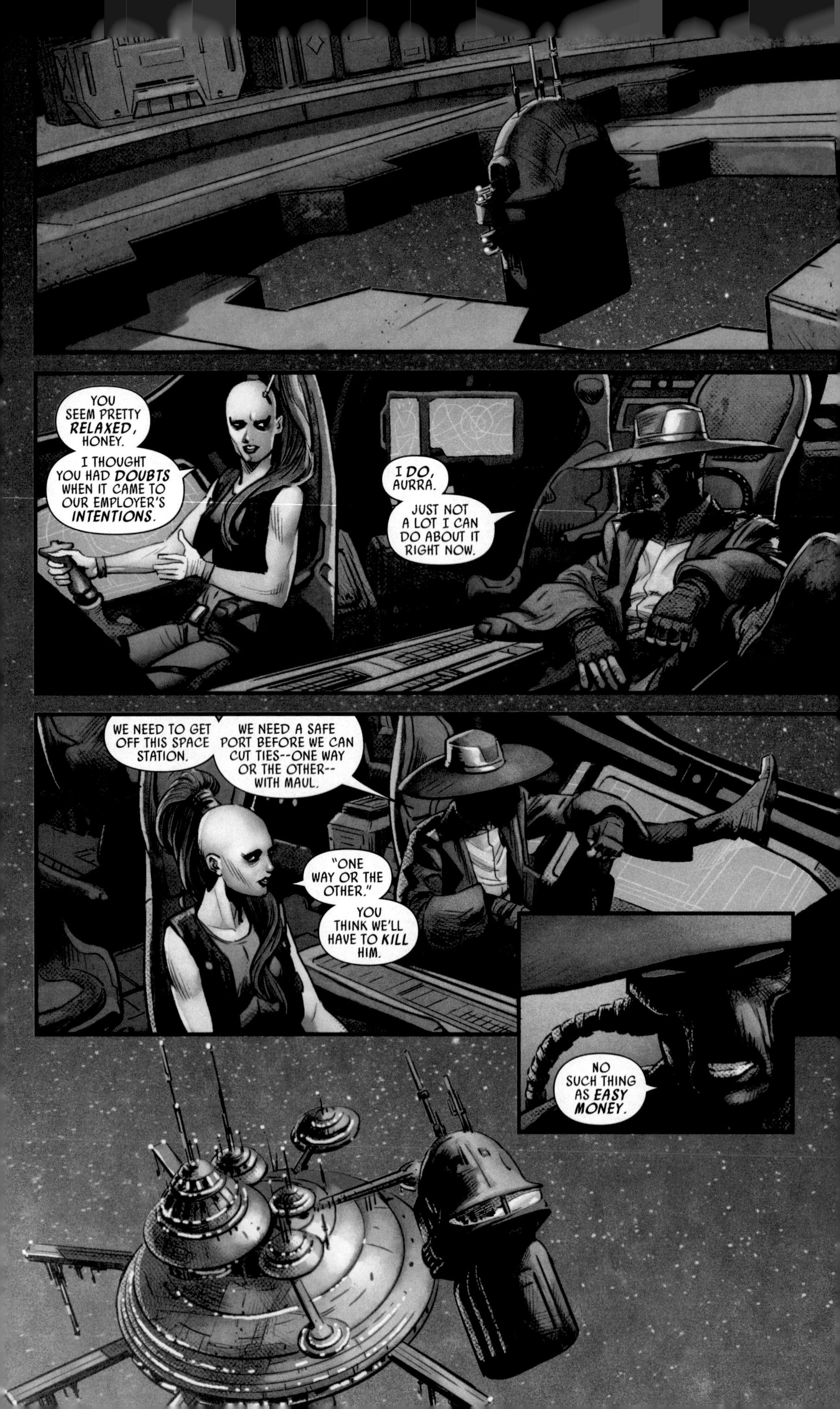
YOU SEEM PRETTY RELAXED, HONEY.
I THOUGHT YOU HAD DOUBTS WHEN IT CAME TO OUR EMPLOYER'S INTENTIONS.
I DO, AURRA.
JUST NOT A LOT I CAN DO ABOUT IT RIGHT NOW.
WE NEED TO GET OFF THIS SPACE STATION.
WE NEED A SAFE PORT BEFORE WE CAN CUT TIES--ONE WAY OR THE OTHER--WITH MAUL.
"ONE WAY OR THE OTHER."
YOU THINK WE'LL HAVE TO KILL HIM.
NO SUCH THING AS EASY MONEY.

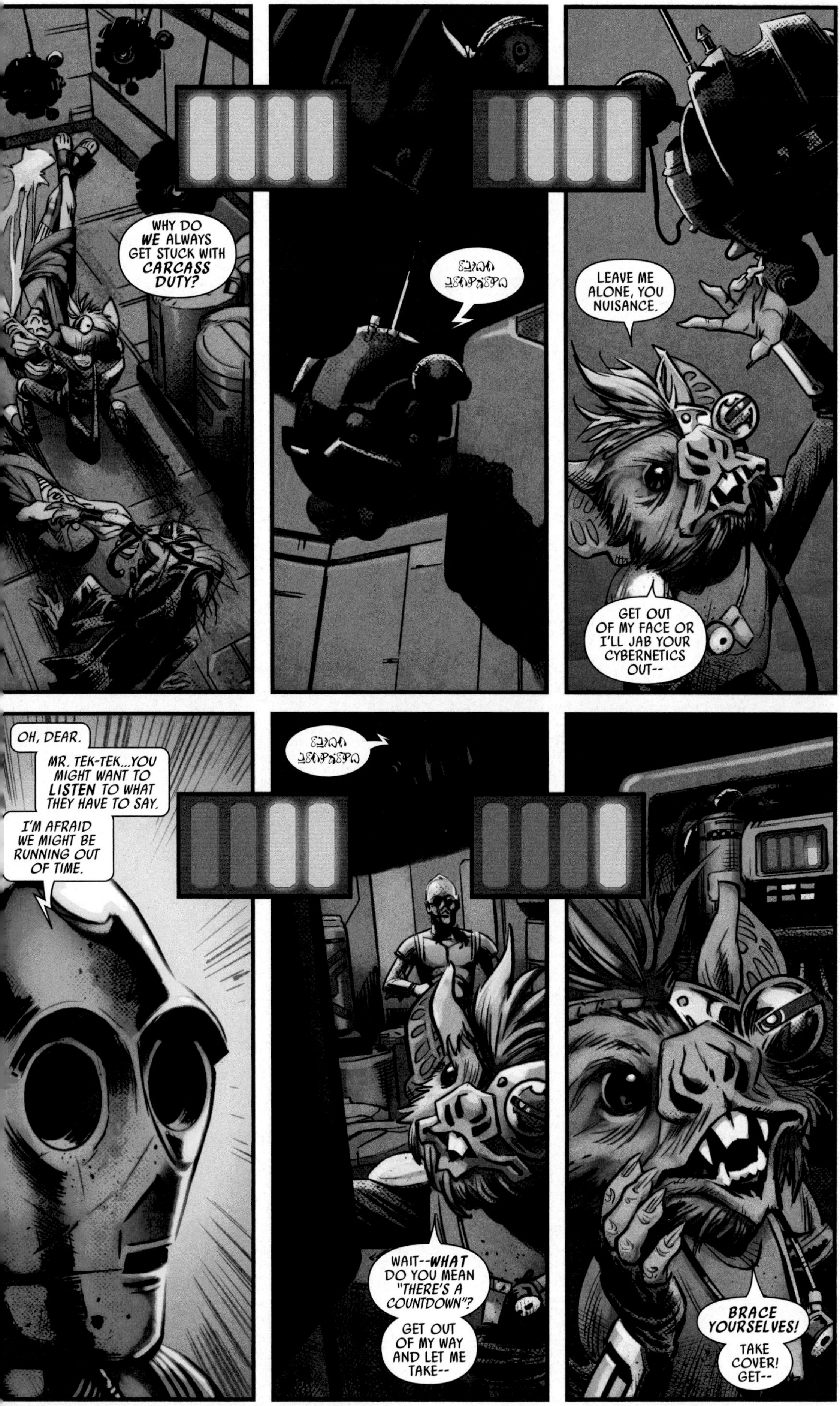

WHY DO WE ALWAYS GET STUCK WITH CARCASS DUTY?
LEAVE ME ALONE, YOU NUISANCE.
GET OUT OF MY FACE OR I'LL JAB YOUR CYBERNETICS OUT--
OH, DEAR.
MR. TEK-TEK...YOU MIGHT WANT TO LISTEN TO WHAT THEY HAVE TO SAY.
I'M AFRAID WE MIGHT BE RUNNING OUT OF TIME.
WAIT--WHAT DO YOU MEAN "THERE'S A COUNTDOWN"?
GET OUT OF MY WAY AND LET ME TAKE--
BRACE YOURSELVES!
TAKE COVER! GET--

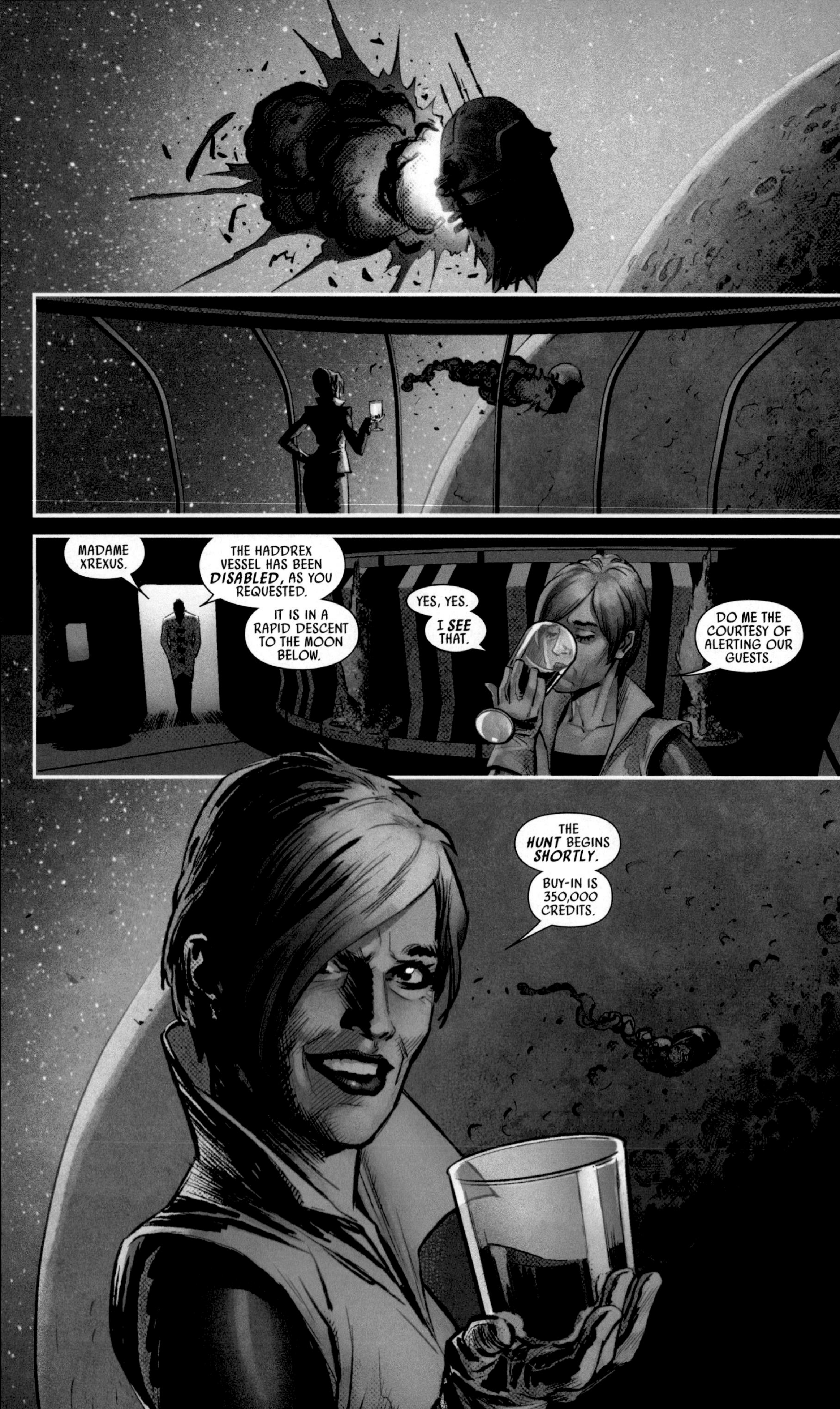
MADAME XREXUS.
THE HADDREX VESSEL HAS BEEN DISABLED, AS YOU REQUESTED.
IT IS IN A RAPID DESCENT TO THE MOON BELOW.
YES, YES.
I SEE THAT.
DO ME THE COURTESY OF ALERTING OUR GUESTS.
THE HUNT BEGINS SHORTLY.
BUY-IN IS 350,000 CREDITS.

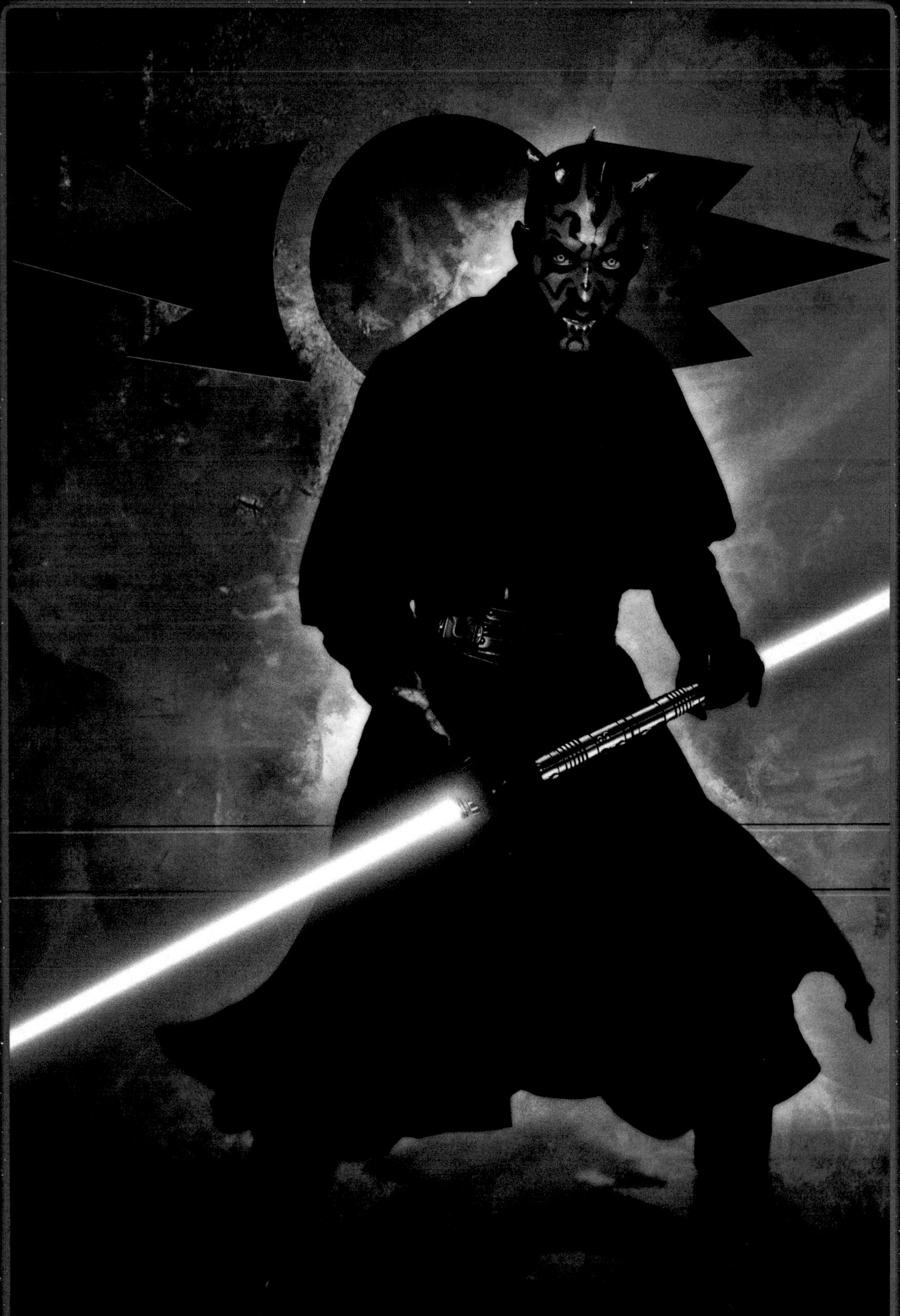

STAR WARS: DARTH MAUL 1
MOVIE VARIANT

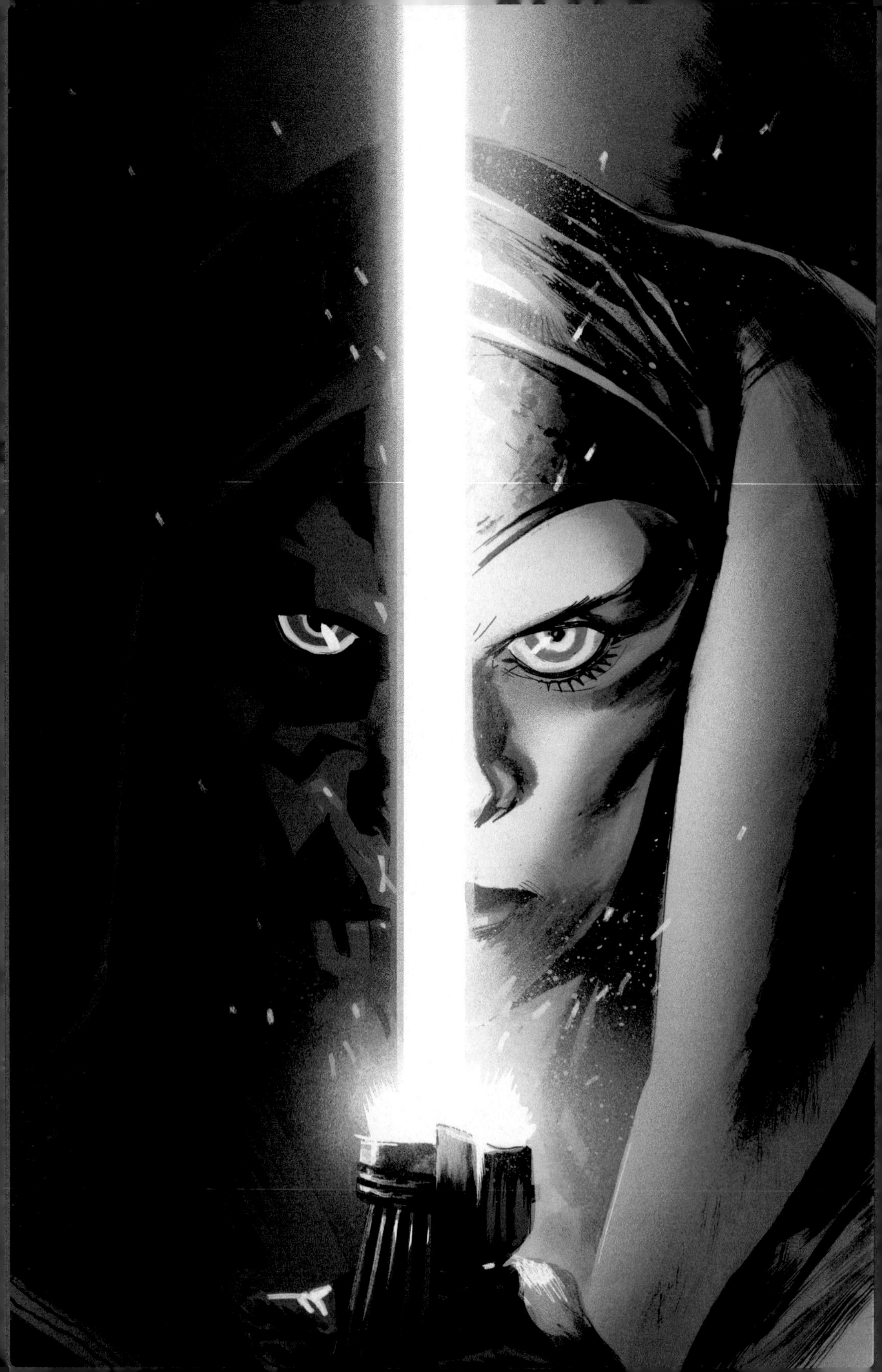

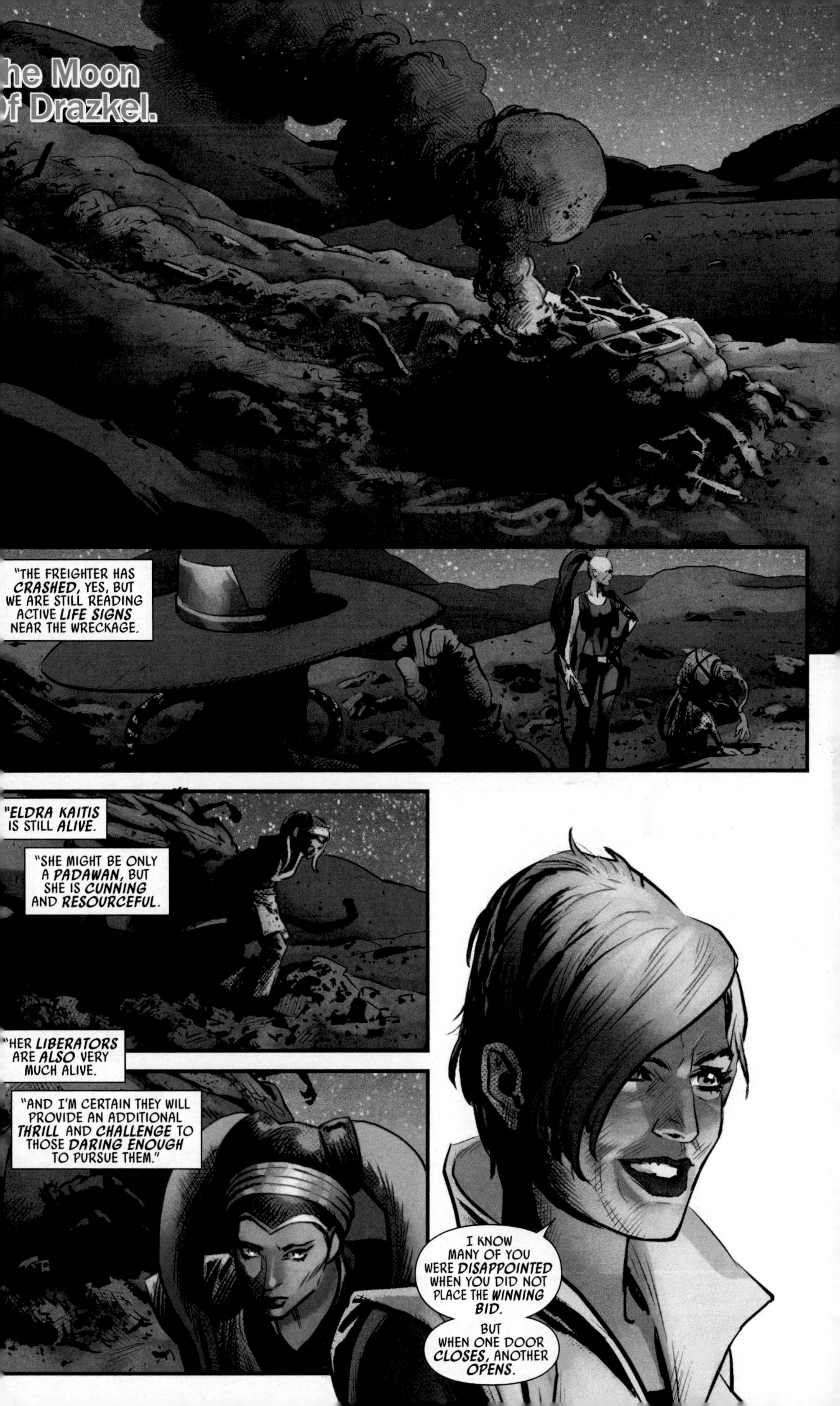

he Moon
Of Drazkel.
"THE FREIGHTER HAS CRASHED, YES, BUT WE ARE STILL READING ACTIVE LIFE SIGNS NEAR THE WRECKAGE.
"ELDRA KAITIS IS STILL ALIVE.
"SHE MIGHT BE ONLY A PADAWAN, BUT SHE IS CUNNING AND RESOURCEFUL.
"HER LIBERATORS ARE ALSO VERY MUCH ALIVE.
"AND I'M CERTAIN THEY WILL PROVIDE AN ADDITIONAL THRILL AND CHALLENGE TO THOSE DARING ENOUGH TO PURSUE THEM."
I KNOW MANY OF YOU WERE DISAPPOINTED WHEN YOU DID NOT PLACE THE WINNING BID.
BUT WHEN ONE DOOR CLOSES, ANOTHER OPENS.

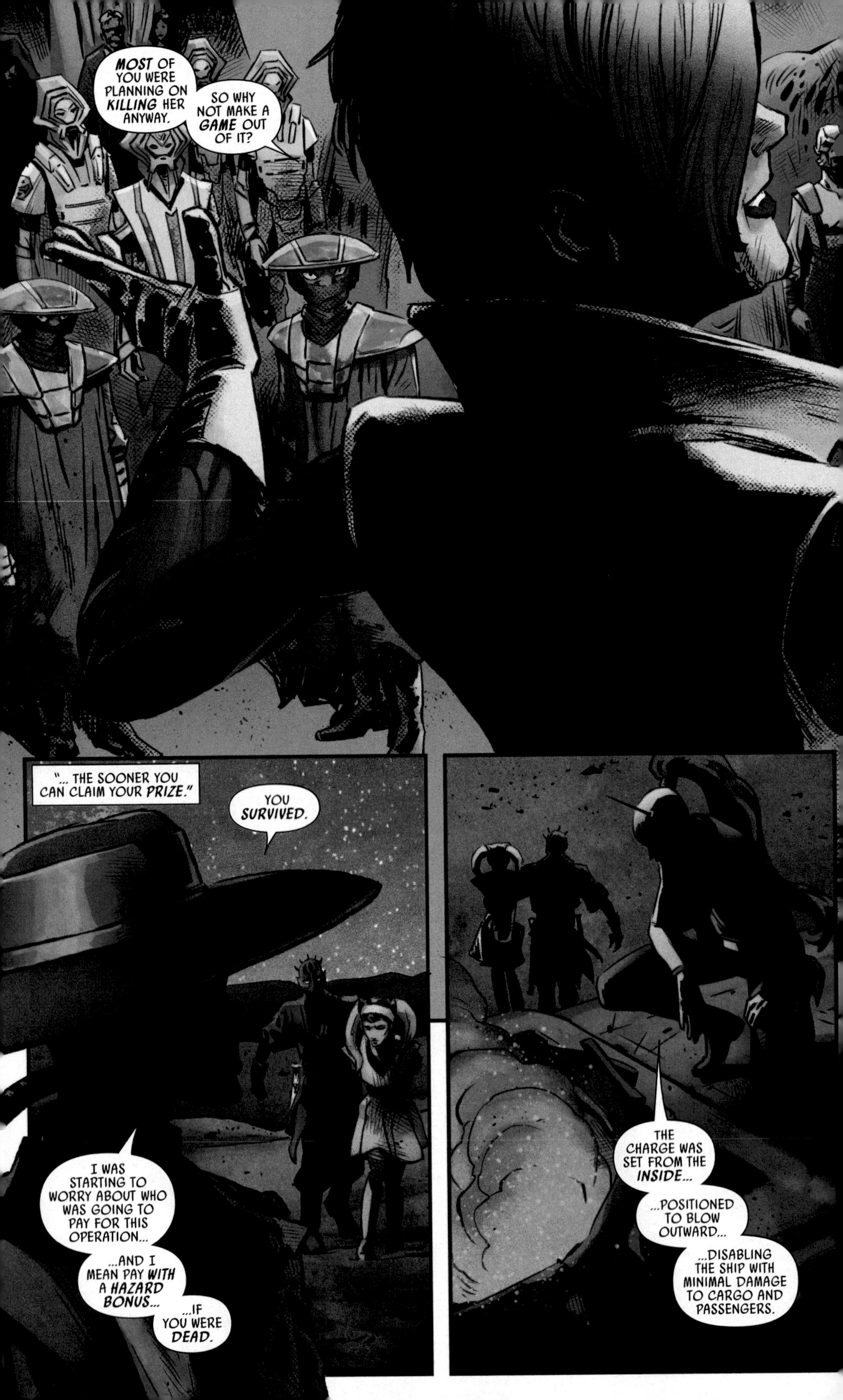
MOST OF YOU WERE PLANNING ON KILLING HER ANYWAY.
SO WHY NOT MAKE A GAME OUT OF IT?
"... THE SOONER YOU CAN CLAIM YOUR PRIZE."
YOU SURVIVED.
I WAS STARTING TO WORRY ABOUT WHO WAS GOING TO PAY FOR THIS OPERATION...
...AND I MEAN PAY WITH A HAZARD BONUS...
...IF YOU WERE DEAD.
THE CHARGE WAS SET FROM THE INSIDE...
...POSITIONED TO BLOW OUTWARD...
...DISABLING THE SHIP WITH MINIMAL DAMAGE TO CARGO AND PASSENGERS.

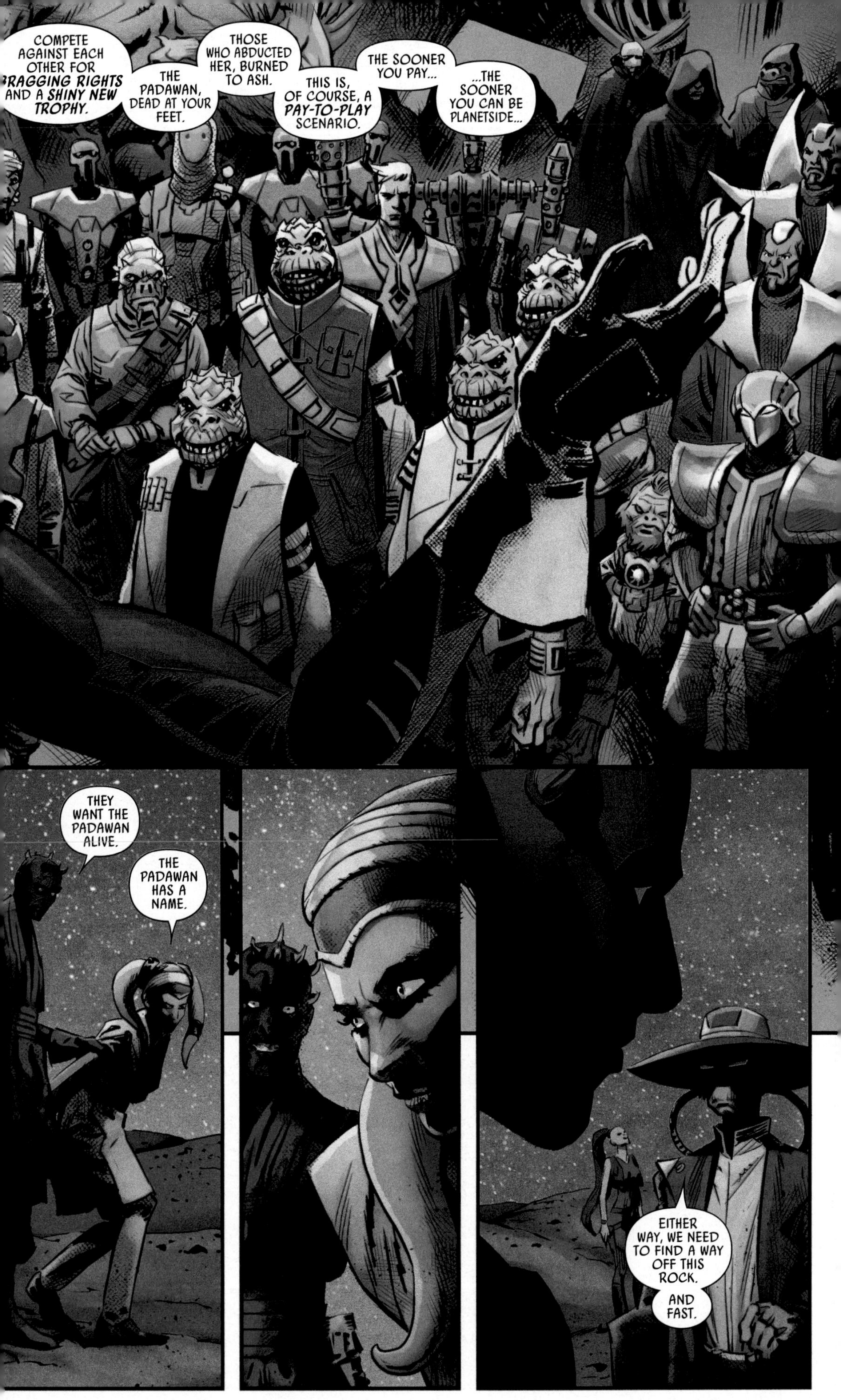
COMPETE AGAINST EACH OTHER FOR BRAGGING RIGHTS AND A SHINY NEW TROPHY.
THE PADAWAN, DEAD AT YOUR FEET.
THOSE WHO ABDUCTED HER, BURNED TO ASH.
THIS IS, OF COURSE, A PAY-TO-PLAY SCENARIO.
THE SOONER YOU PAY...
...THE SOONER YOU CAN BE PLANETSIDE...
THEY WANT THE PADAWAN ALIVE.
THE PADAWAN HAS A NAME.
EITHER WAY, WE NEED TO FIND A WAY OFF THIS ROCK.
AND FAST.

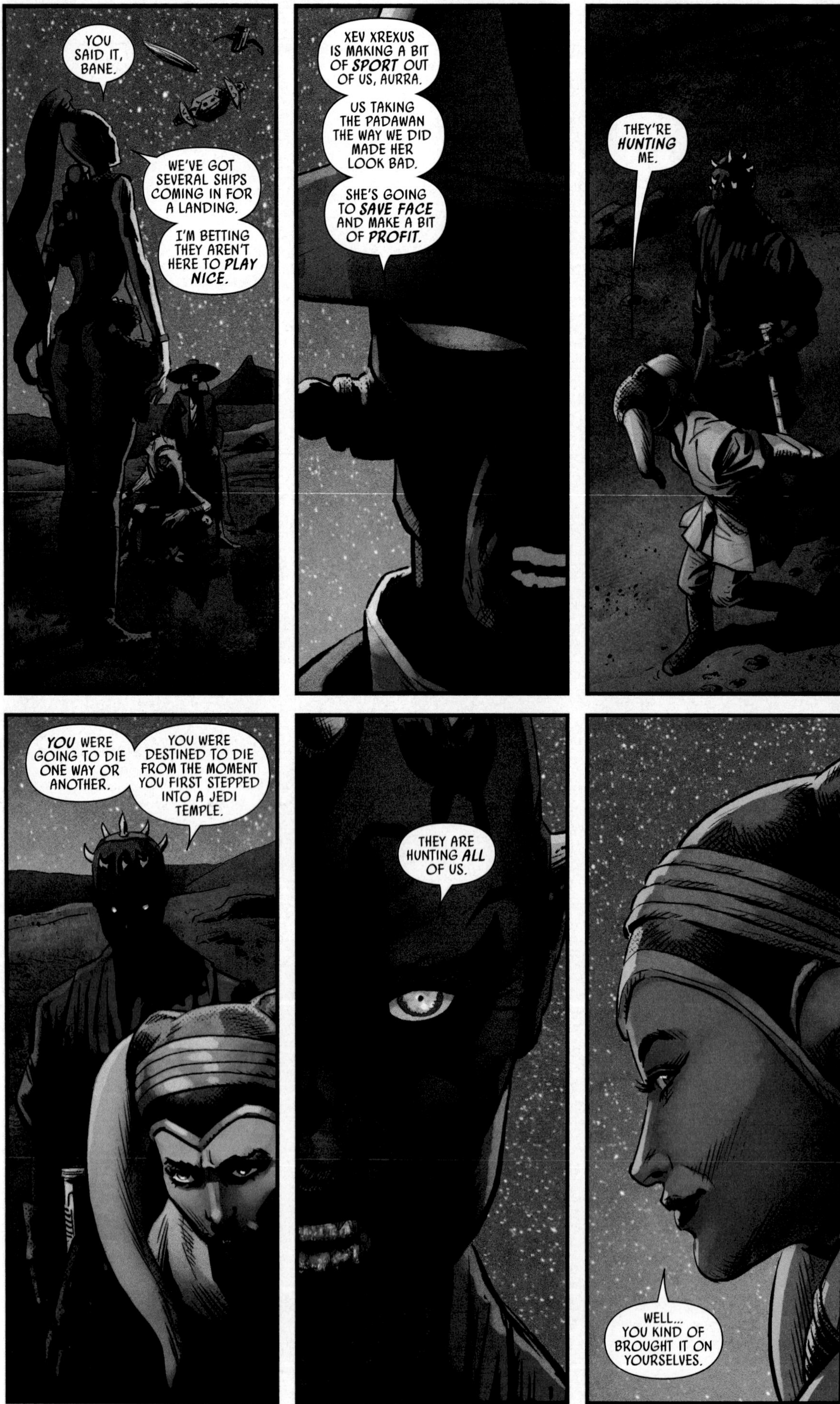
YOU SAID IT, BANE.
WE'VE GOT SEVERAL SHIPS COMING IN FOR A LANDING.
I'M BETTING THEY AREN'T HERE TO PLAY NICE.
XEV XREXUS IS MAKING A BIT OF SPORT OUT OF US, AURRA.
US TAKING THE PADAWAN THE WAY WE DID MADE HER LOOK BAD.
SHE'S GOING TO SAVE FACE AND MAKE A BIT OF PROFIT.
THEY'RE HUNTING ME.
YOU WERE GOING TO DIE ONE WAY OR ANOTHER.
YOU WERE DESTINED TO DIE FROM THE MOMENT YOU FIRST STEPPED INTO A JEDI TEMPLE.
THEY ARE HUNTING ALL OF US.
WELL... YOU KIND OF BROUGHT IT ON YOURSELVES.

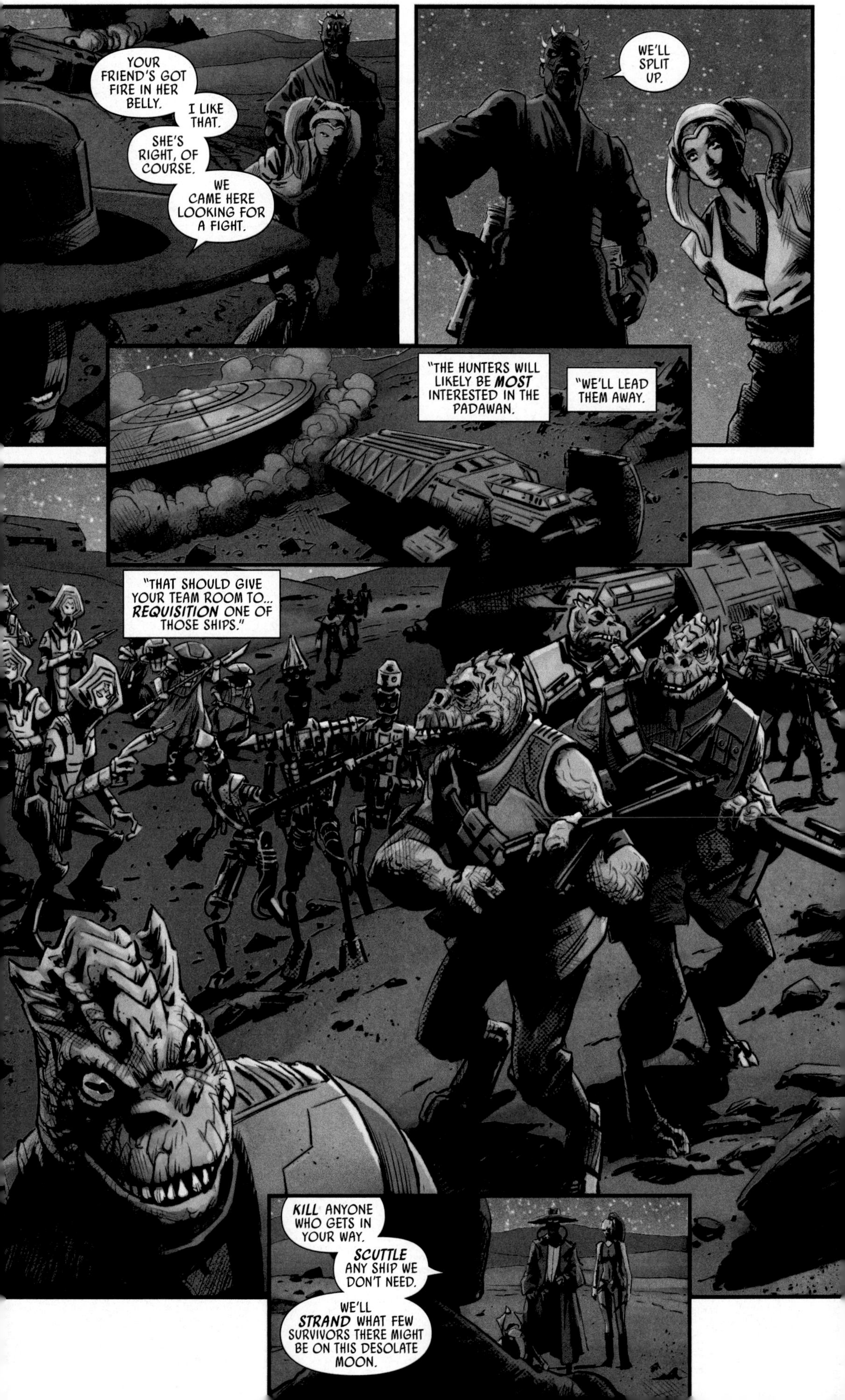
YOUR FRIEND'S GOT FIRE IN HER BELLY.
I LIKE THAT.
SHE'S RIGHT, OF COURSE.
WE CAME HERE LOOKING FOR A FIGHT.
WE'LL SPLIT UP.
"THE HUNTERS WILL LIKELY BE MOST INTERESTED IN THE PADAWAN.
"WE'LL LEAD THEM AWAY.
"THAT SHOULD GIVE YOUR TEAM ROOM TO... REQUISITION ONE OF THOSE SHIPS."
KILL ANYONE WHO GETS IN YOUR WAY.
SCUTTLE ANY SHIP WE DON'T NEED.
WE'LL STRAND WHAT FEW SURVIVORS THERE MIGHT BE ON THIS DESOLATE MOON.

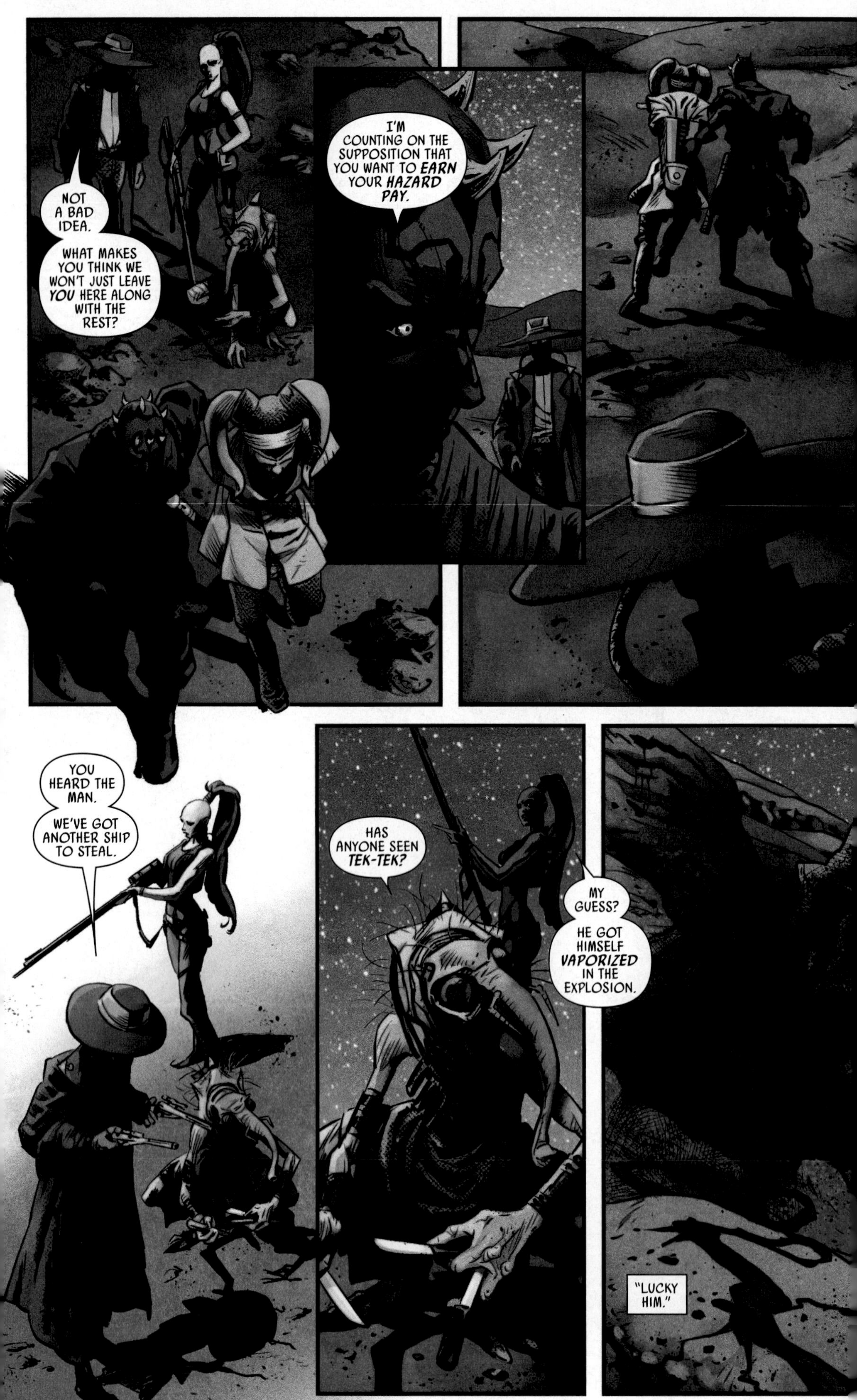
NOT A BAD IDEA.
WHAT MAKES YOU THINK WE WON'T JUST LEAVE YOU HERE ALONG WITH THE REST?
I'M COUNTING ON THE SUPPOSITION THAT YOU WANT TO EARN YOUR HAZARD PAY.
YOU HEARD THE MAN.
WE'VE GOT ANOTHER SHIP TO STEAL.
HAS ANYONE SEEN TEK-TEK?
MY GUESS?
HE GOT HIMSELF VAPORIZED IN THE EXPLOSION.
"LUCKY HIM."

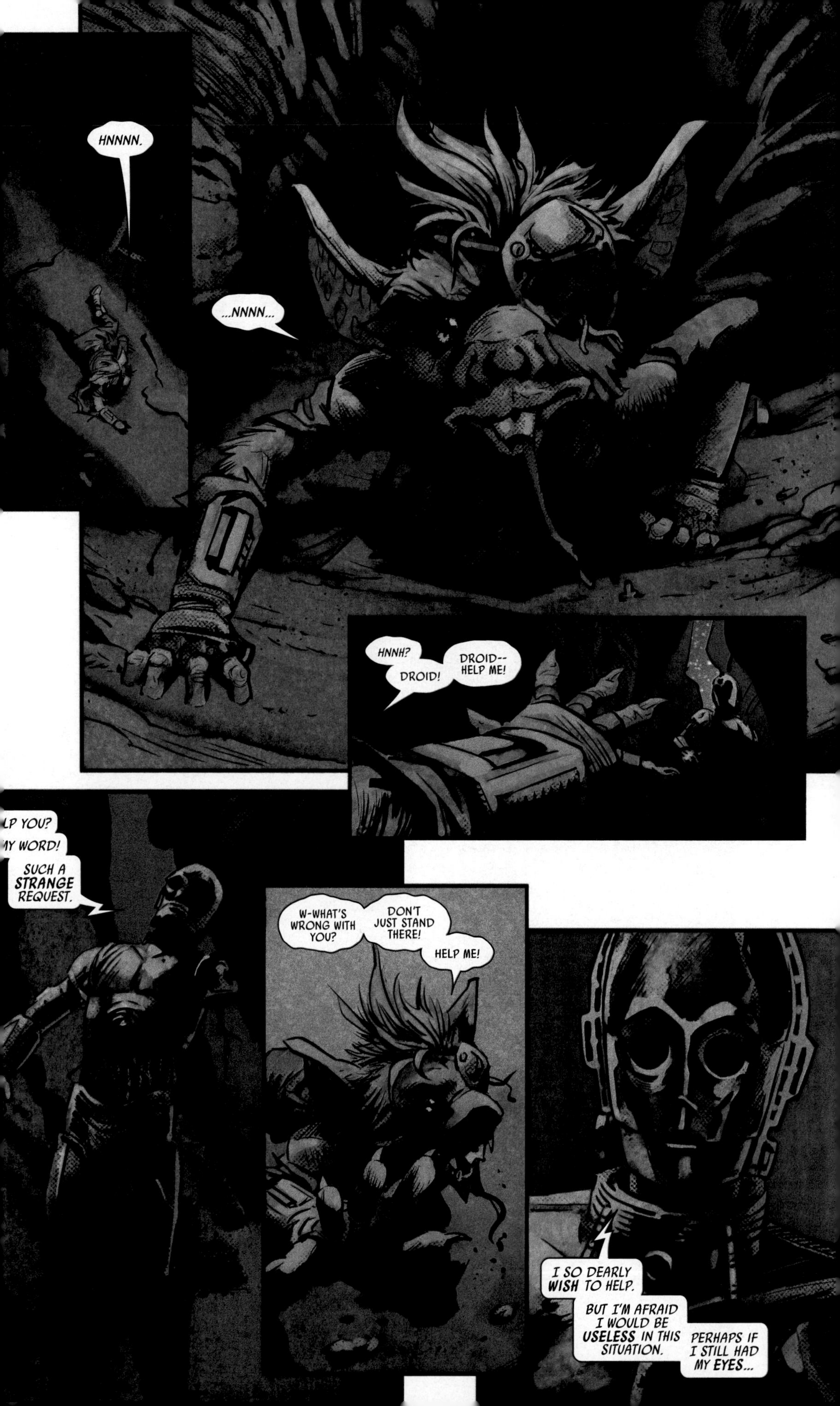
HNNNN.
...NNNN...
HNNH?
DROID!
DROID-- HELP ME!
LP YOU?
MY WORD!
SUCH A STRANGE REQUEST.
W-WHAT'S WRONG WITH YOU?
DON'T JUST STAND THERE!
HELP ME!
I SO DEARLY WISH TO HELP.
BUT I'M AFRAID I WOULD BE USELESS IN THIS SITUATION.
PERHAPS IF I STILL HAD MY EYES...

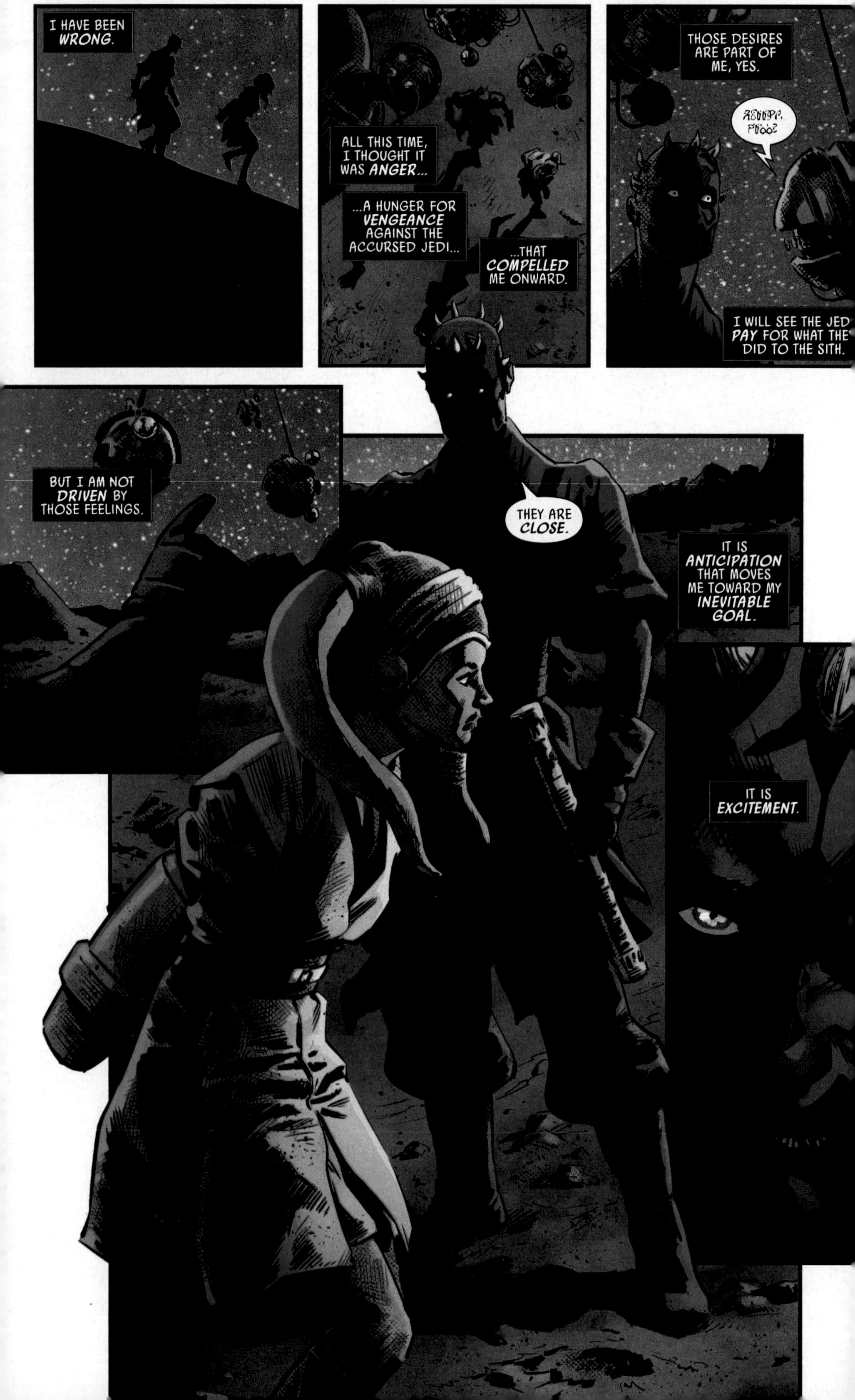
I HAVE BEEN WRONG.
ALL THIS TIME, I THOUGHT IT WAS ANGER...
...A HUNGER FOR VENGEANCE AGAINST THE ACCURSED JEDI...
...THAT COMPELLED ME ONWARD.
THOSE DESIRES ARE PART OF ME, YES.
I WILL SEE THE JED PAY FOR WHAT THE DID TO THE SITH.
BUT I AM NOT DRIVEN BY THOSE FEELINGS.
THEY ARE CLOSE.
IT IS ANTICIPATION THAT MOVES ME TOWARD MY INEVITABLE GOAL.
IT IS EXCITEMENT.

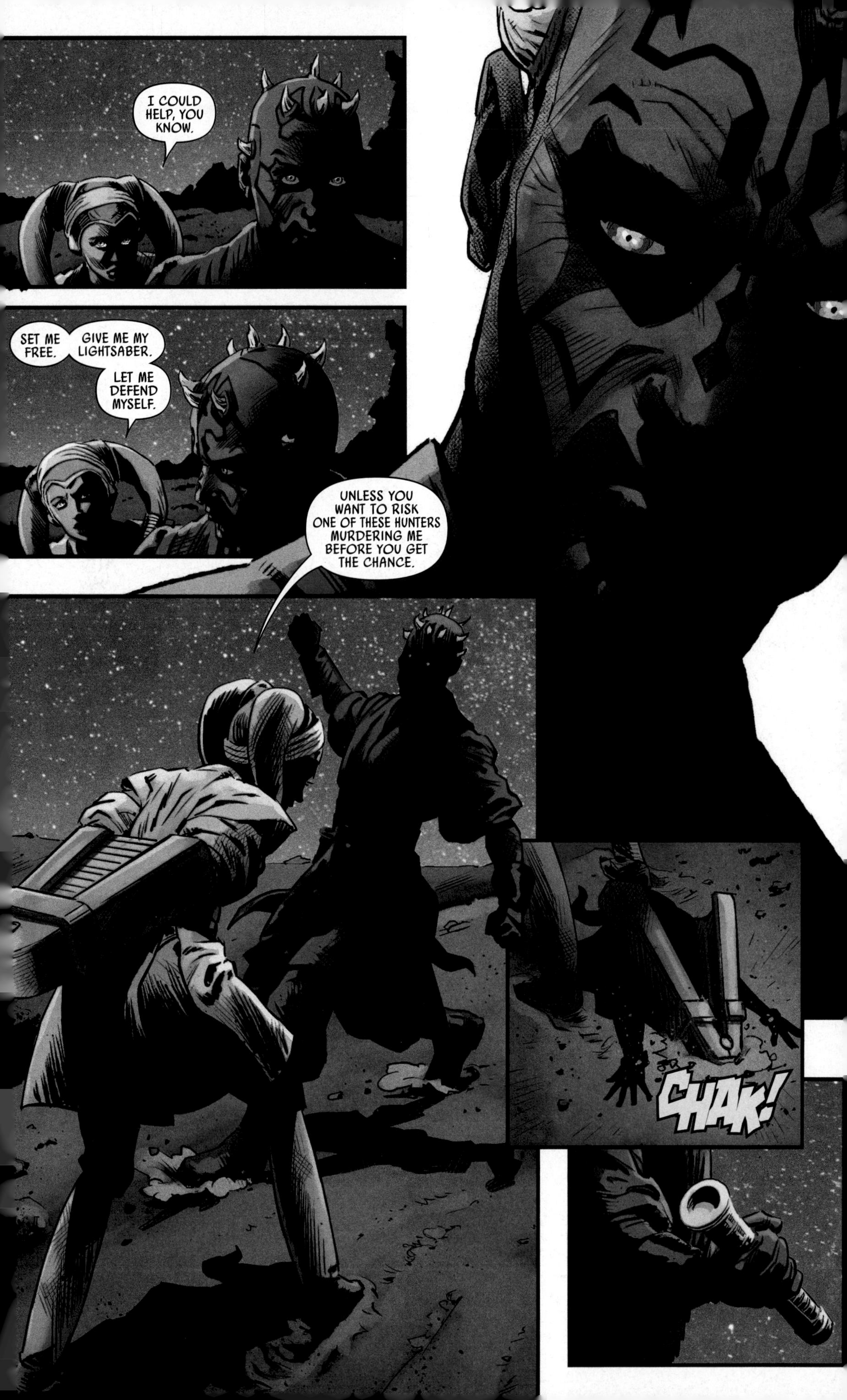

I COULD HELP, YOU KNOW.
SET ME FREE.
GIVE ME MY LIGHTSABER.
LET ME DEFEND MYSELF.
UNLESS YOU WANT TO RISK ONE OF THESE HUNTERS MURDERING ME BEFORE YOU GET THE CHANCE.
CHAK!

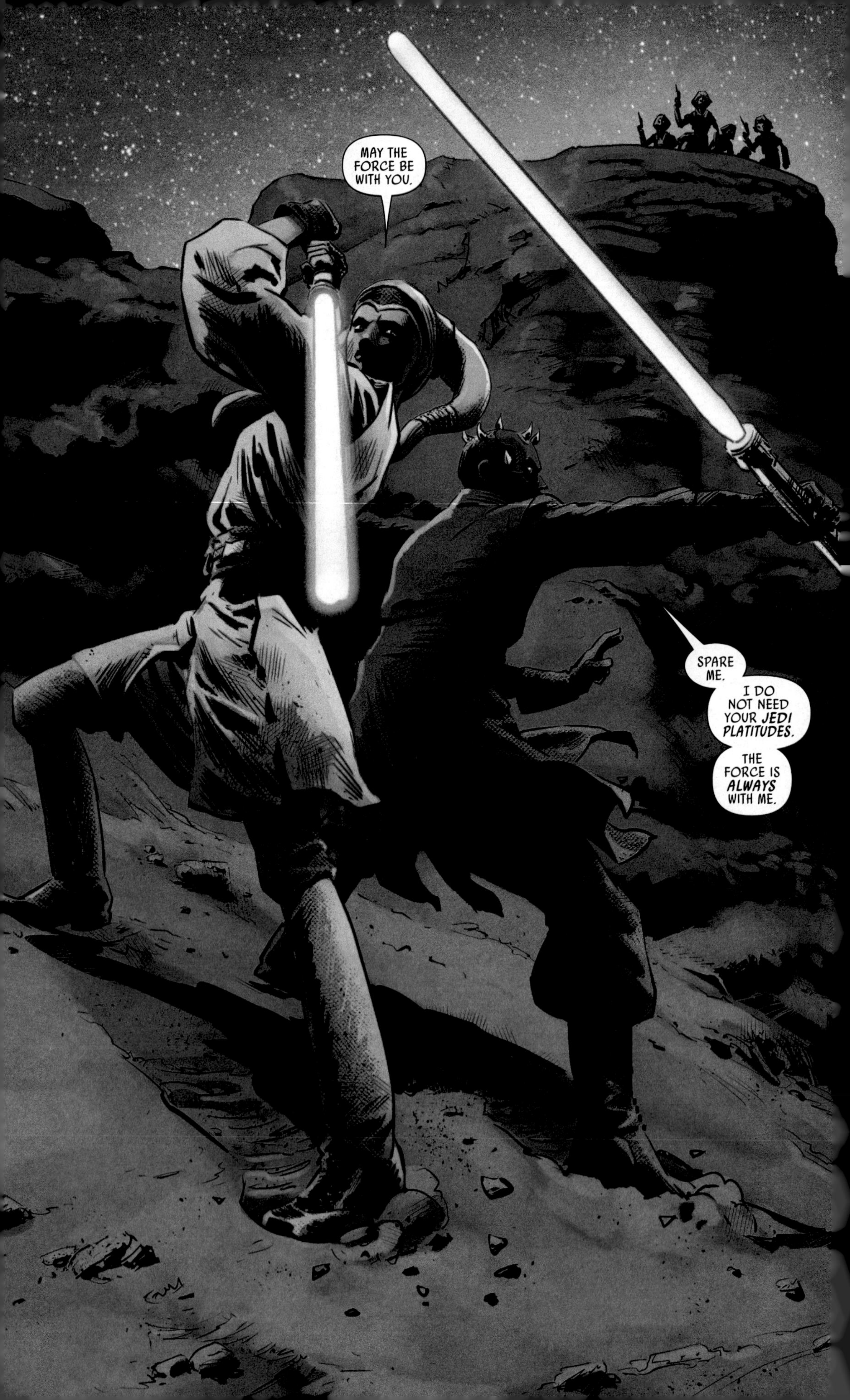
MAY THE FORCE BE WITH YOU.
SPARE ME.
I DO NOT NEED YOUR *JEDI PLATITUDES.*
THE FORCE IS *ALWAYS* WITH ME.

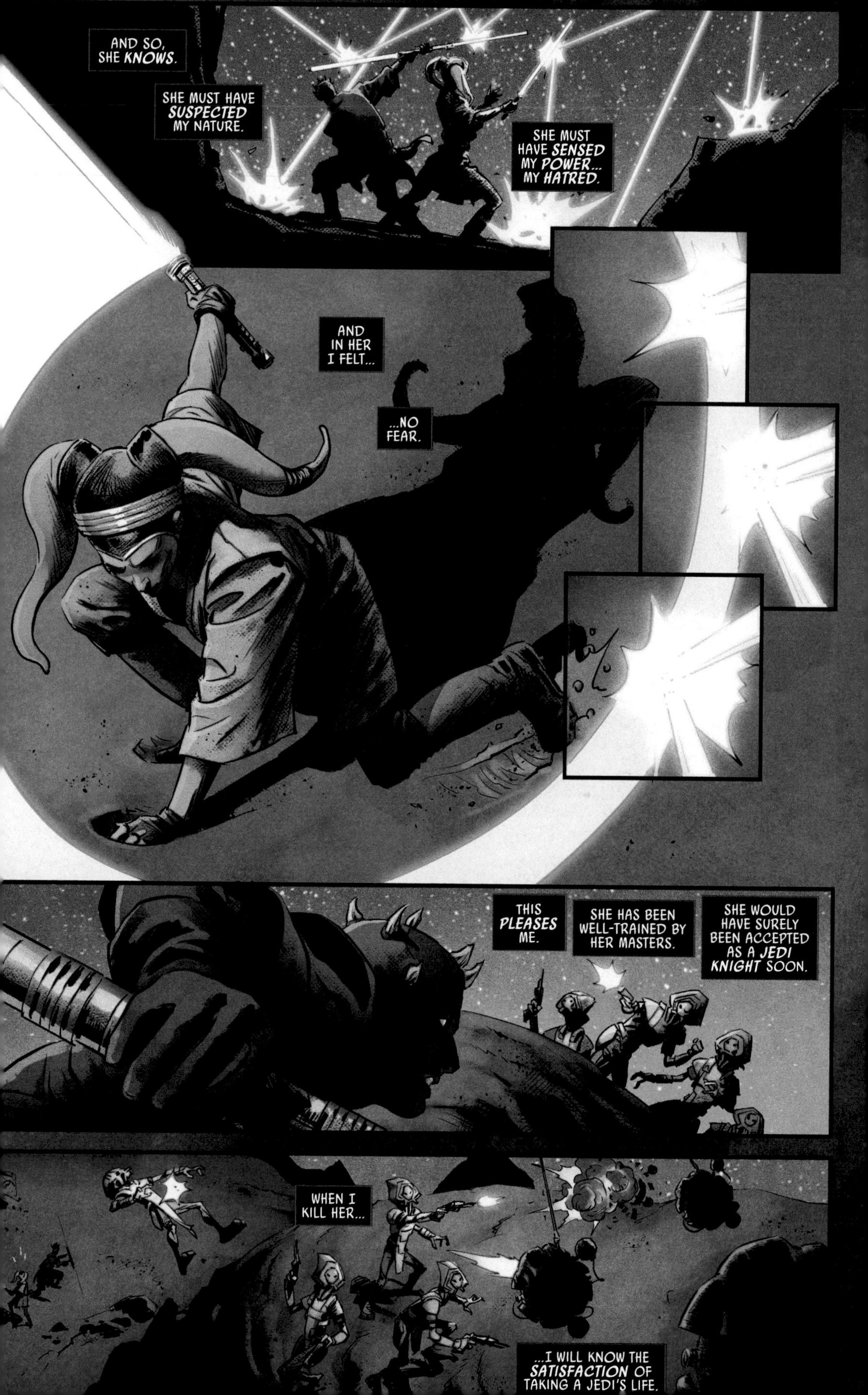
AND SO, SHE KNOWS.
SHE MUST HAVE SUSPECTED MY NATURE.
SHE MUST HAVE SENSED MY POWER... MY HATRED.
AND IN HER I FELT...
...NO FEAR.
THIS PLEASES ME.
SHE HAS BEEN WELL-TRAINED BY HER MASTERS.
SHE WOULD HAVE SURELY BEEN ACCEPTED AS A JEDI KNIGHT SOON.
WHEN I KILL HER...
...I WILL KNOW THE SATISFACTION OF TAKING A JEDI'S LIFE.

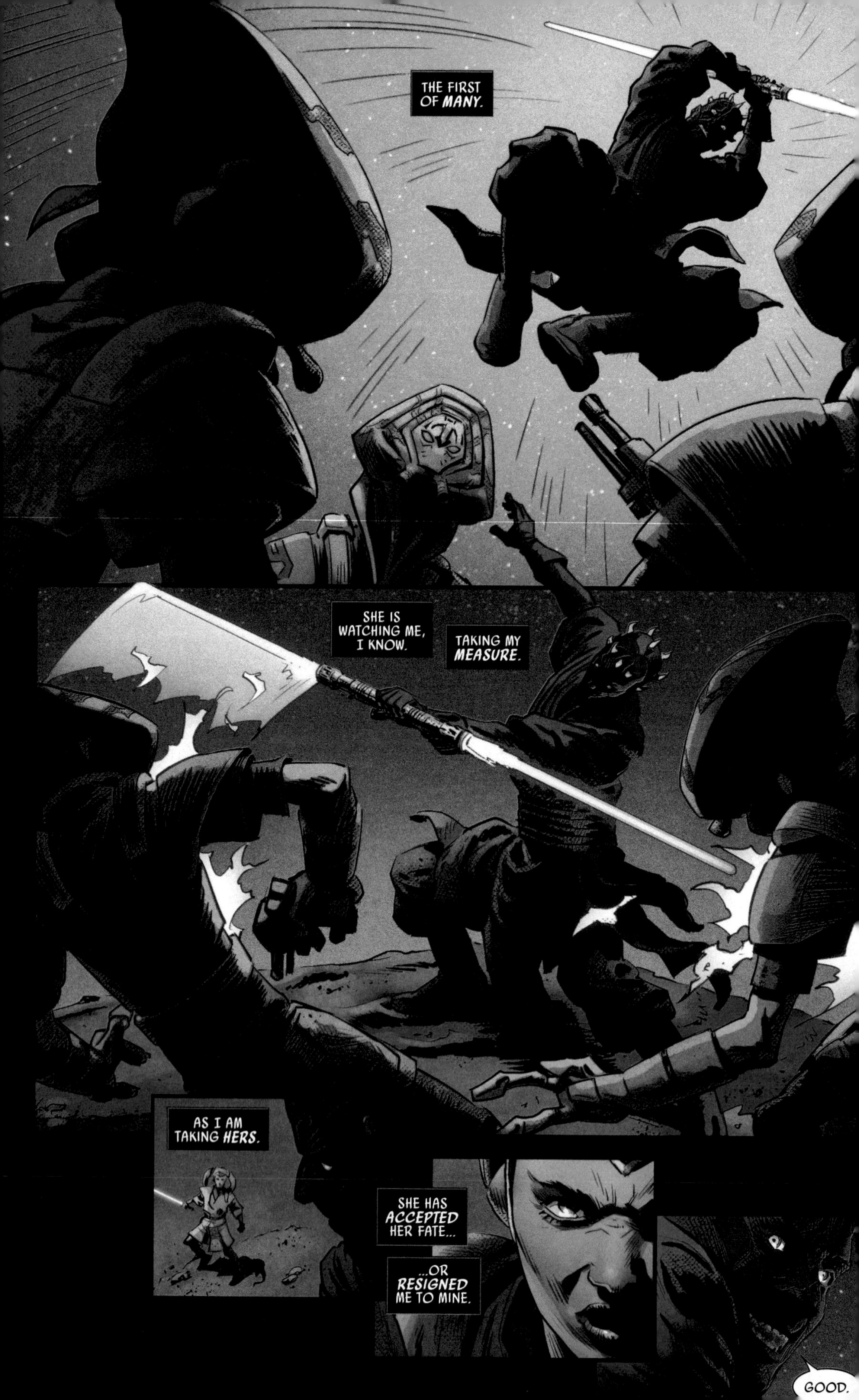
THE FIRST OF MANY.
SHE IS WATCHING ME, I KNOW.
TAKING MY MEASURE.
AS I AM TAKING HERS.
SHE HAS ACCEPTED HER FATE...
...OR RESIGNED ME TO MINE.
GOOD.

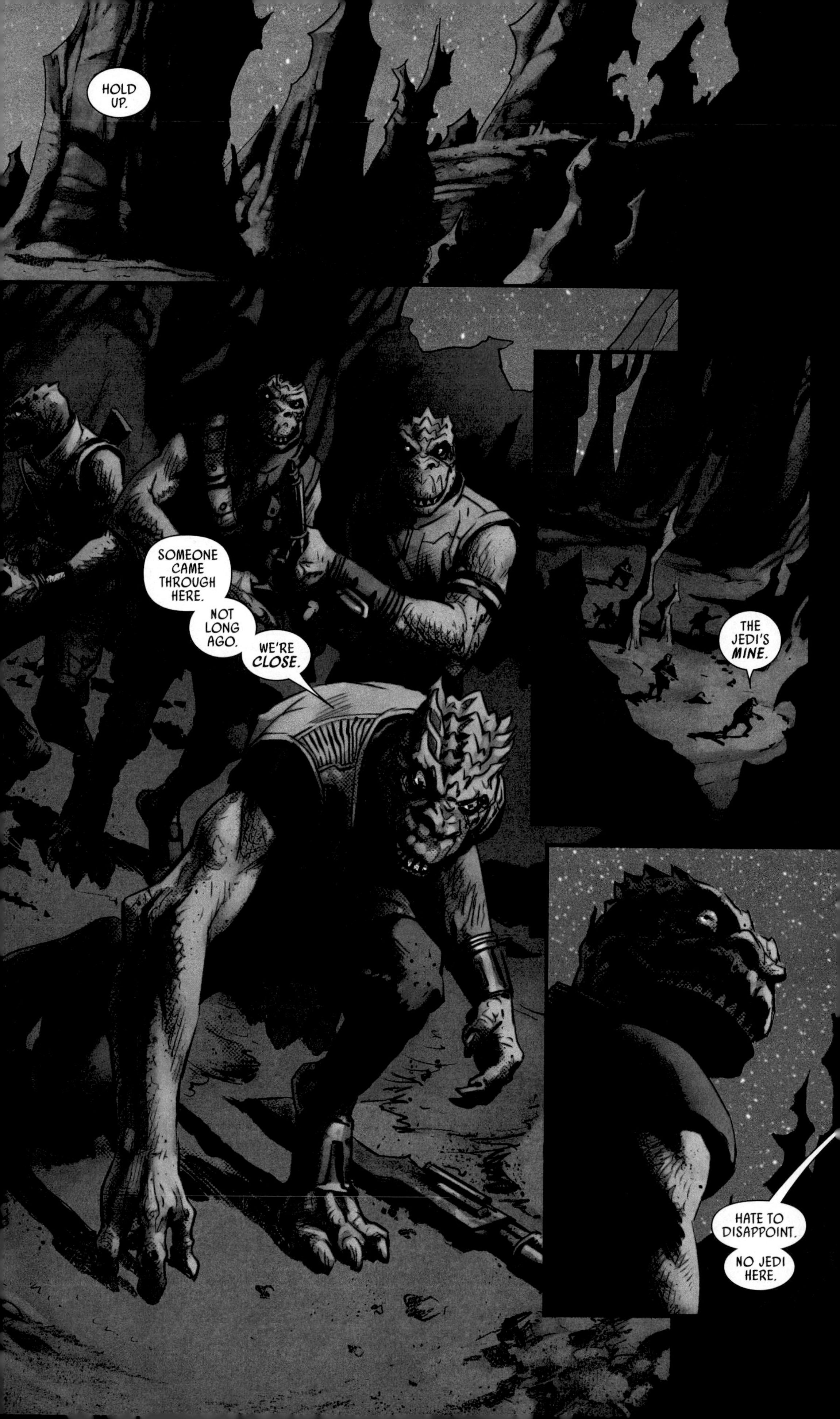
HOLD UP.
SOMEONE CAME THROUGH HERE.
NOT LONG AGO.
WE'RE *CLOSE.*
THE JEDI'S *MINE.*
HATE TO DISAPPOINT.
NO JEDI HERE.

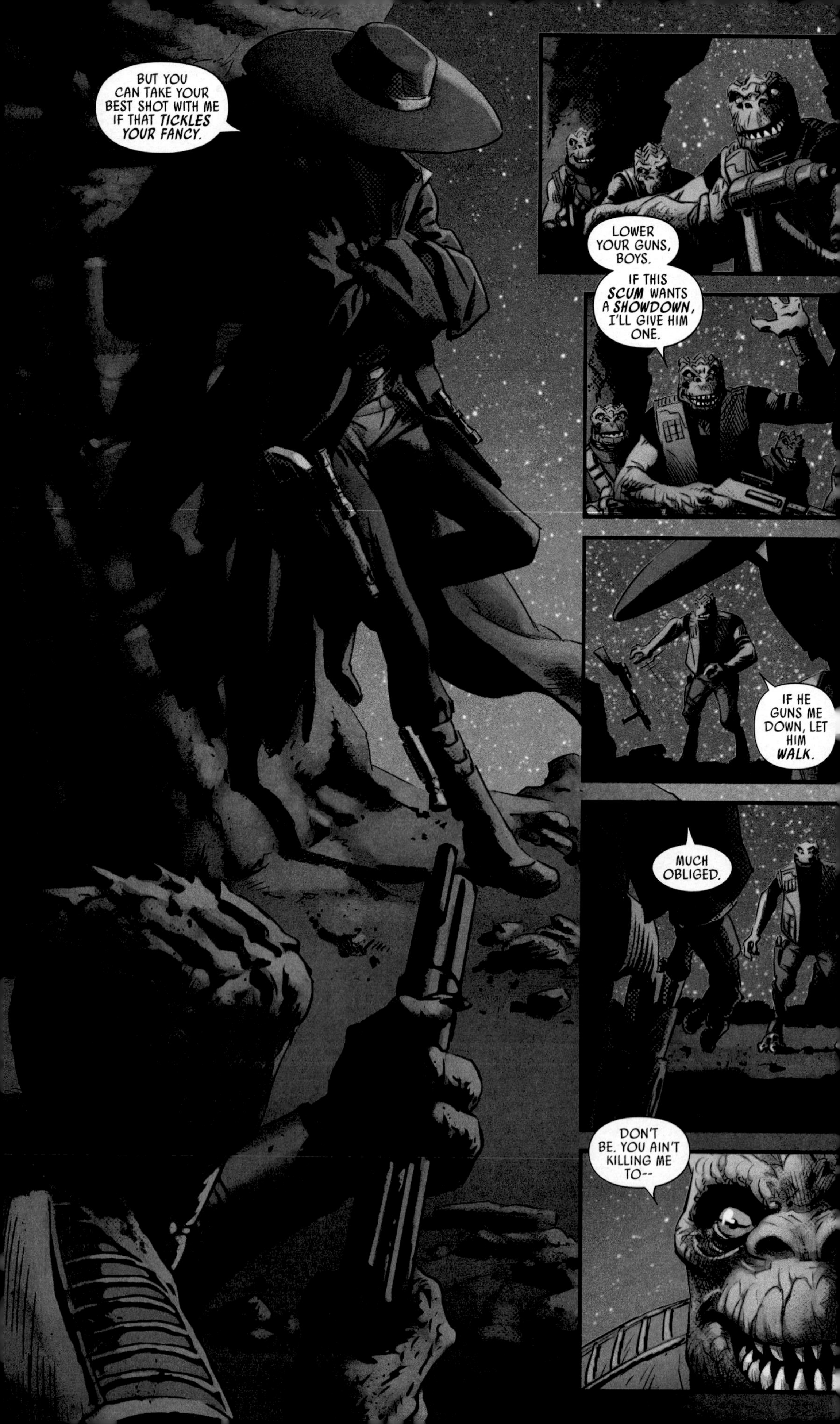
BUT YOU CAN TAKE YOUR BEST SHOT WITH ME IF THAT *TICKLES YOUR FANCY.*
LOWER YOUR GUNS, BOYS.
IF THIS ***SCUM*** WANTS A ***SHOWDOWN***, I'LL GIVE HIM ONE.
IF HE GUNS ME DOWN, LET HIM ***WALK.***
MUCH OBLIGED.
DON'T BE. YOU AIN'T KILLING ME TO--

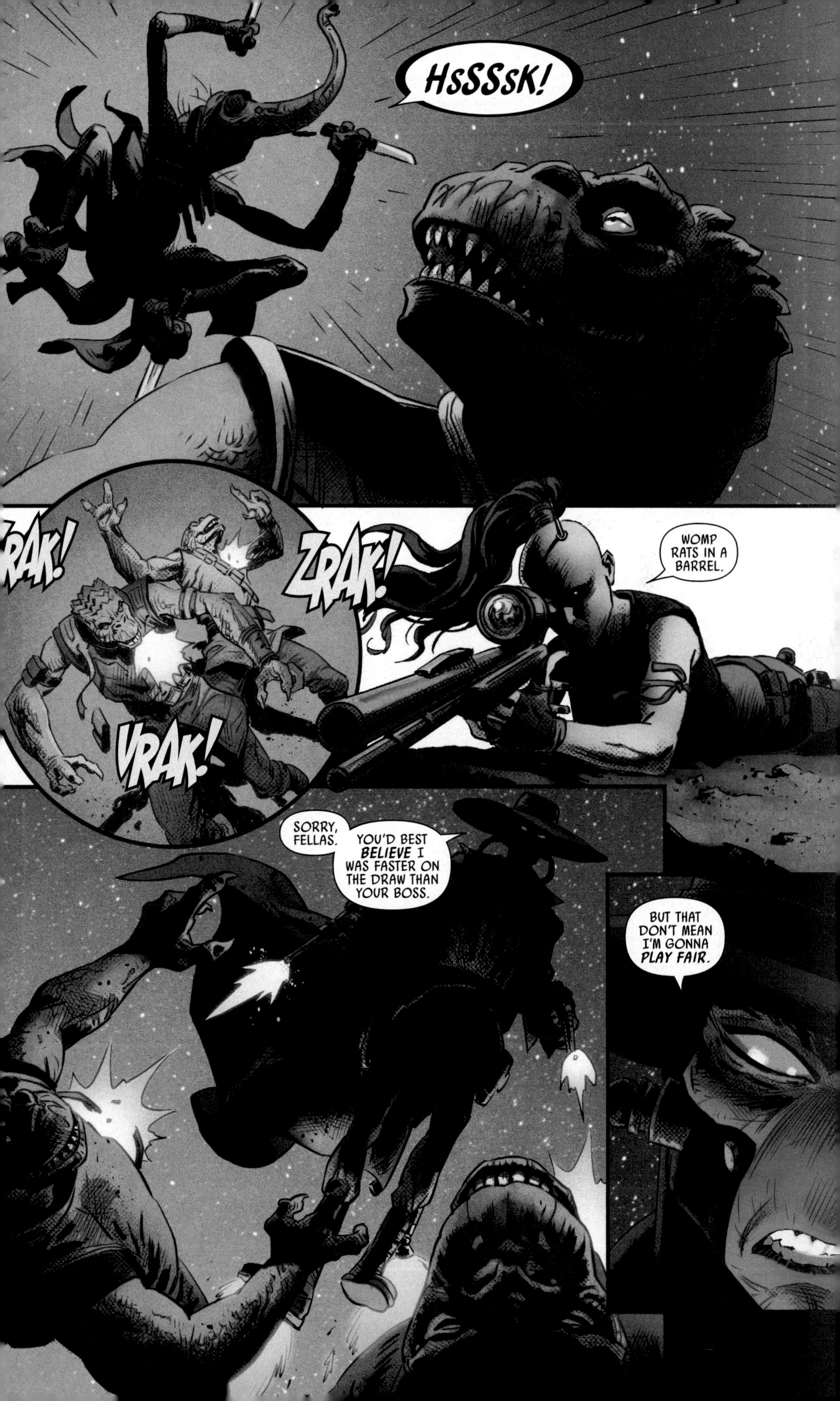
HsSSsK!
RAK!
ZRAK!
VRAK!
WOMP RATS IN A BARREL.
SORRY, FELLAS.
YOU'D BEST BELIEVE I WAS FASTER ON THE DRAW THAN YOUR BOSS.
BUT THAT DON'T MEAN I'M GONNA PLAY FAIR.

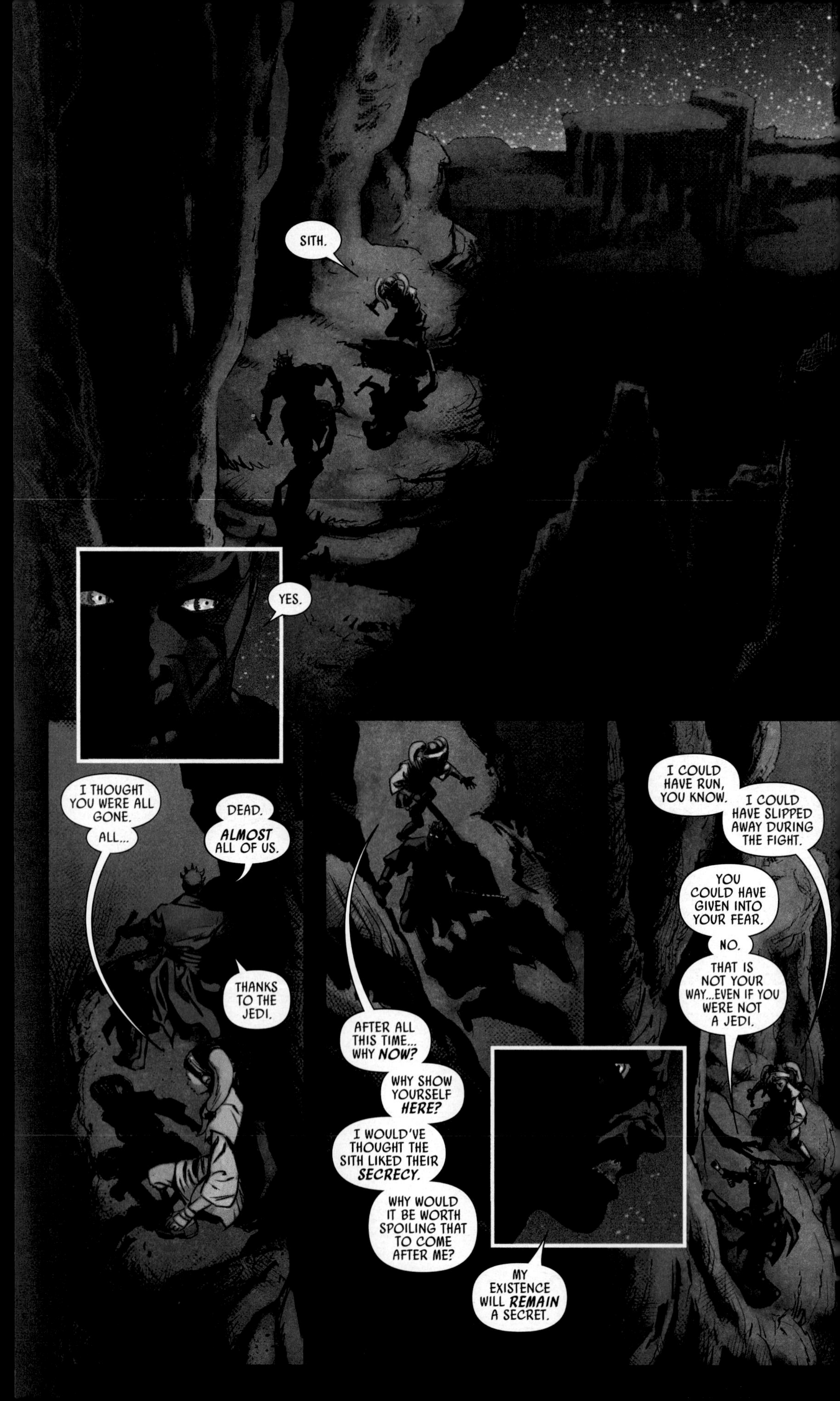
SITH.
YES.
I THOUGHT YOU WERE ALL GONE.
ALL...
DEAD.
ALMOST ALL OF US.
THANKS TO THE JEDI.
AFTER ALL THIS TIME... WHY *NOW?*
WHY SHOW YOURSELF *HERE?*
I WOULD'VE THOUGHT THE SITH LIKED THEIR *SECRECY.*
WHY WOULD IT BE WORTH SPOILING THAT TO COME AFTER ME?
MY EXISTENCE WILL *REMAIN* A SECRET.
I COULD HAVE RUN, YOU KNOW.
I COULD HAVE SLIPPED AWAY DURING THE FIGHT.
YOU COULD HAVE GIVEN INTO YOUR FEAR.
NO.
THAT IS NOT YOUR WAY...EVEN IF YOU WERE NOT A JEDI.

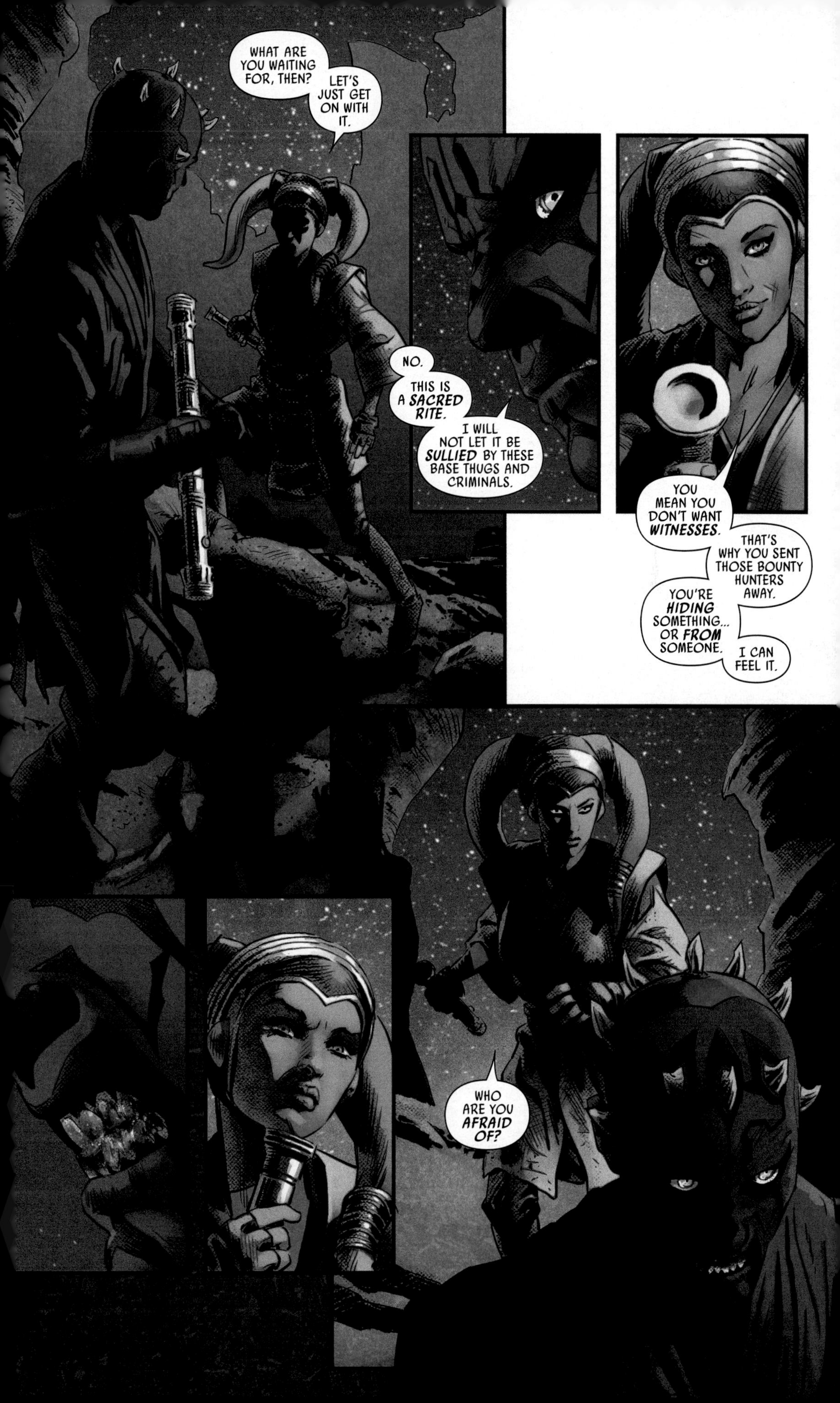
WHAT ARE YOU WAITING FOR, THEN?
LET'S JUST GET ON WITH IT.
NO.
THIS IS A SACRED RITE.
I WILL NOT LET IT BE SULLIED BY THESE BASE THUGS AND CRIMINALS.
YOU MEAN YOU DON'T WANT WITNESSES.
THAT'S WHY YOU SENT THOSE BOUNTY HUNTERS AWAY.
YOU'RE HIDING SOMETHING... OR FROM SOMEONE.
I CAN FEEL IT.
WHO ARE YOU AFRAID OF?

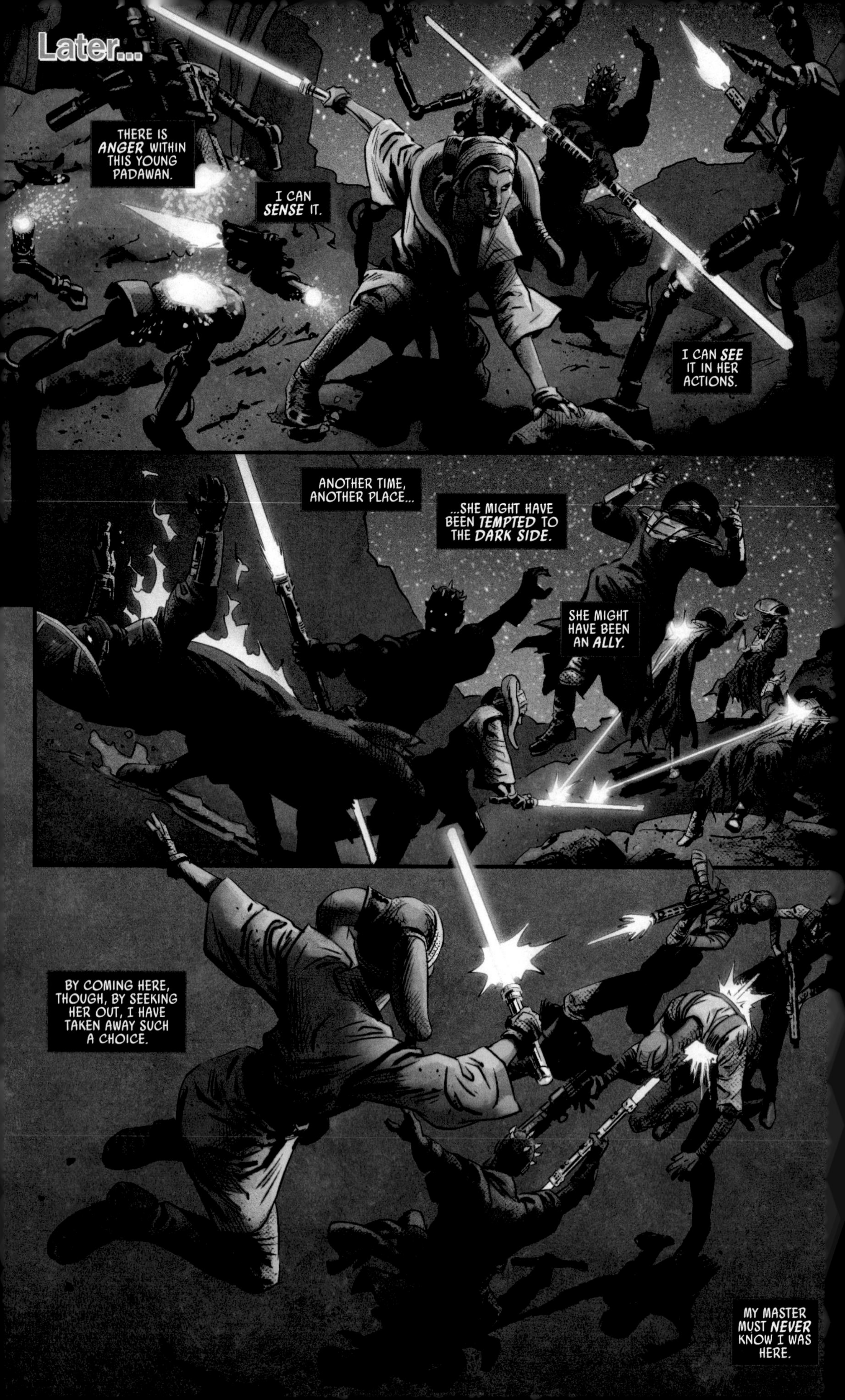
Later...
THERE IS ANGER WITHIN THIS YOUNG PADAWAN.
I CAN SENSE IT.
I CAN SEE IT IN HER ACTIONS.
ANOTHER TIME, ANOTHER PLACE...
...SHE MIGHT HAVE BEEN TEMPTED TO THE DARK SIDE.
SHE MIGHT HAVE BEEN AN ALLY.
BY COMING HERE, THOUGH, BY SEEKING HER OUT, I HAVE TAKEN AWAY SUCH A CHOICE.
MY MASTER MUST NEVER KNOW I WAS HERE.

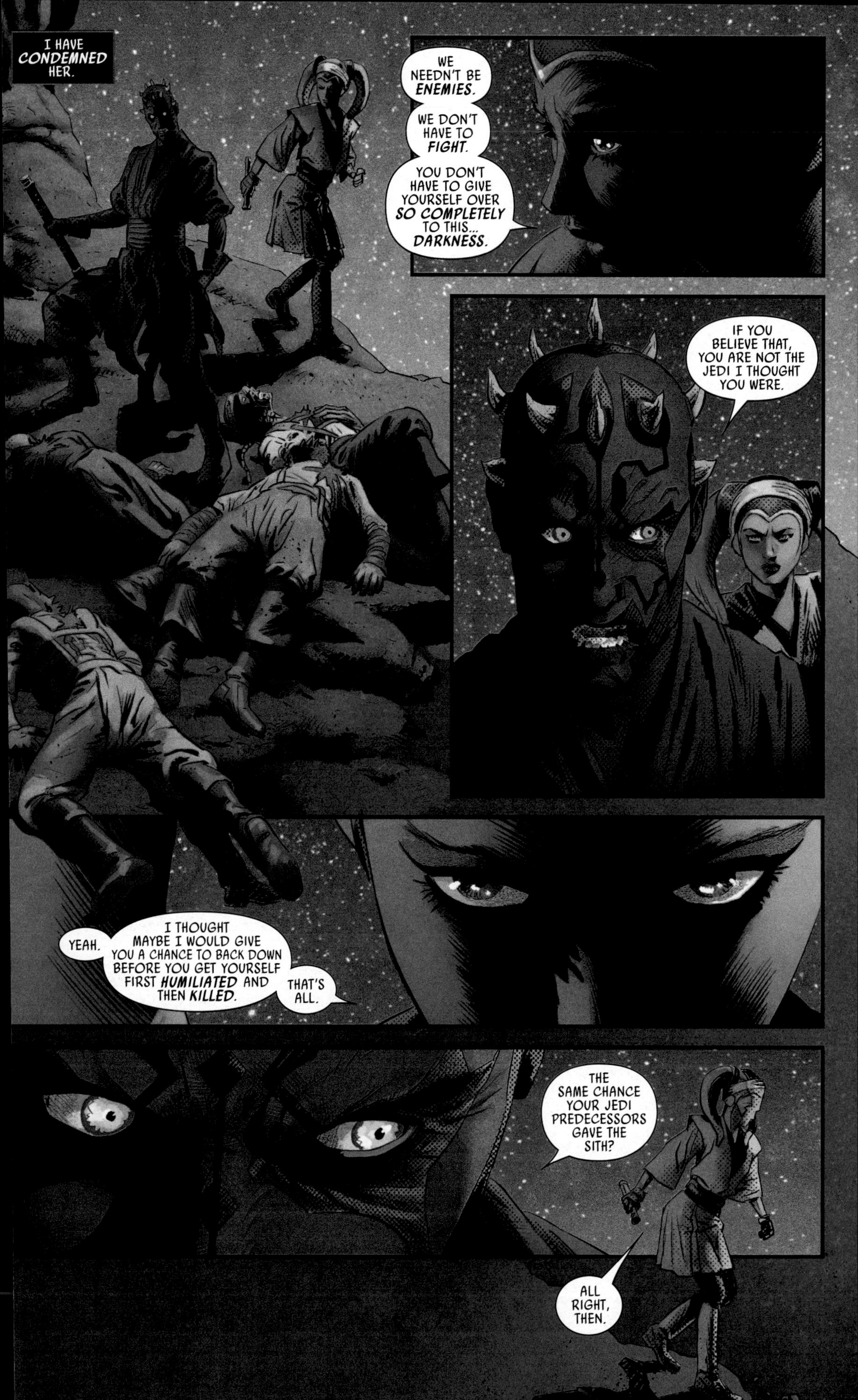

I HAVE *CONDEMNED* HER.
WE NEEDN'T BE *ENEMIES*.
WE DON'T HAVE TO *FIGHT*.
YOU DON'T HAVE TO GIVE YOURSELF OVER *SO COMPLETELY* TO THIS... *DARKNESS*.
IF YOU BELIEVE THAT, YOU ARE NOT THE JEDI I THOUGHT YOU WERE.
YEAH.
I THOUGHT MAYBE I WOULD GIVE YOU A CHANCE TO BACK DOWN BEFORE YOU GET YOURSELF FIRST *HUMILIATED* AND THEN *KILLED*.
THAT'S ALL.
THE SAME CHANCE YOUR JEDI PREDECESSORS GAVE THE SITH?
ALL RIGHT, THEN.

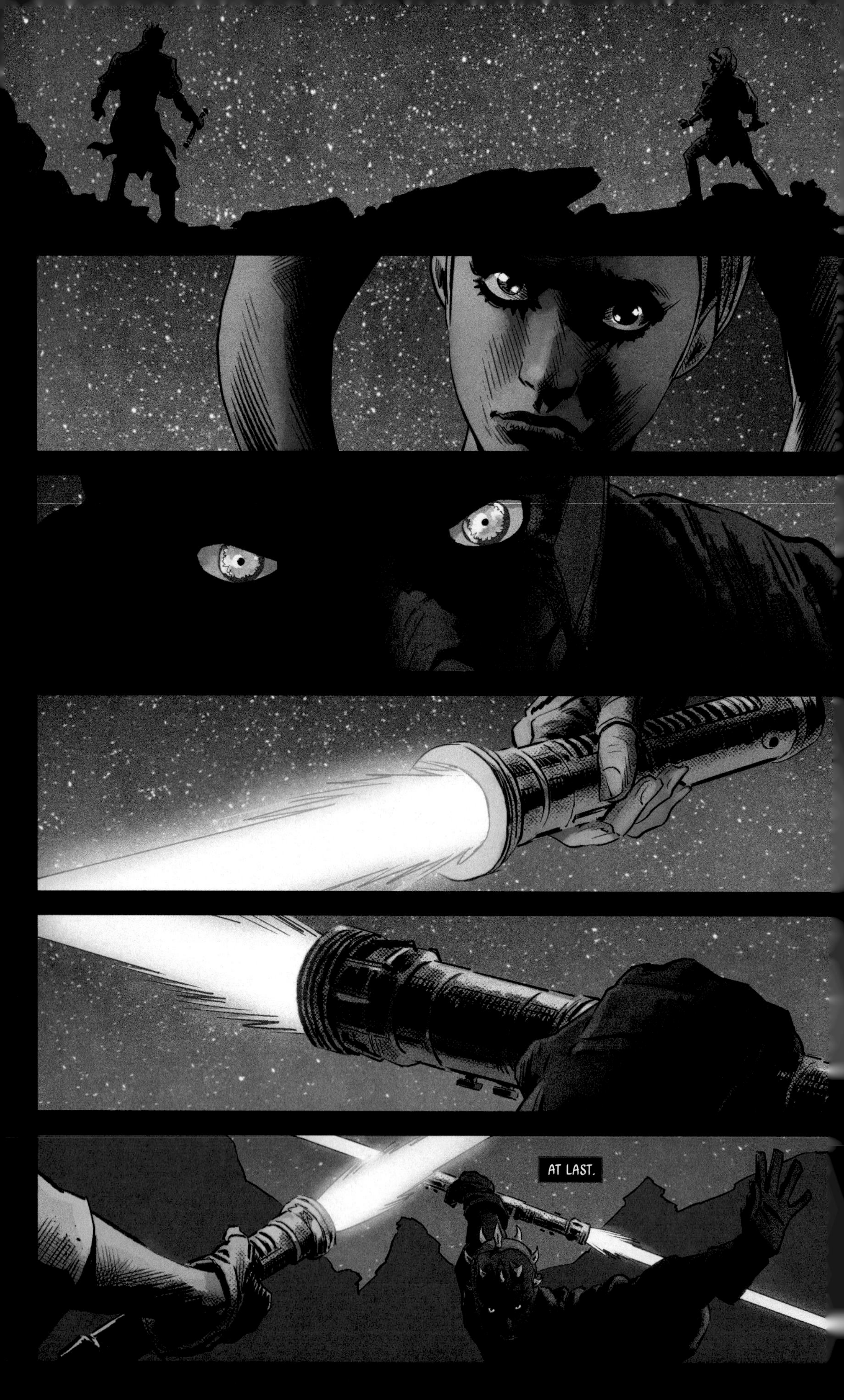
AT LAST.

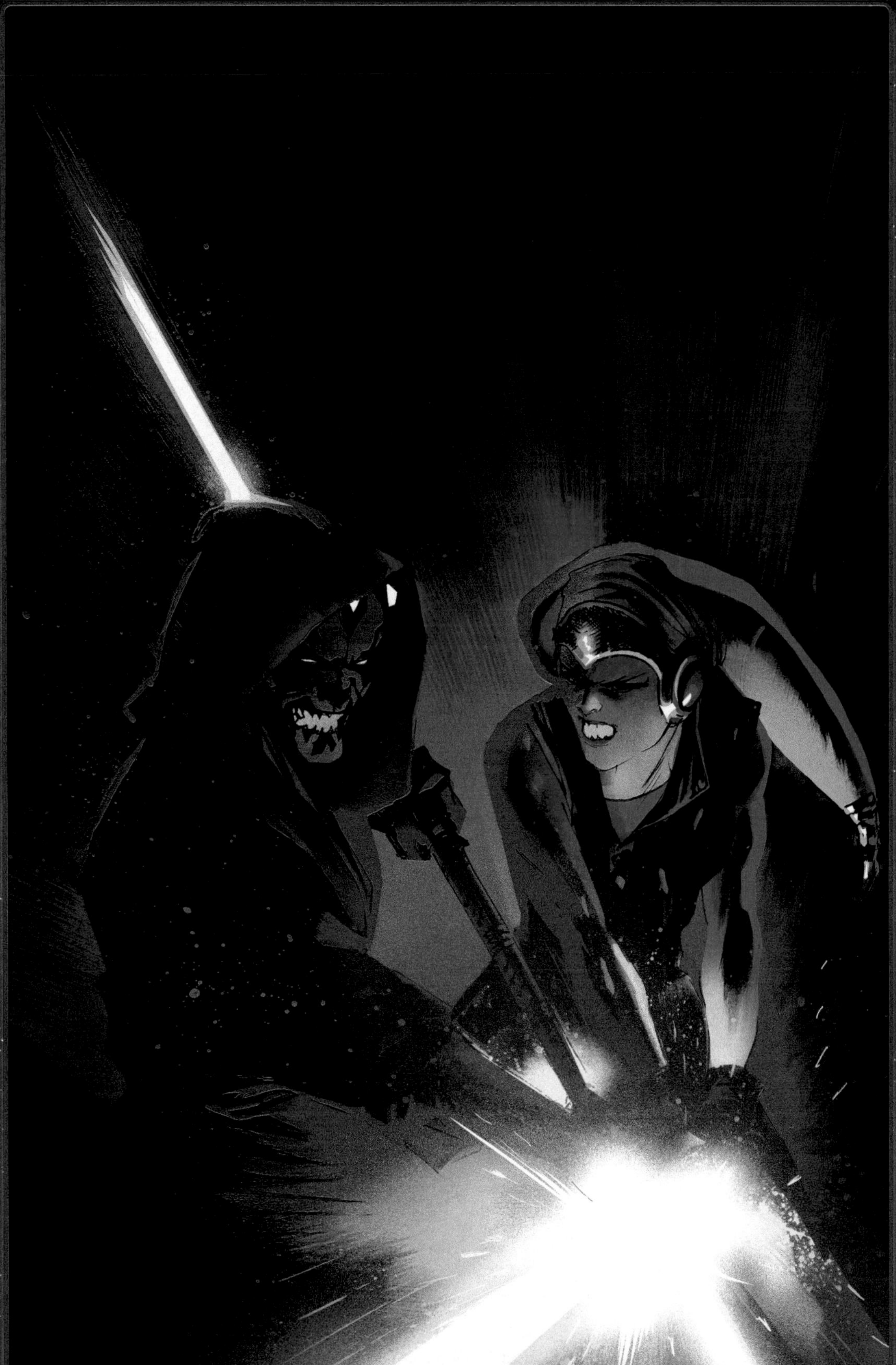

5

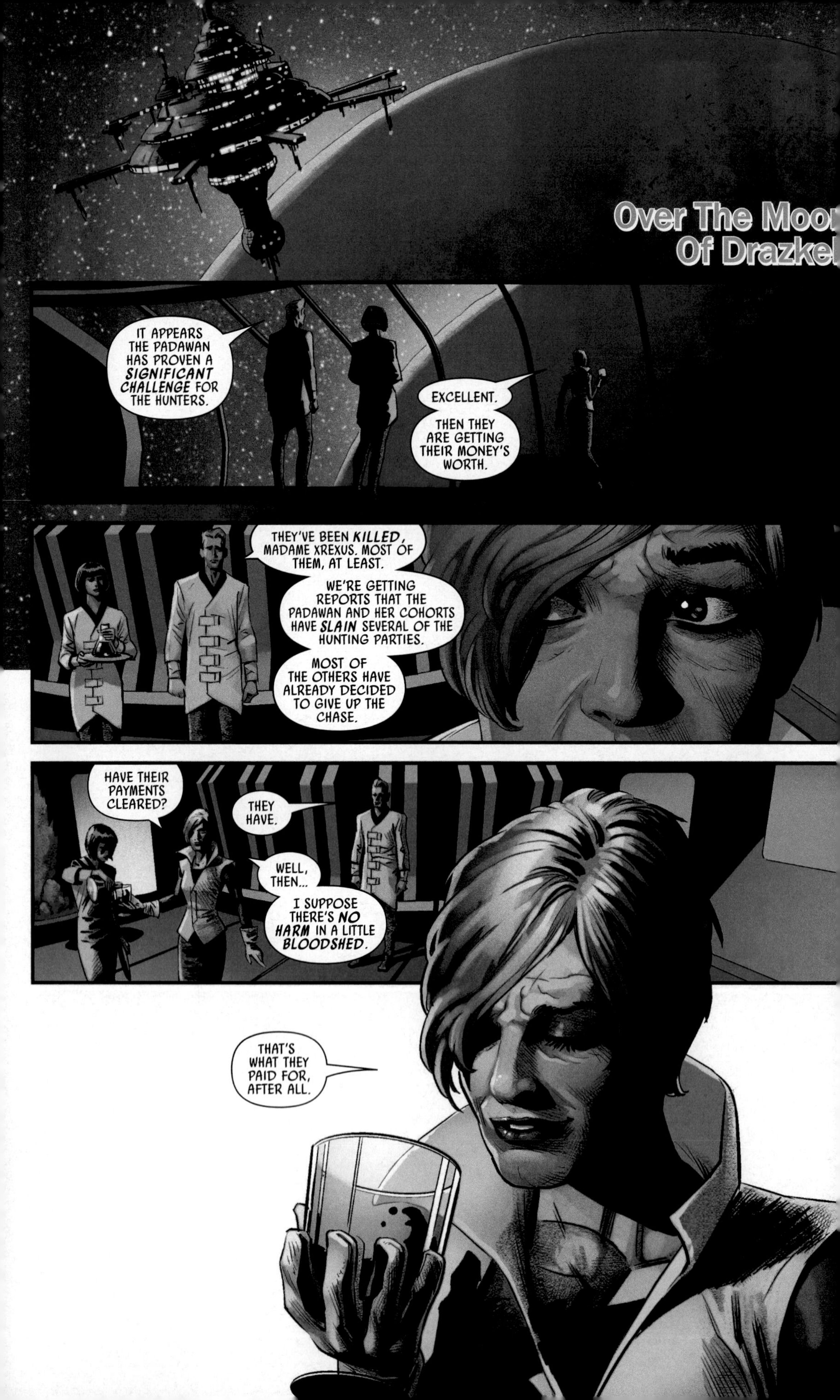
Over The Moon
Of Drazkel
IT APPEARS THE PADAWAN HAS PROVEN A SIGNIFICANT CHALLENGE FOR THE HUNTERS.
EXCELLENT.
THEN THEY ARE GETTING THEIR MONEY'S WORTH.
THEY'VE BEEN KILLED, MADAME XREXUS. MOST OF THEM, AT LEAST.
WE'RE GETTING REPORTS THAT THE PADAWAN AND HER COHORTS HAVE SLAIN SEVERAL OF THE HUNTING PARTIES.
MOST OF THE OTHERS HAVE ALREADY DECIDED TO GIVE UP THE CHASE.
HAVE THEIR PAYMENTS CLEARED?
THEY HAVE.
WELL, THEN...
I SUPPOSE THERE'S NO HARM IN A LITTLE BLOODSHED.
THAT'S WHAT THEY PAID FOR, AFTER ALL.

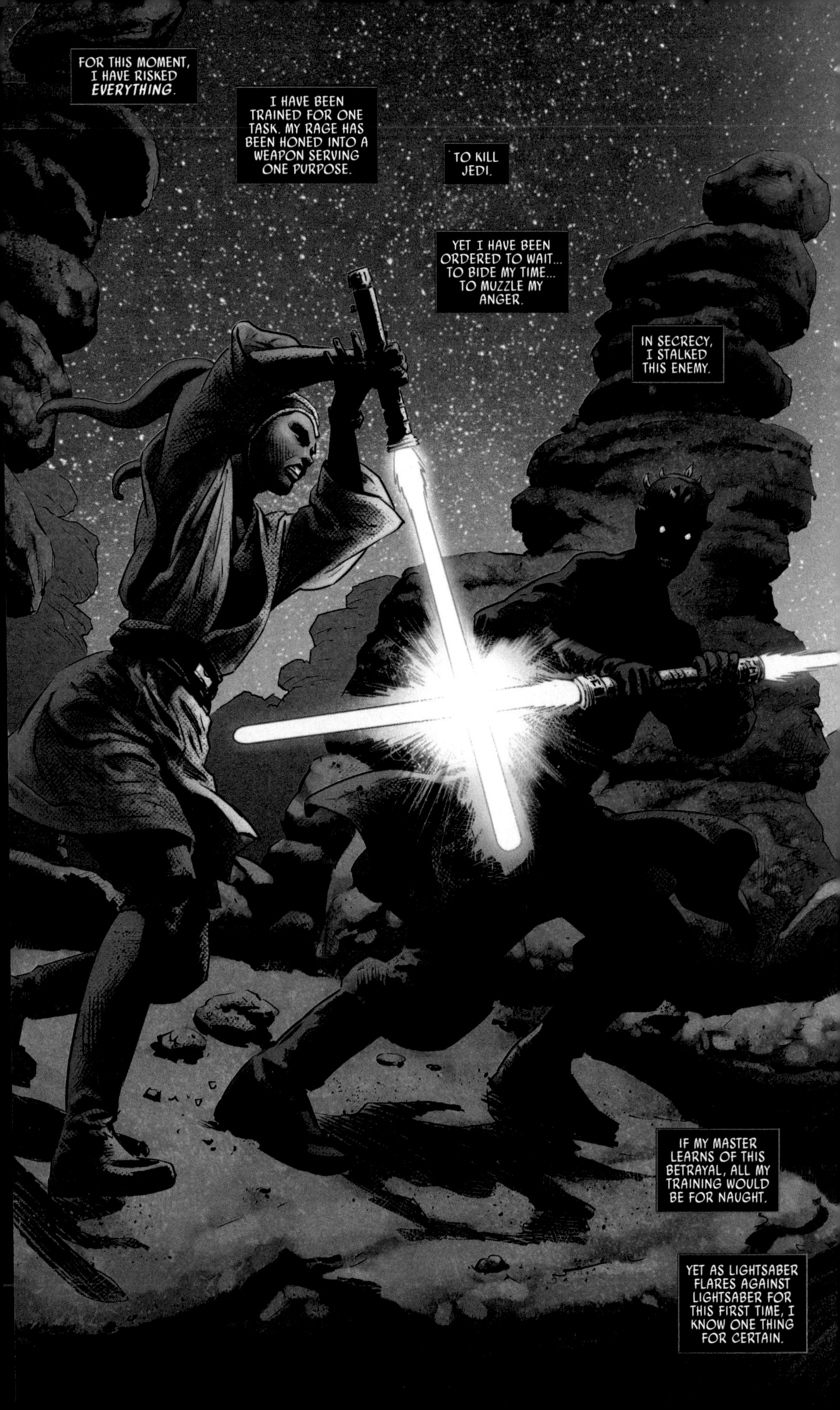
FOR THIS MOMENT, I HAVE RISKED *EVERYTHING*.
I HAVE BEEN TRAINED FOR ONE TASK. MY RAGE HAS BEEN HONED INTO A WEAPON SERVING ONE PURPOSE.
TO KILL JEDI.
YET I HAVE BEEN ORDERED TO WAIT... TO BIDE MY TIME... TO MUZZLE MY ANGER.
IN SECRECY, I STALKED THIS ENEMY.
IF MY MASTER LEARNS OF THIS BETRAYAL, ALL MY TRAINING WOULD BE FOR NAUGHT.
YET AS LIGHTSABER FLARES AGAINST LIGHTSABER FOR THIS FIRST TIME, I KNOW ONE THING FOR CERTAIN.

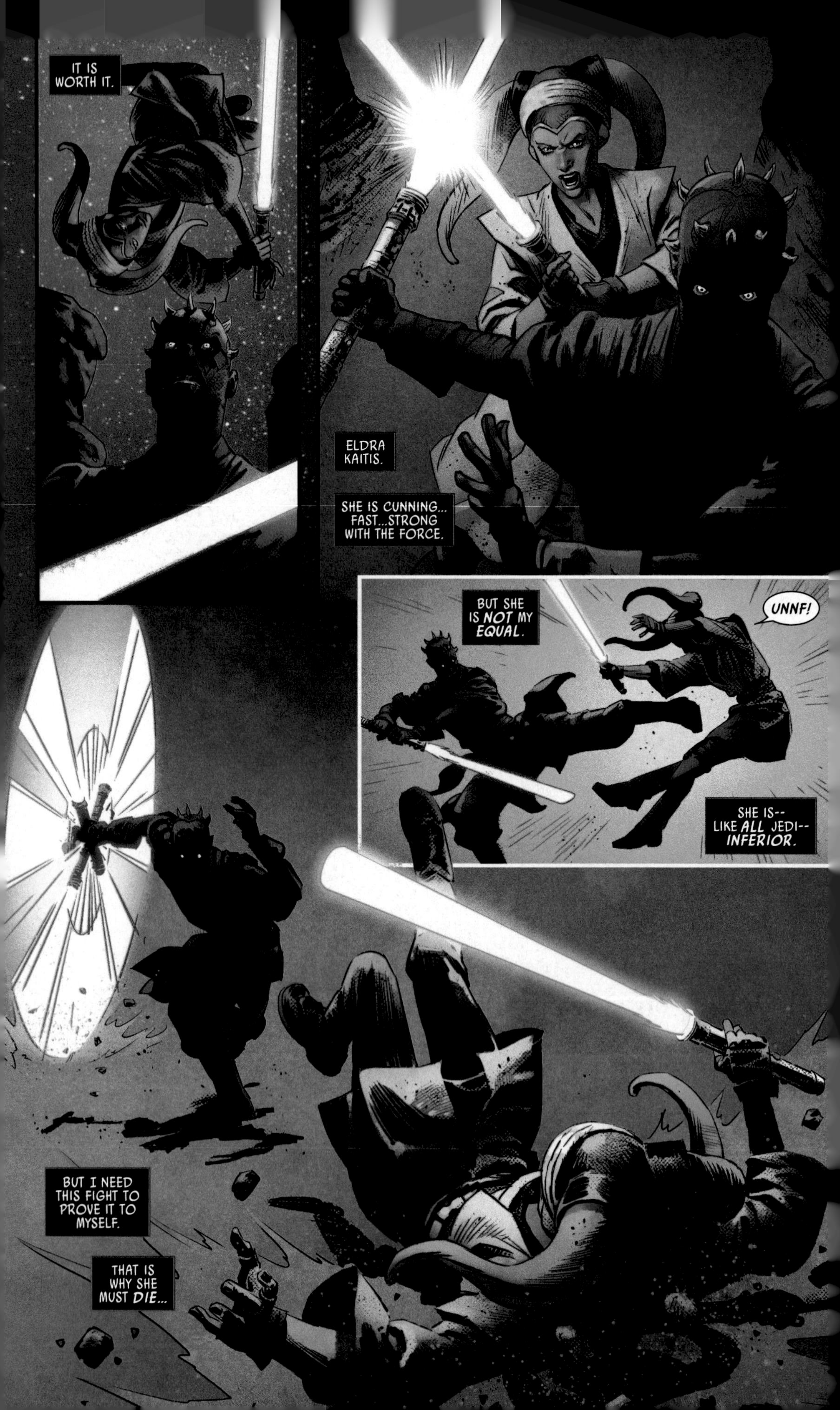

IT IS WORTH IT.
ELDRA KAITIS.
SHE IS CUNNING... FAST...STRONG WITH THE FORCE.
BUT SHE IS NOT MY EQUAL.
UNNF!
SHE IS-- LIKE ALL JEDI-- INFERIOR.
BUT I NEED THIS FIGHT TO PROVE IT TO MYSELF.
THAT IS WHY SHE MUST DIE...

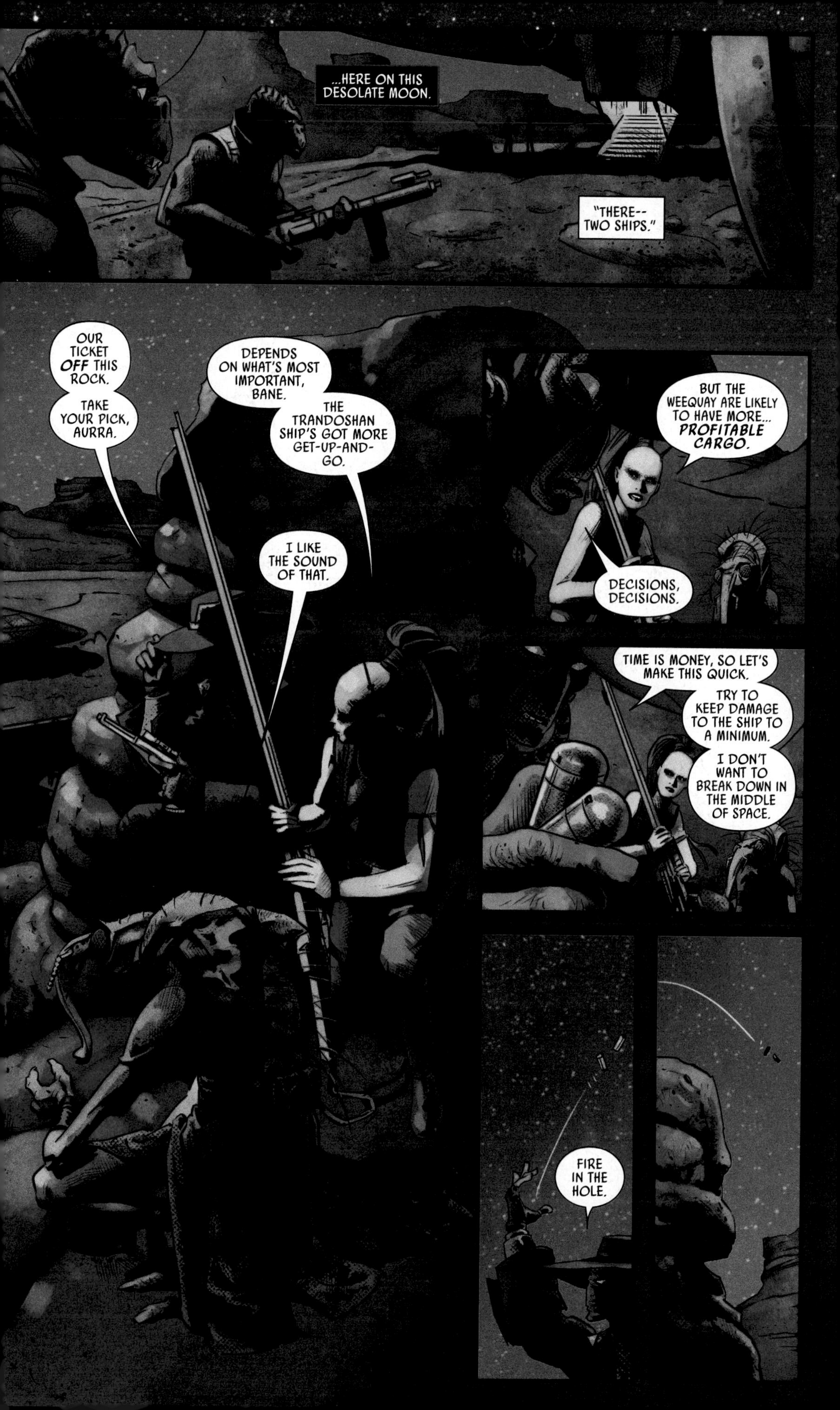
...HERE ON THIS DESOLATE MOON.
"THERE-- TWO SHIPS."
OUR TICKET OFF THIS ROCK.
TAKE YOUR PICK, AURRA.
DEPENDS ON WHAT'S MOST IMPORTANT, BANE.
THE TRANDOSHAN SHIP'S GOT MORE GET-UP-AND-GO.
I LIKE THE SOUND OF THAT.
BUT THE WEEQUAY ARE LIKELY TO HAVE MORE... PROFITABLE CARGO.
DECISIONS, DECISIONS.
TIME IS MONEY, SO LET'S MAKE THIS QUICK.
TRY TO KEEP DAMAGE TO THE SHIP TO A MINIMUM.
I DON'T WANT TO BREAK DOWN IN THE MIDDLE OF SPACE.
FIRE IN THE HOLE.

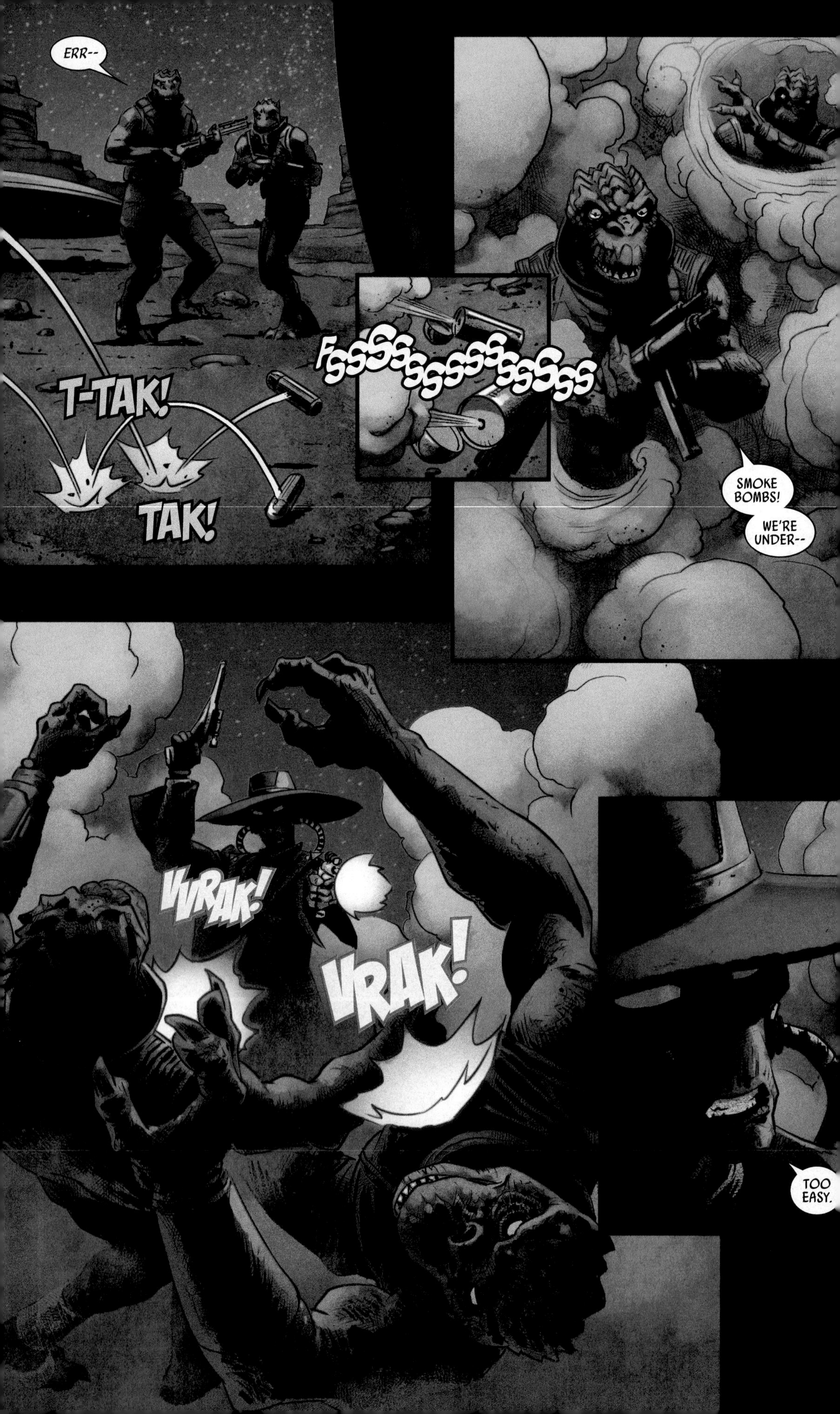
ERR--
T-TAK!
TAK!
FSSSSSSSSSSSSSSSS
SMOKE BOMBS!
WE'RE UNDER--
VVRAK!
VRAK!
TOO EASY.

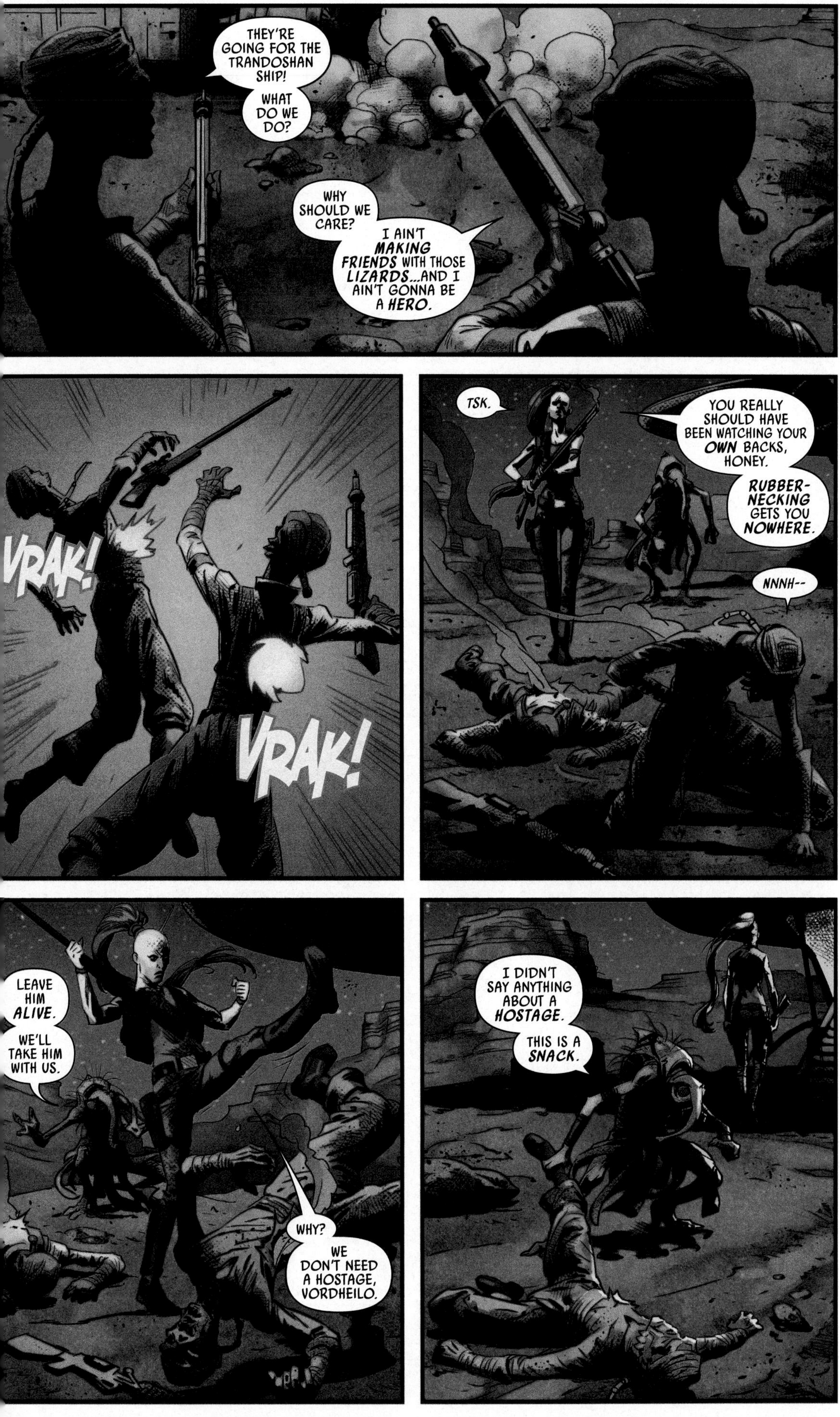

THEY'RE GOING FOR THE TRANDOSHAN SHIP!
WHAT DO WE DO?
WHY SHOULD WE CARE?
I AIN'T MAKING FRIENDS WITH THOSE LIZARDS...AND I AIN'T GONNA BE A HERO.
VRAK!
VRAK!
TSK.
YOU REALLY SHOULD HAVE BEEN WATCHING YOUR OWN BACKS, HONEY.
RUBBER-NECKING GETS YOU NOWHERE.
NNNH--
LEAVE HIM ALIVE.
WE'LL TAKE HIM WITH US.
WHY?
WE DON'T NEED A HOSTAGE, VORDHEILO.
I DIDN'T SAY ANYTHING ABOUT A HOSTAGE.
THIS IS A SNACK.

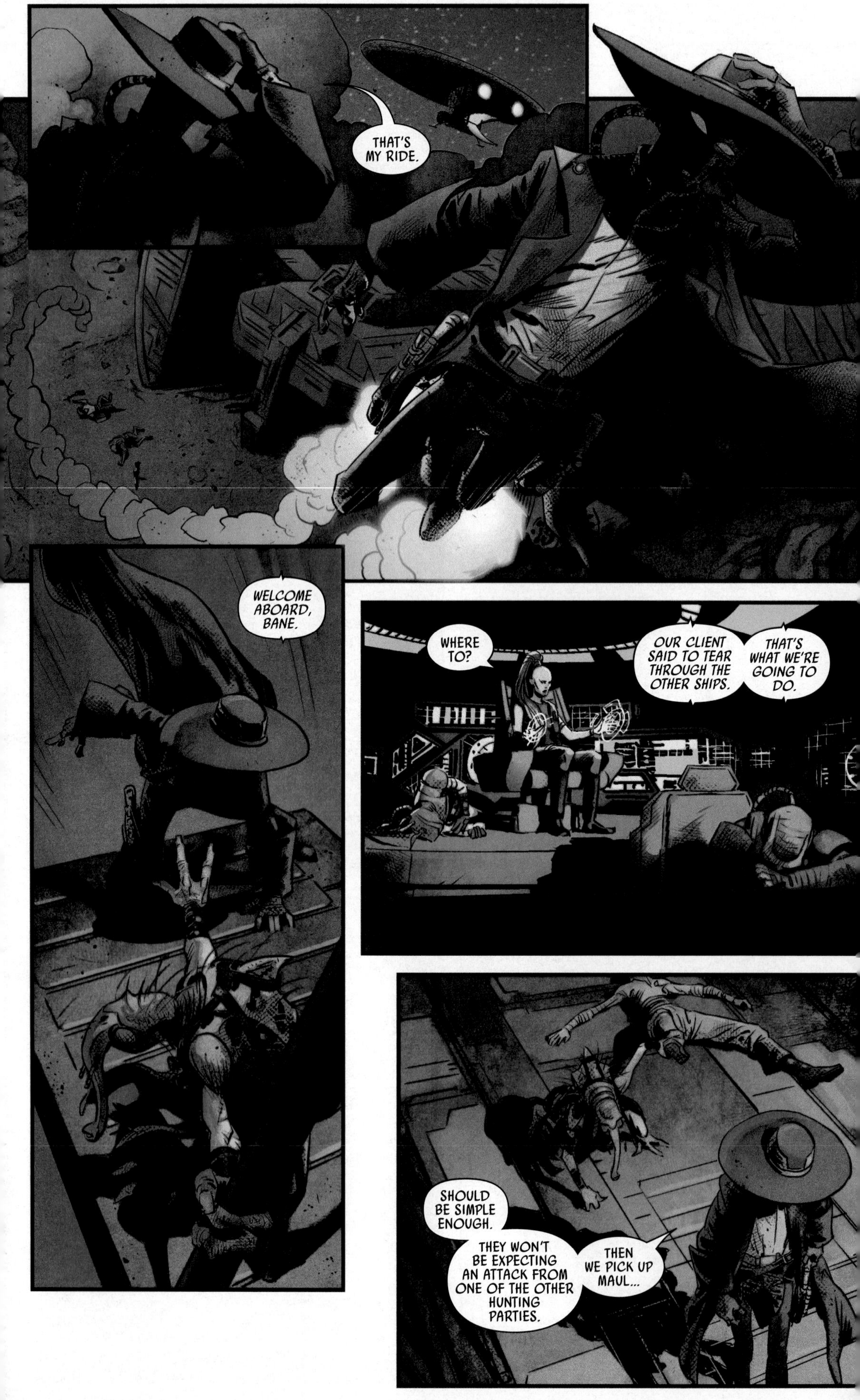
THAT'S MY RIDE.
WELCOME ABOARD, BANE.
WHERE TO?
OUR CLIENT SAID TO TEAR THROUGH THE OTHER SHIPS.
THAT'S WHAT WE'RE GOING TO DO.
SHOULD BE SIMPLE ENOUGH.
THEY WON'T BE EXPECTING AN ATTACK FROM ONE OF THE OTHER HUNTING PARTIES.
THEN WE PICK UP MAUL...

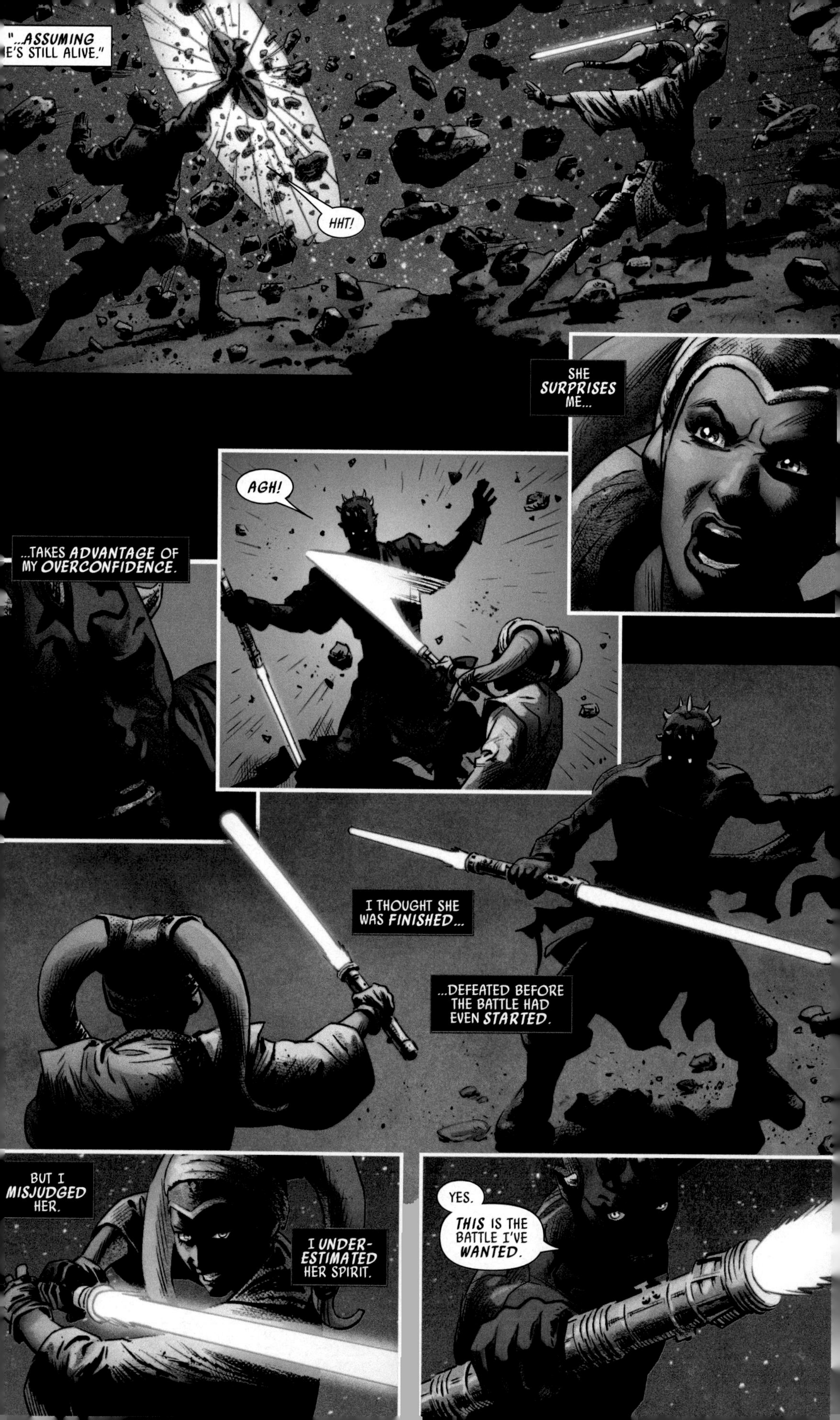
"...ASSUMING
E'S STILL ALIVE."
HHT!
SHE SURPRISES ME...
AGH!
...TAKES ADVANTAGE OF MY OVERCONFIDENCE.
I THOUGHT SHE WAS FINISHED...
...DEFEATED BEFORE THE BATTLE HAD EVEN STARTED.
BUT I MISJUDGED HER.
I UNDER-ESTIMATED HER SPIRIT.
YES.
THIS IS THE BATTLE I'VE WANTED.

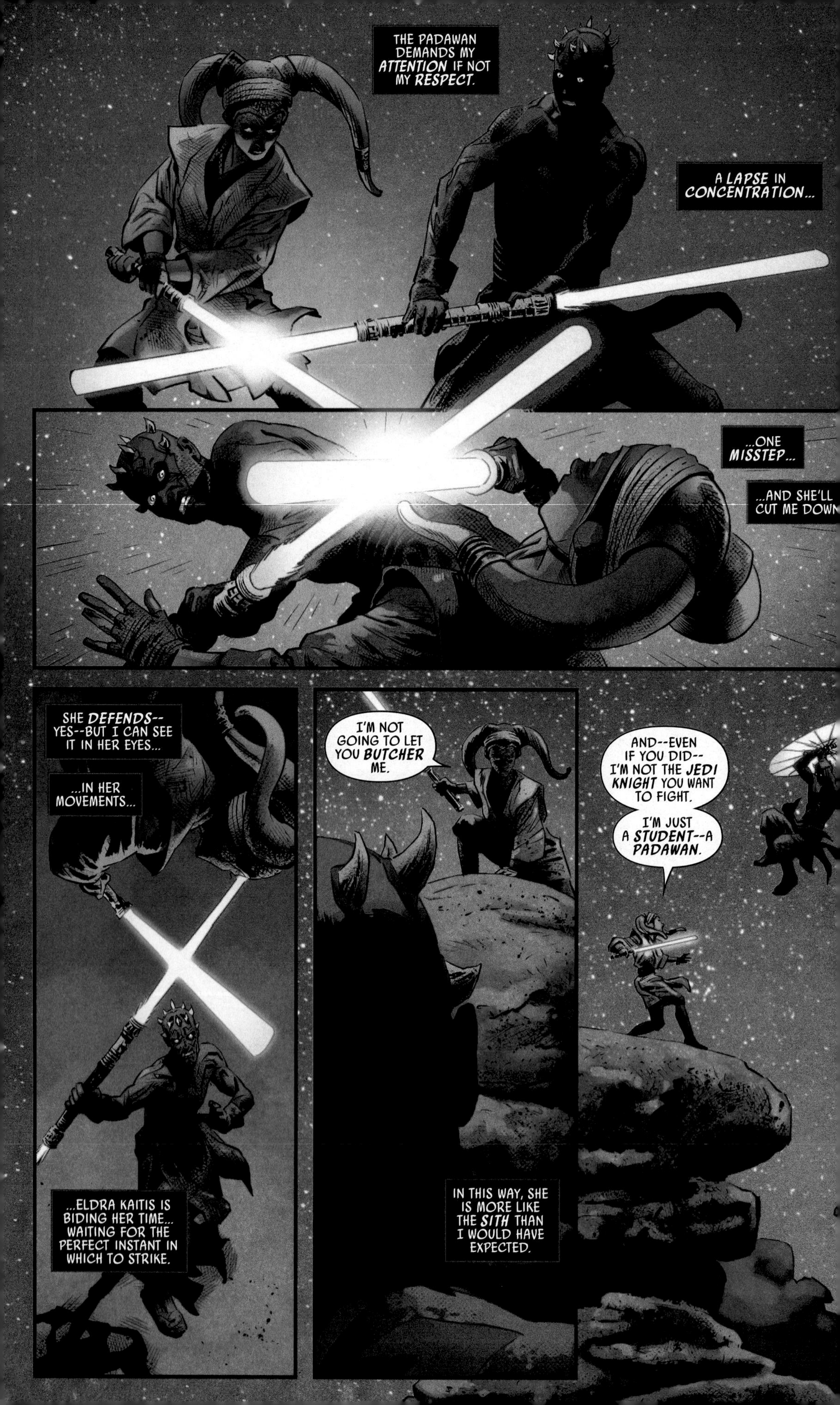
THE PADAWAN DEMANDS MY ATTENTION IF NOT MY RESPECT.
A LAPSE IN CONCENTRATION...
...ONE MISSTEP...
...AND SHE'LL CUT ME DOWN
SHE DEFENDS--YES--BUT I CAN SEE IT IN HER EYES...
...IN HER MOVEMENTS...
...ELDRA KAITIS IS BIDING HER TIME... WAITING FOR THE PERFECT INSTANT IN WHICH TO STRIKE.
I'M NOT GOING TO LET YOU BUTCHER ME.
AND--EVEN IF YOU DID--I'M NOT THE JEDI KNIGHT YOU WANT TO FIGHT.
I'M JUST A STUDENT--A PADAWAN.
IN THIS WAY, SHE IS MORE LIKE THE SITH THAN I WOULD HAVE EXPECTED.

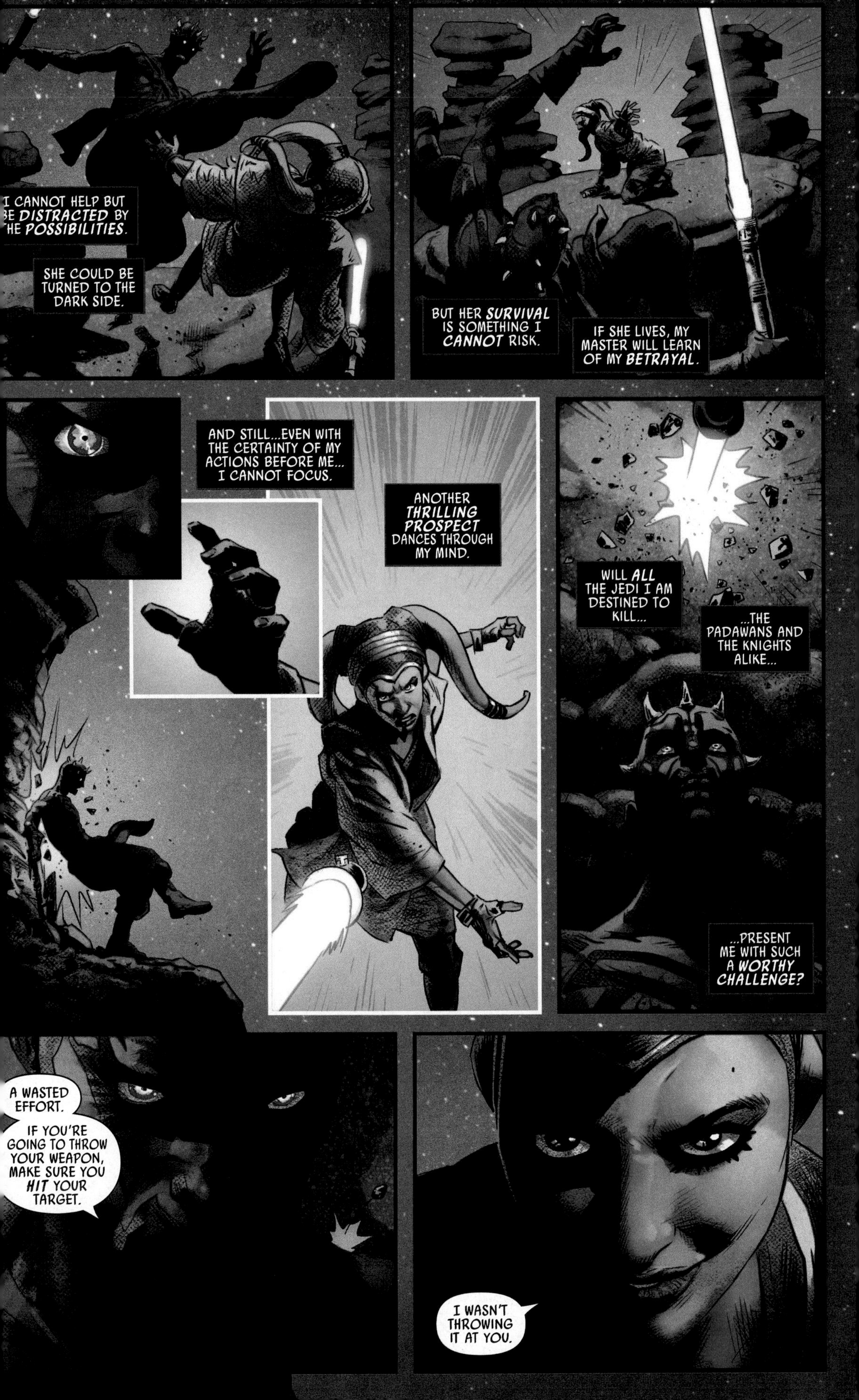
I CANNOT HELP BUT BE DISTRACTED BY THE POSSIBILITIES.
SHE COULD BE TURNED TO THE DARK SIDE.
BUT HER SURVIVAL IS SOMETHING I CANNOT RISK.
IF SHE LIVES, MY MASTER WILL LEARN OF MY BETRAYAL.
AND STILL...EVEN WITH THE CERTAINTY OF MY ACTIONS BEFORE ME... I CANNOT FOCUS.
ANOTHER THRILLING PROSPECT DANCES THROUGH MY MIND.
WILL ALL THE JEDI I AM DESTINED TO KILL...
...THE PADAWANS AND THE KNIGHTS ALIKE...
...PRESENT ME WITH SUCH A WORTHY CHALLENGE?
A WASTED EFFORT.
IF YOU'RE GOING TO THROW YOUR WEAPON, MAKE SURE YOU HIT YOUR TARGET.
I WASN'T THROWING IT AT YOU.

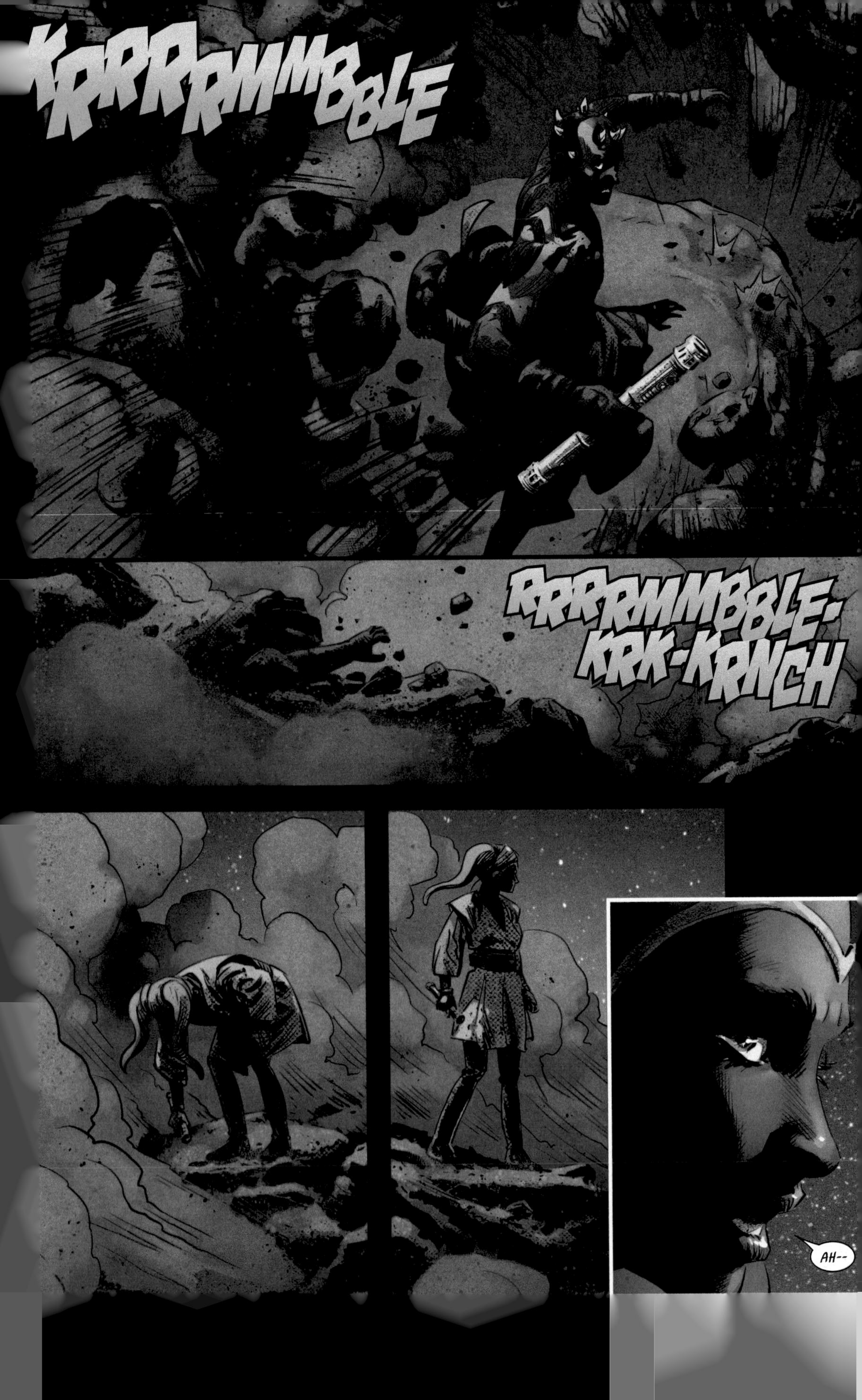
KRRRRMMBBLE
RRRRMMBBLE-
KRK-KRNCH
AH--

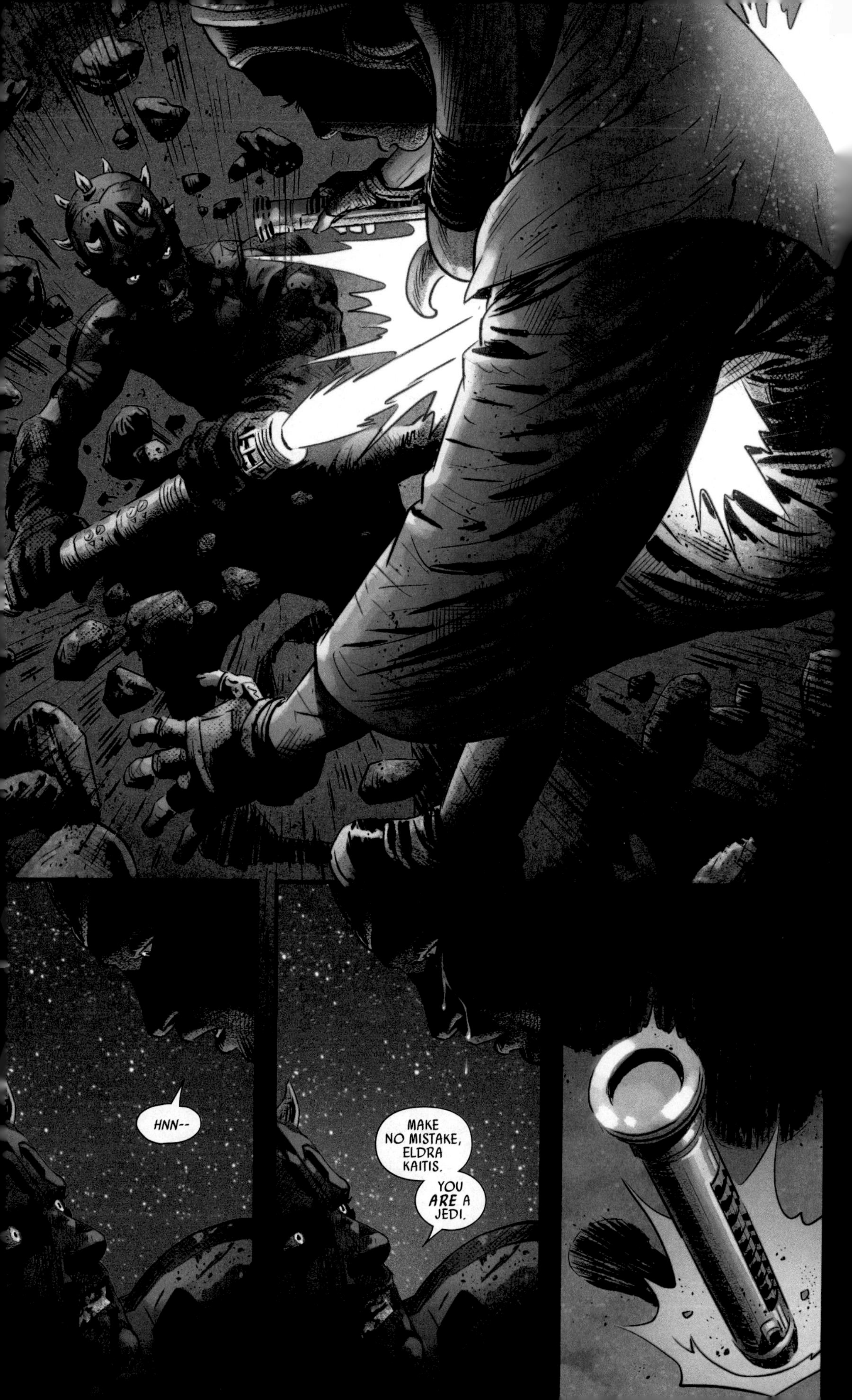
HNN--
MAKE NO MISTAKE, ELDRA KAITIS.
YOU ARE A JEDI.

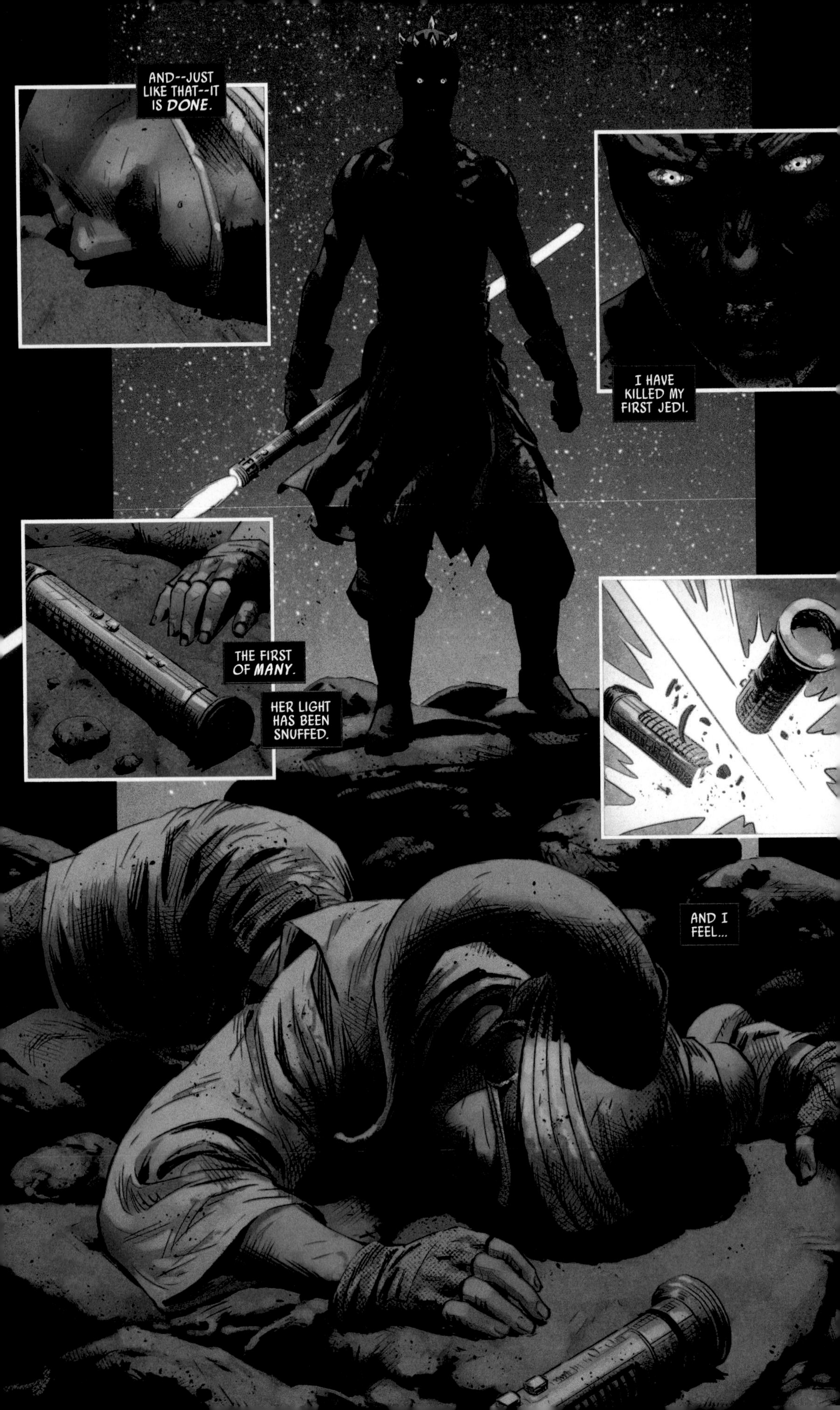
AND--JUST LIKE THAT--IT IS DONE.
I HAVE KILLED MY FIRST JEDI.
THE FIRST OF MANY.
HER LIGHT HAS BEEN SNUFFED.
AND I FEEL...

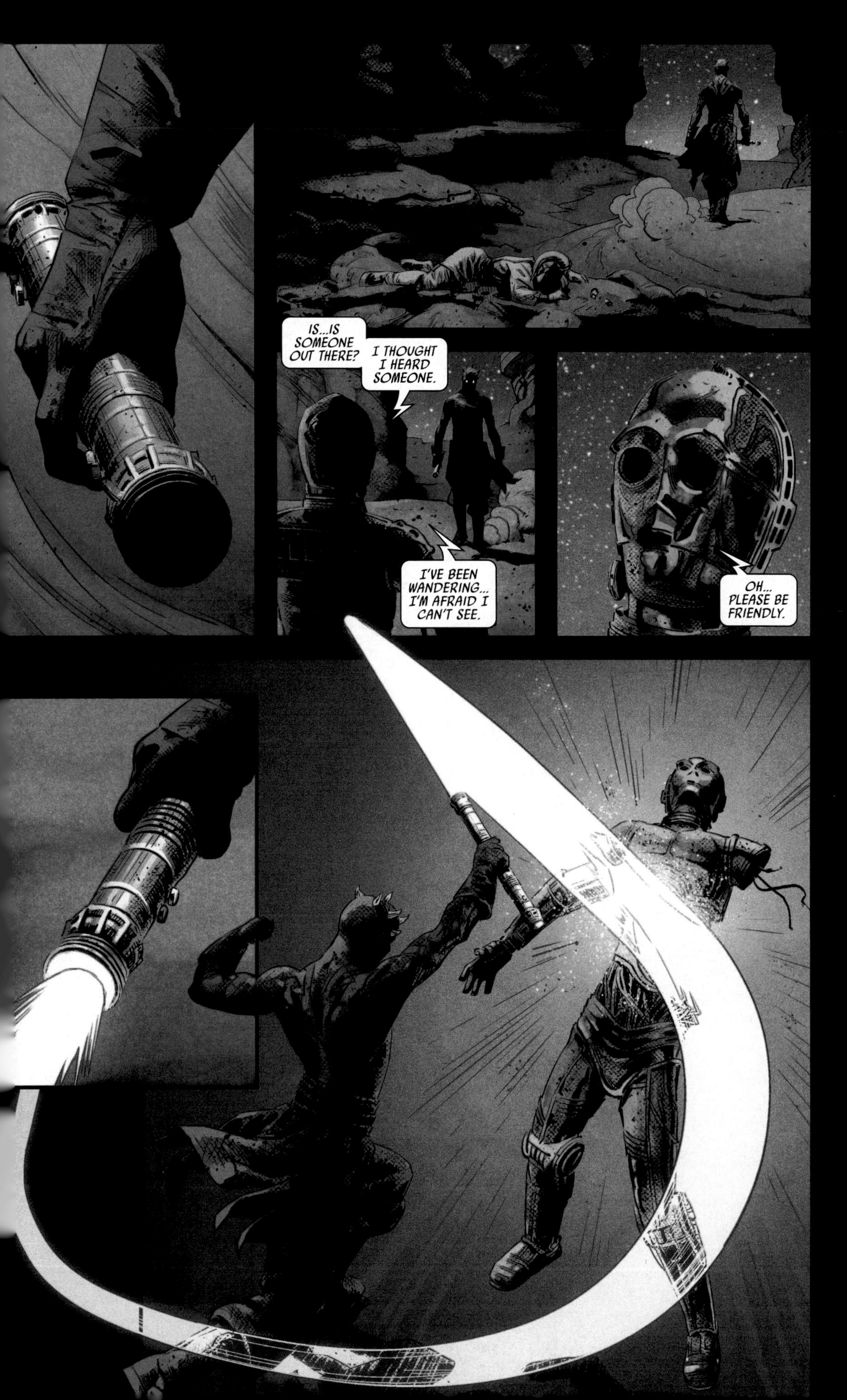
IS...IS SOMEONE OUT THERE?
I THOUGHT I HEARD SOMEONE.
I'VE BEEN WANDERING... I'M AFRAID I CAN'T SEE.
OH... PLEASE BE FRIENDLY.

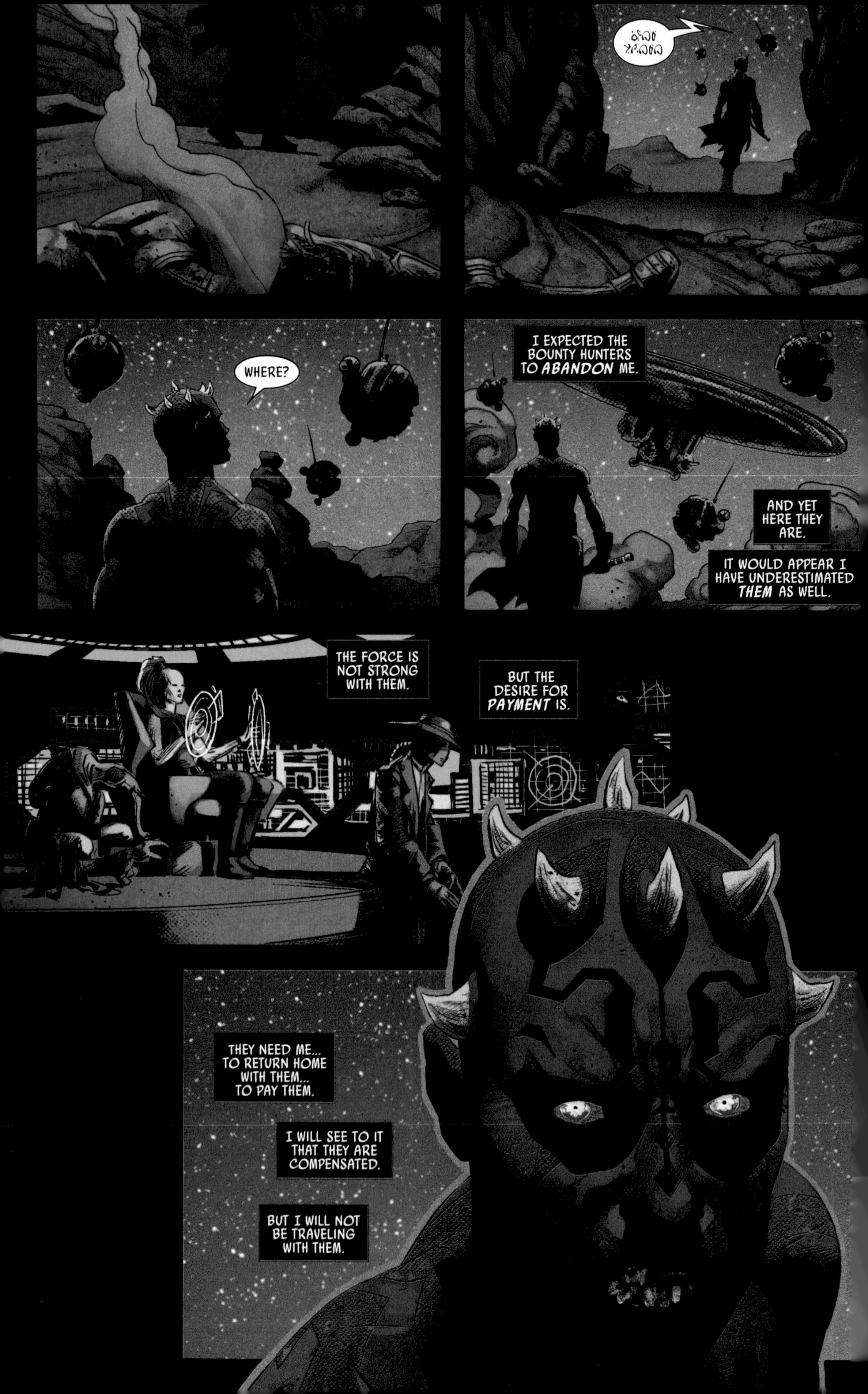
WHERE?
I EXPECTED THE BOUNTY HUNTERS TO ABANDON ME.
AND YET HERE THEY ARE.
IT WOULD APPEAR I HAVE UNDERESTIMATED THEM AS WELL.
THE FORCE IS NOT STRONG WITH THEM.
BUT THE DESIRE FOR PAYMENT IS.
THEY NEED ME... TO RETURN HOME WITH THEM... TO PAY THEM.
I WILL SEE TO IT THAT THEY ARE COMPENSATED.
BUT I WILL NOT BE TRAVELING WITH THEM.

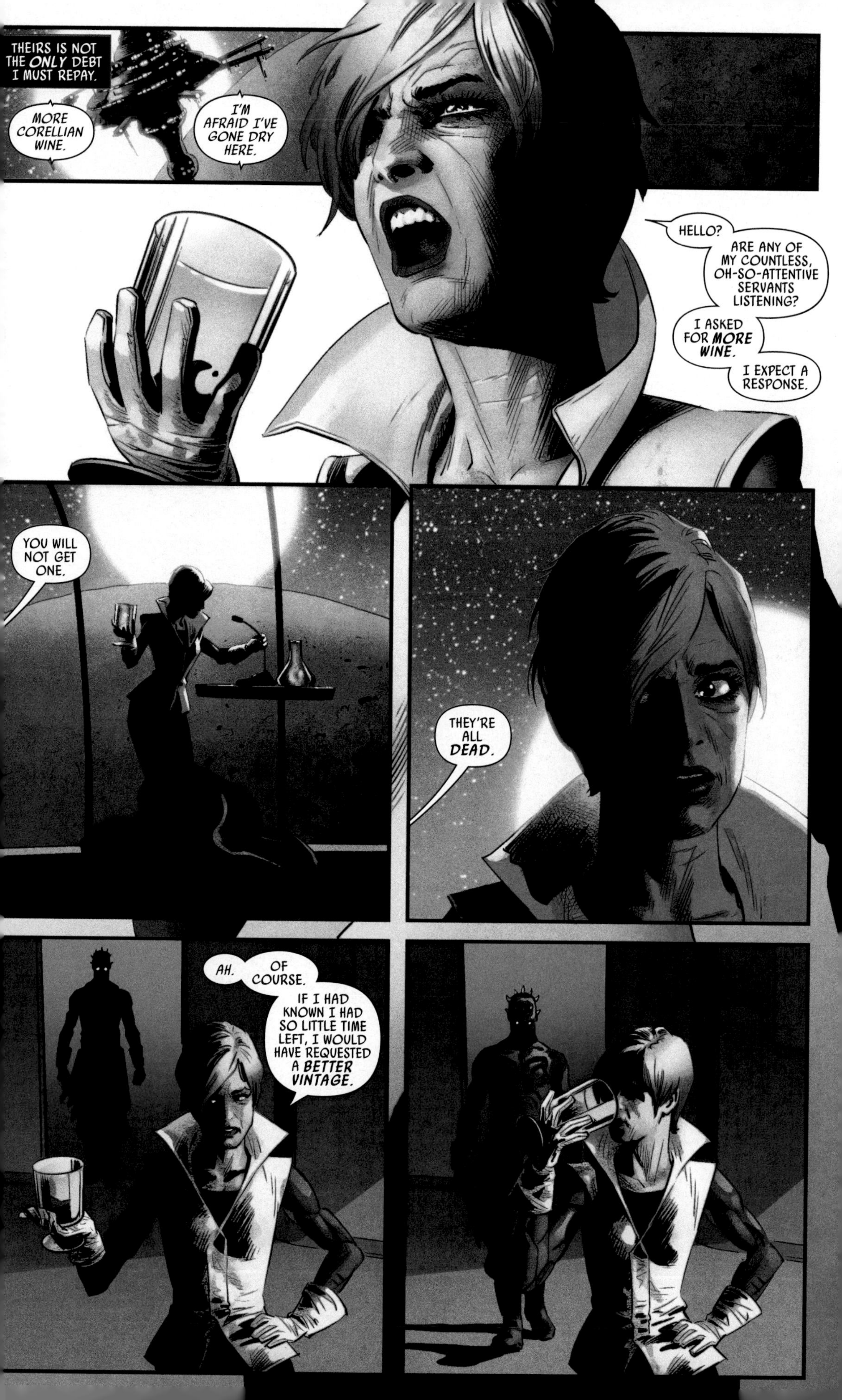

THEIRS IS NOT THE *ONLY* DEBT I MUST REPAY.
MORE CORELLIAN WINE.
I'M AFRAID I'VE GONE DRY HERE.
HELLO?
ARE ANY OF MY COUNTLESS, OH-SO-ATTENTIVE SERVANTS LISTENING?
I ASKED FOR **MORE WINE.**
I EXPECT A RESPONSE.
YOU WILL NOT GET ONE.
THEY'RE ALL **DEAD.**
AH.
OF COURSE.
IF I HAD KNOWN I HAD SO LITTLE TIME LEFT, I WOULD HAVE REQUESTED A **BETTER VINTAGE.**

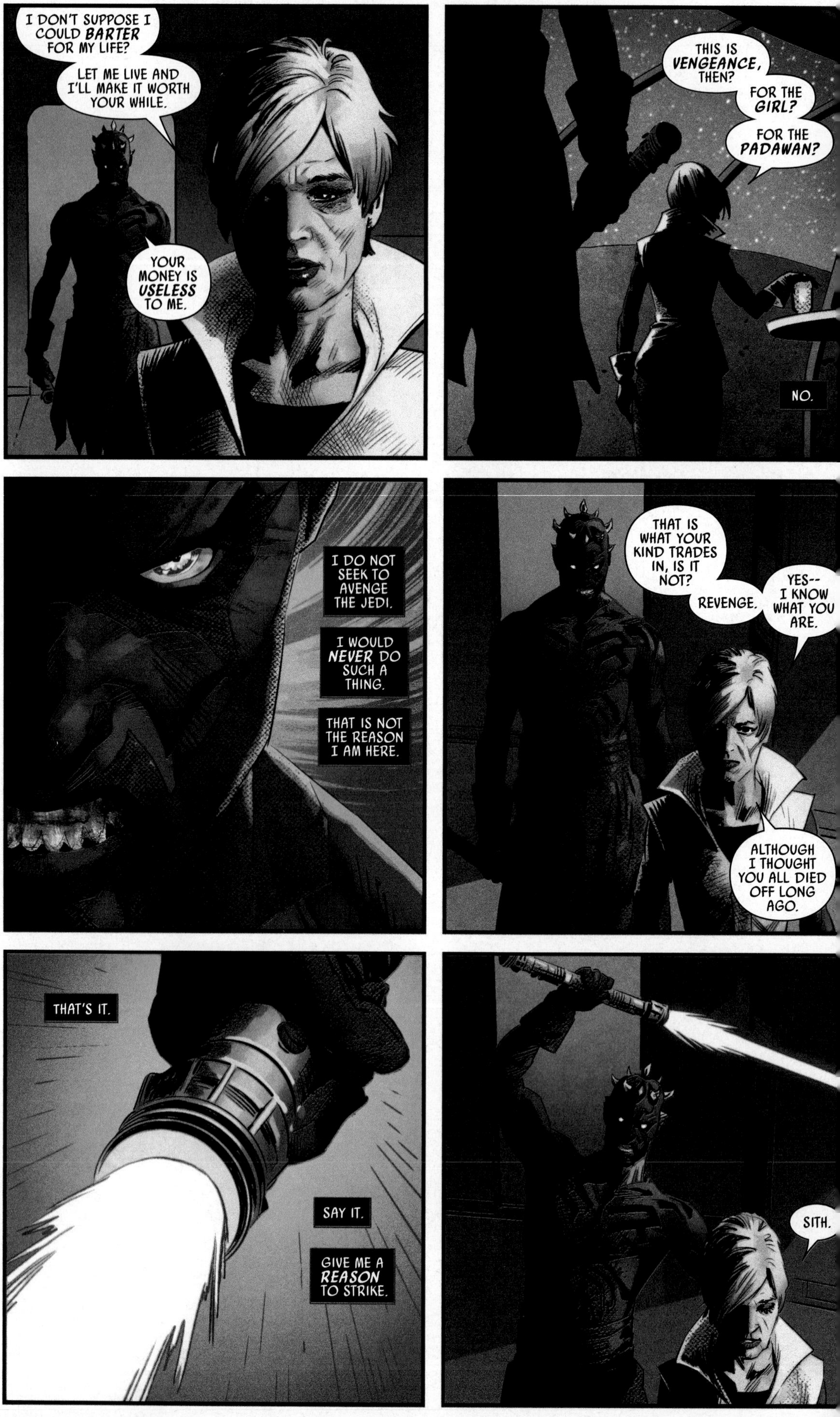

I DON'T SUPPOSE I COULD BARTER FOR MY LIFE?
LET ME LIVE AND I'LL MAKE IT WORTH YOUR WHILE.
YOUR MONEY IS USELESS TO ME.
THIS IS VENGEANCE, THEN?
FOR THE GIRL?
FOR THE PADAWAN?
NO.
I DO NOT SEEK TO AVENGE THE JEDI.
I WOULD NEVER DO SUCH A THING.
THAT IS NOT THE REASON I AM HERE.
THAT IS WHAT YOUR KIND TRADES IN, IS IT NOT?
REVENGE.
YES-- I KNOW WHAT YOU ARE.
ALTHOUGH I THOUGHT YOU ALL DIED OFF LONG AGO.
THAT'S IT.
SAY IT.
GIVE ME A REASON TO STRIKE.
SITH.

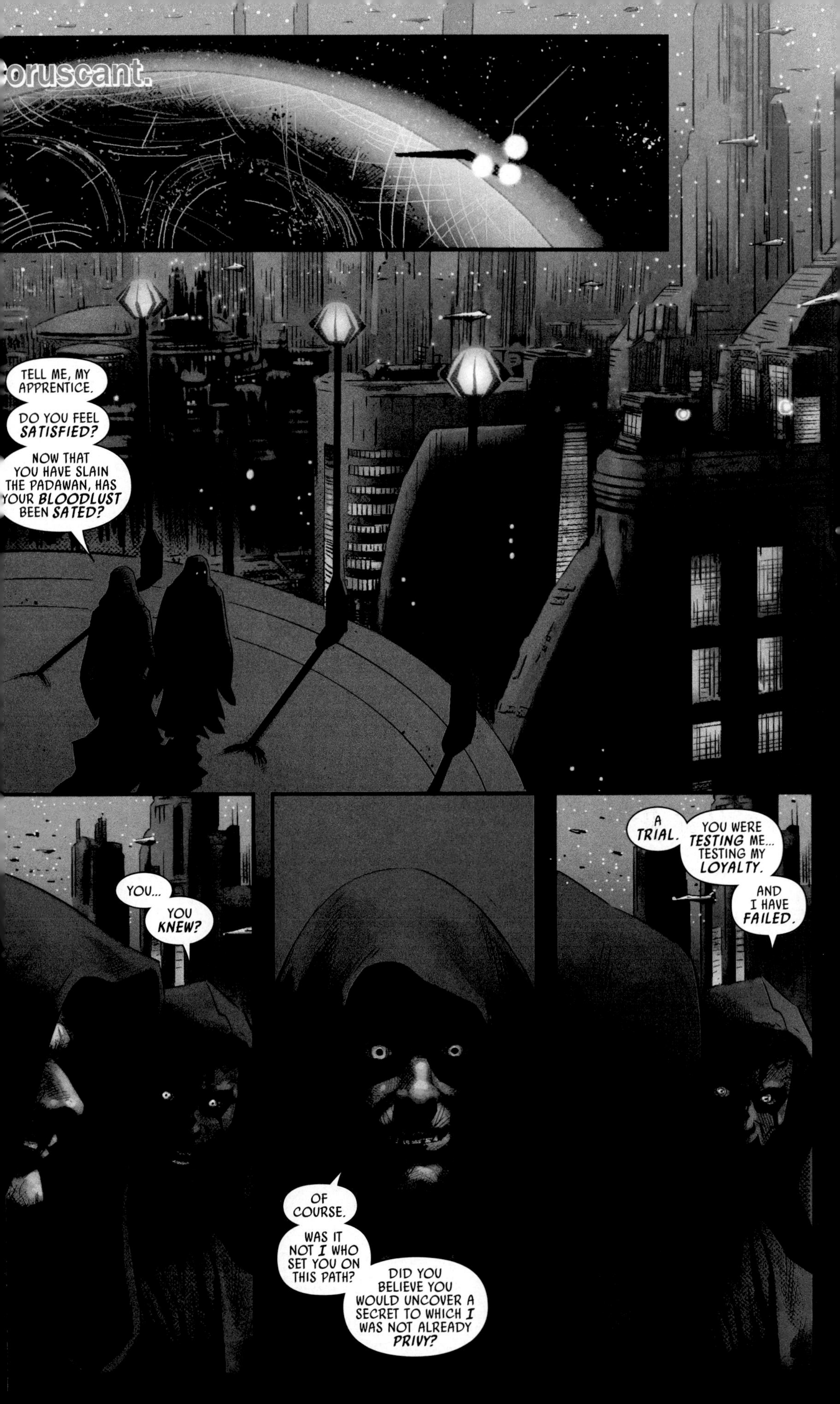
oruscant.
TELL ME, MY APPRENTICE.
DO YOU FEEL SATISFIED?
NOW THAT YOU HAVE SLAIN THE PADAWAN, HAS YOUR BLOODLUST BEEN SATED?
YOU...
YOU KNEW?
OF COURSE.
WAS IT NOT I WHO SET YOU ON THIS PATH?
DID YOU BELIEVE YOU WOULD UNCOVER A SECRET TO WHICH I WAS NOT ALREADY PRIVY?
A TRIAL.
YOU WERE TESTING ME... TESTING MY LOYALTY.
AND I HAVE FAILED.

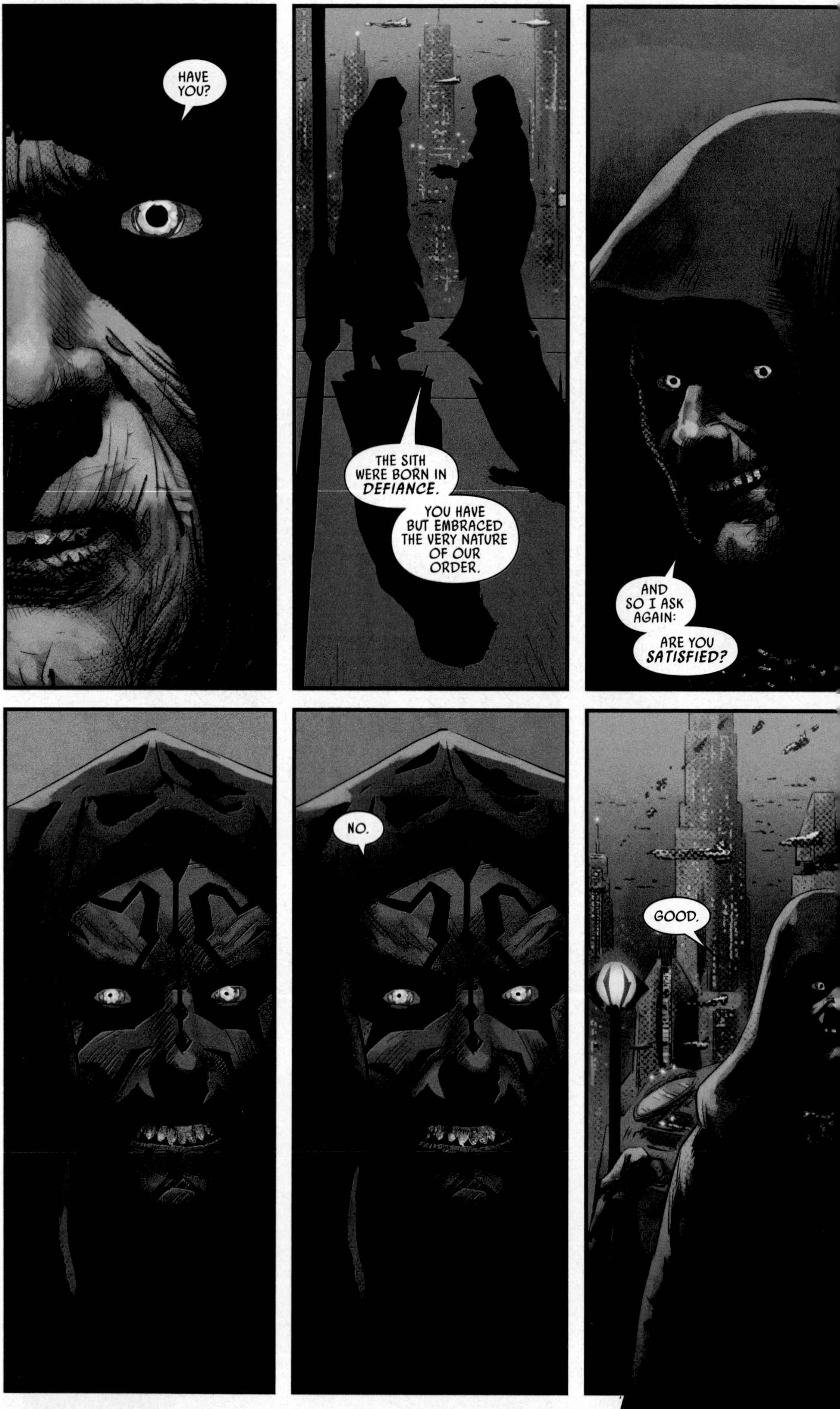
HAVE YOU?
THE SITH WERE BORN IN *DEFIANCE.*
YOU HAVE BUT EMBRACED THE VERY NATURE OF OUR ORDER.
AND SO I ASK AGAIN:
ARE YOU *SATISFIED?*
NO.
GOOD.

AT LAST I KNOW HOW IT FEELS, TAKING A JEDI LIFE.
I DID NOT FORESEE THIS.
I EXPECTED TO BE FULFILLED--AT LEAST MOMENTARILY--BY THE ACT.
BUT MY RAGE... MY HATRED... HAS ONLY INTENSIFIED.
ELDRA KAITIS DIED...AND I ONLY FEEL MORE EMPTY.
AN EMPTINESS I HAVE BEEN TRAINED TO FILL IN ONLY ONE WAY...
...BY SLAYING THE JEDI.
ELDRA KAITIS WAS BUT THE FIRST.
NOW I MUST ONLY... WAIT.
The End

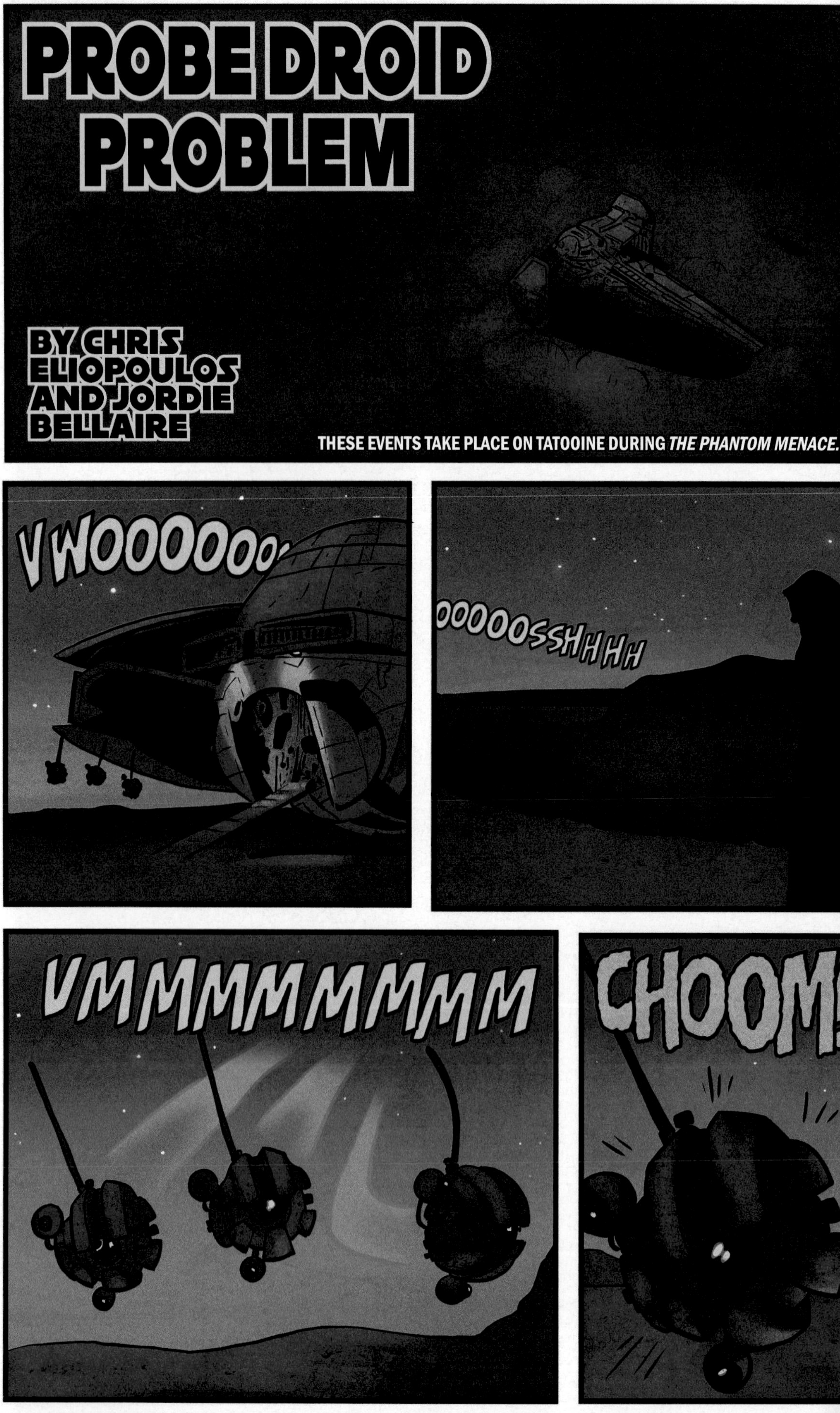
PROBE DROID PROBLEM
BY CHRIS ELIOPOULOS AND JORDIE BELLAIRE
THESE EVENTS TAKE PLACE ON TATOOINE DURING *THE PHANTOM MENACE.*
VWOOOOOO
OOOOOOSSHHHH
VMMMMMMMMM
CHOOM!

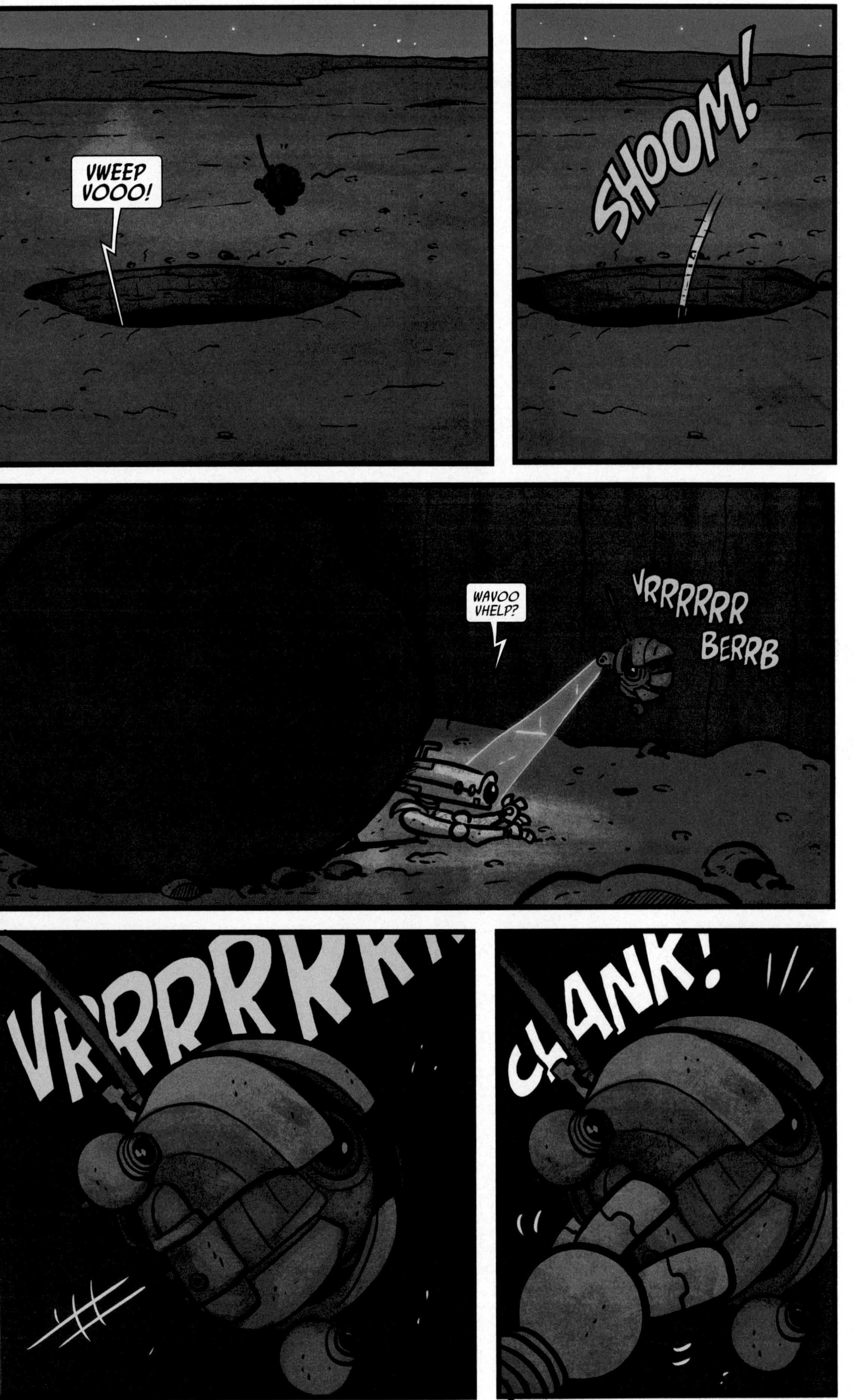
VWEEP VOOO!
SHOOM!
WAVOO VHELP?
VRRRRRRR BERRB
VRRRRRR
CLANK!

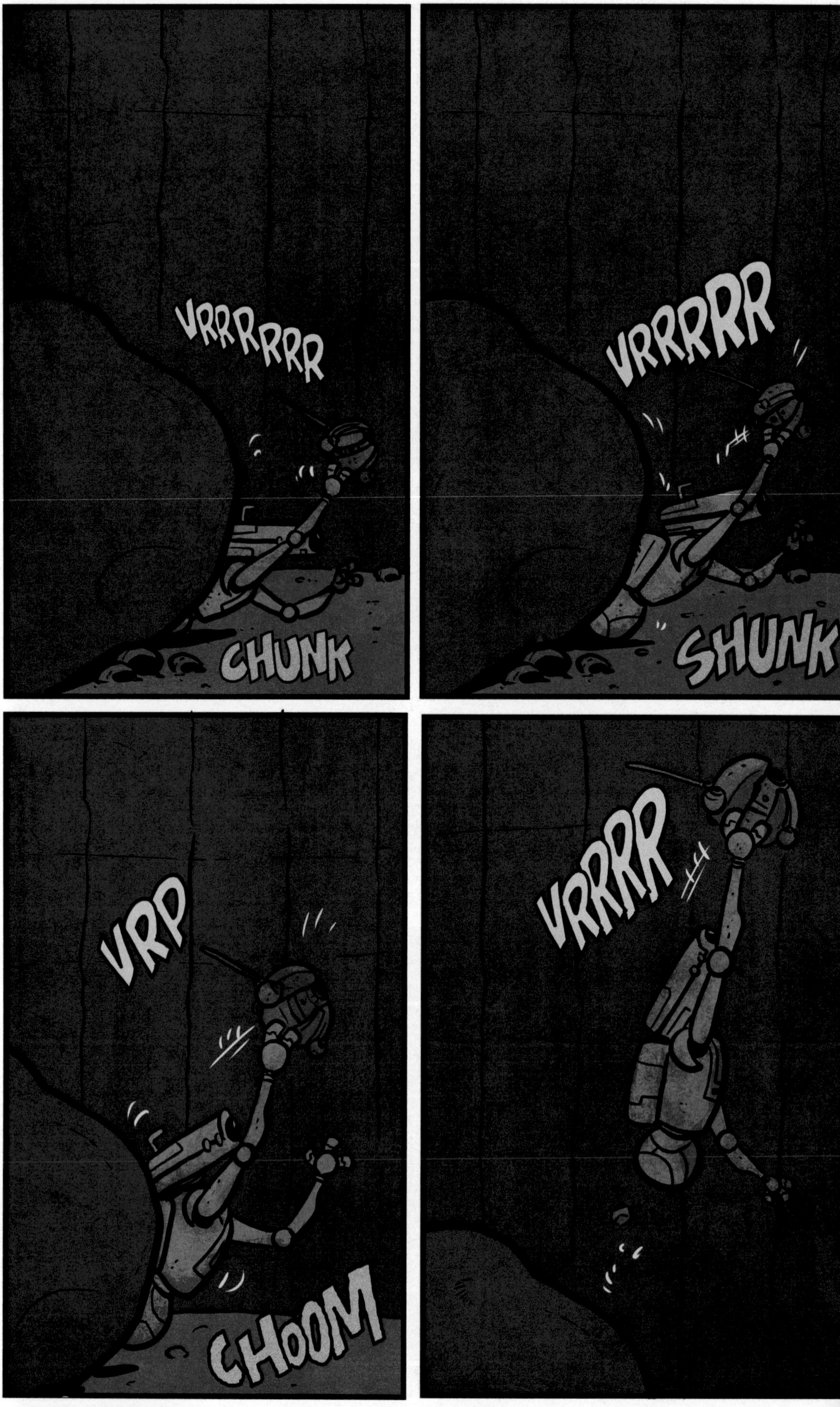
VRRRRRR
CHUNK
VRRRRR
SHUNK
VRP
CHOOM
VRRRR

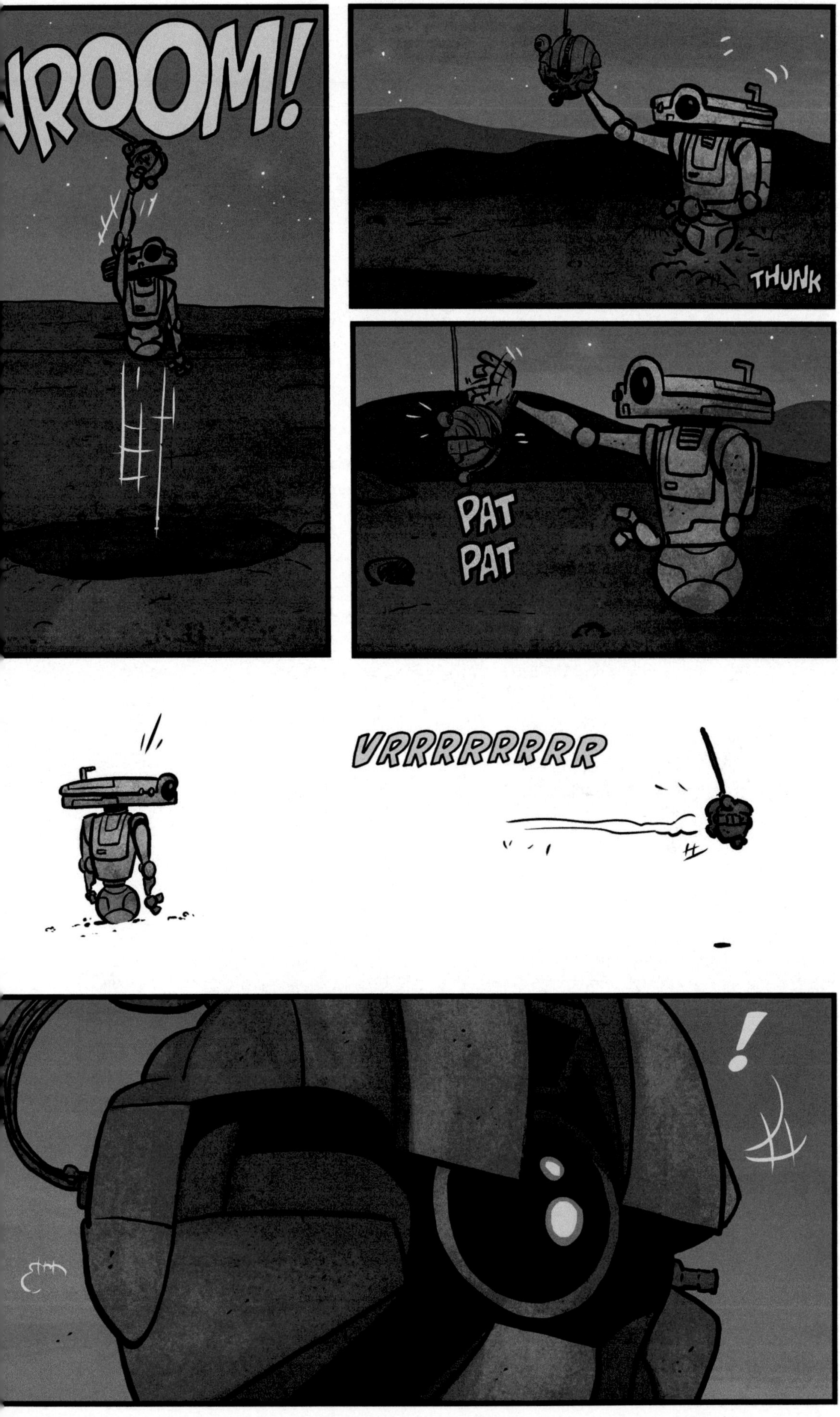
VROOM!
THUNK
PAT
PAT
VRRRRRRRR

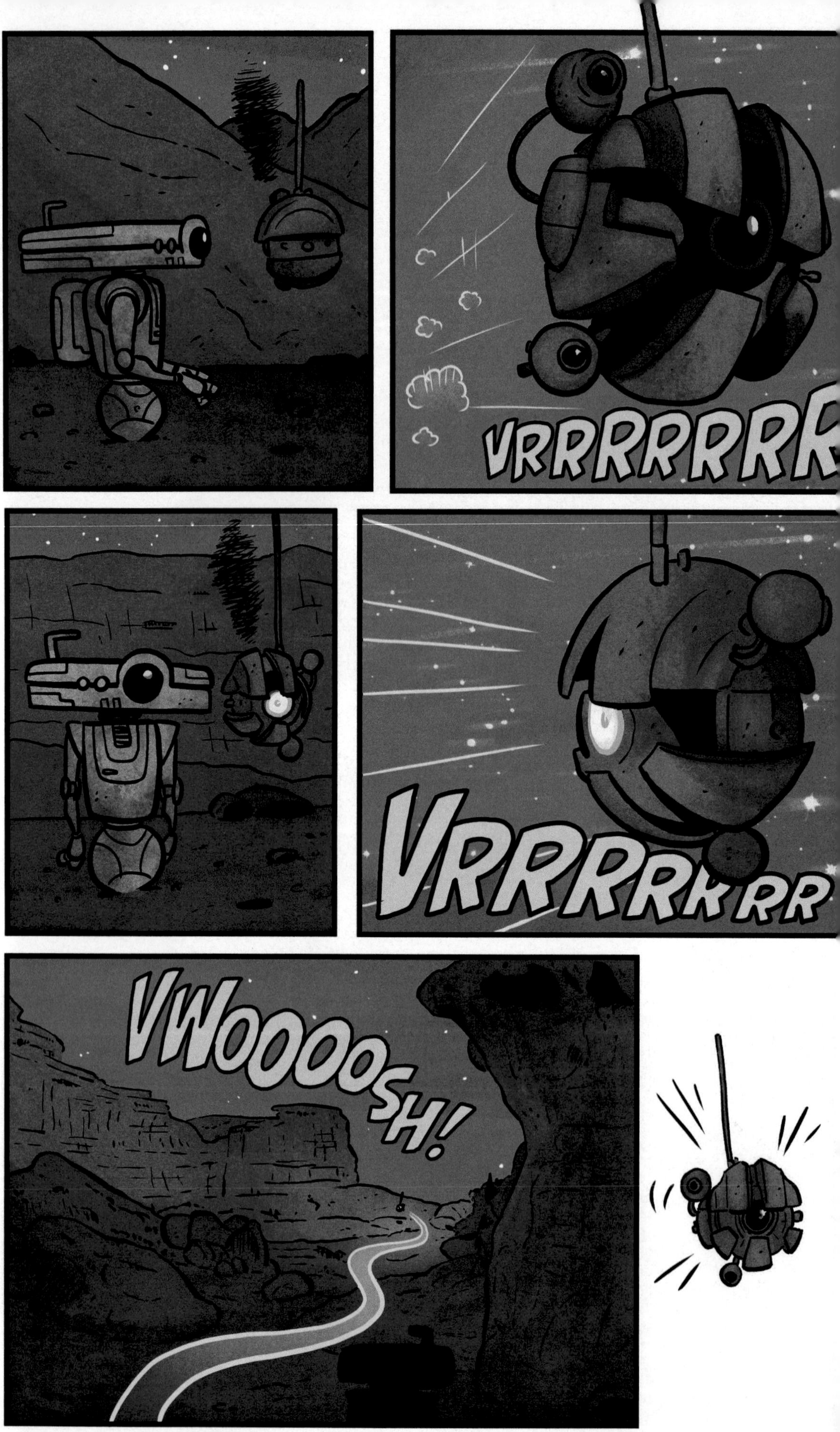

VRRRRRRR
VRRRRRRR
VWOOOOSH!

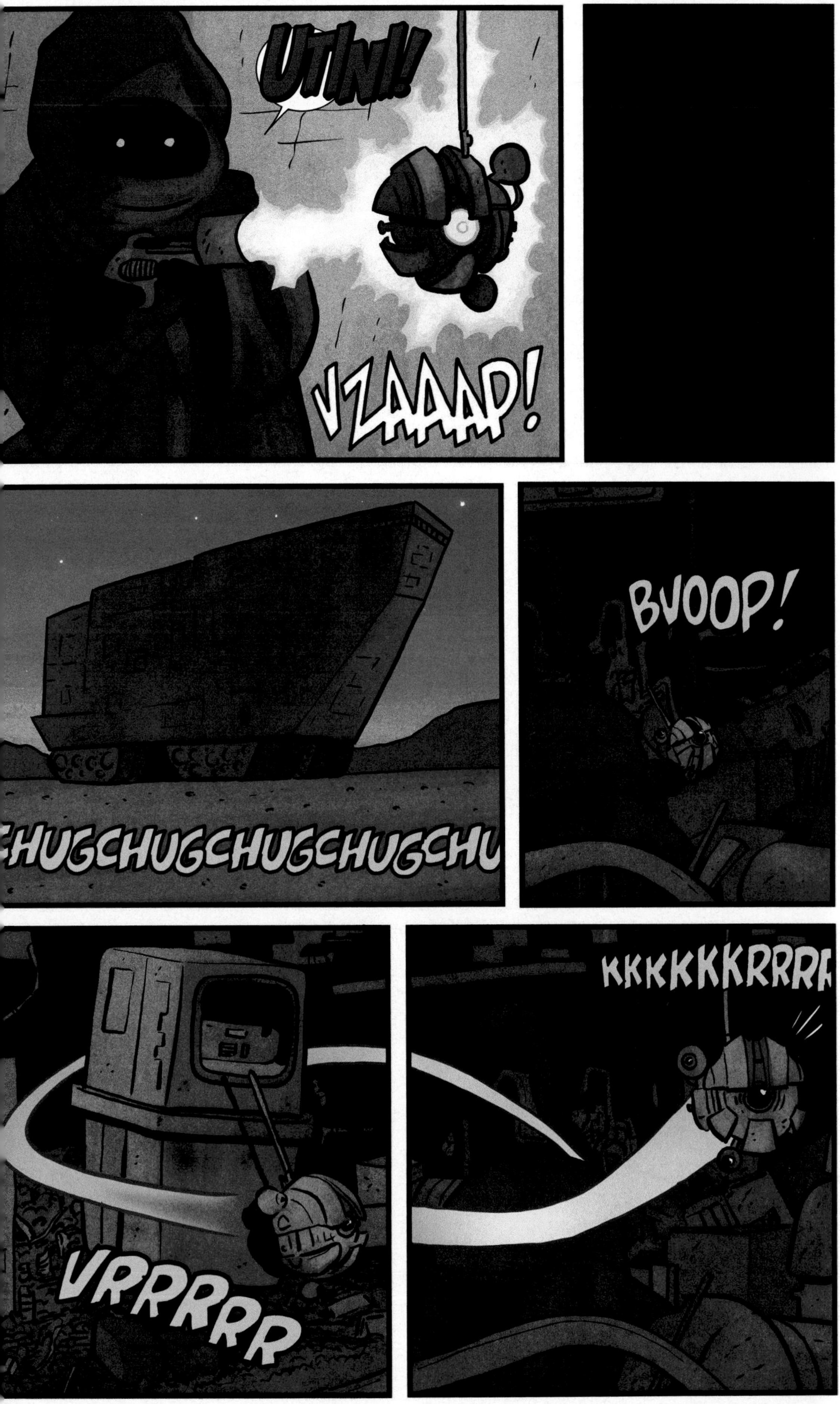
UTINI!
VZAAAP!
CHUGCHUGCHUGCHUGCHU
BVOOP!
VRRRRRR
KKKKKKRRRR

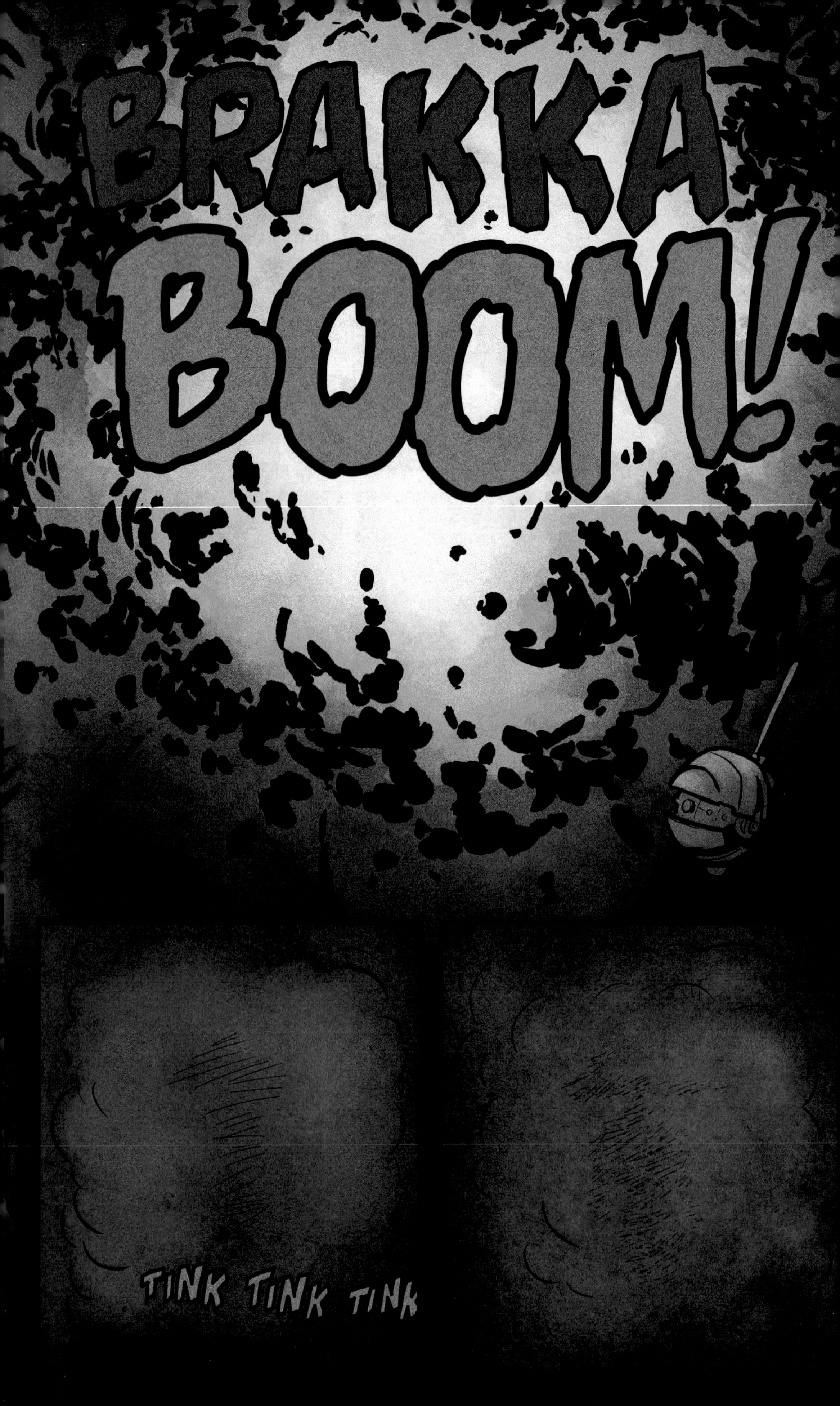
BRAKKA
BOOM!
TINK TINK TINK

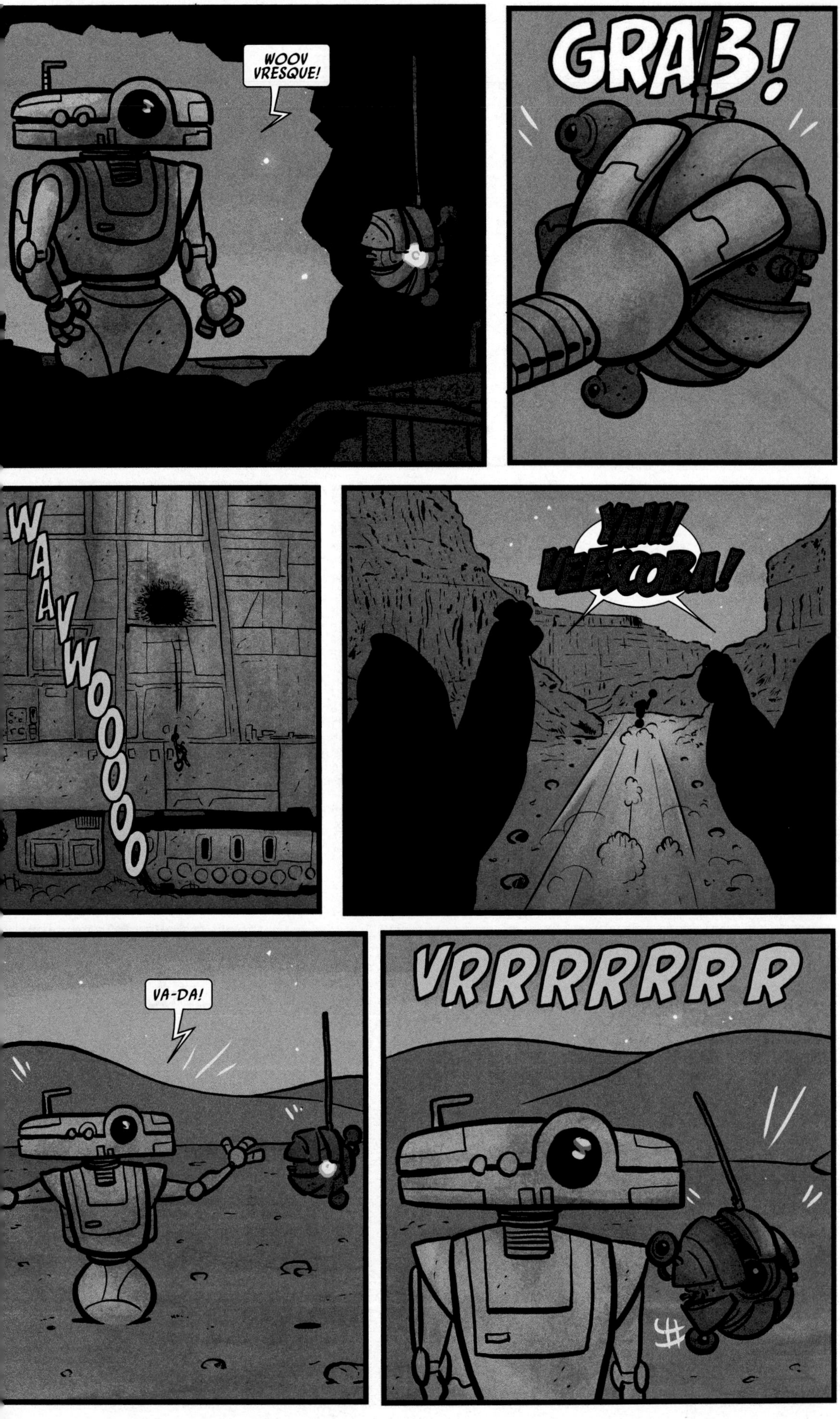
WOOV VRESQUE!
GRAB!
WAAVWOOOOOO
YAH! VEESCOBA!
VA-DA!
VRRRRRRR

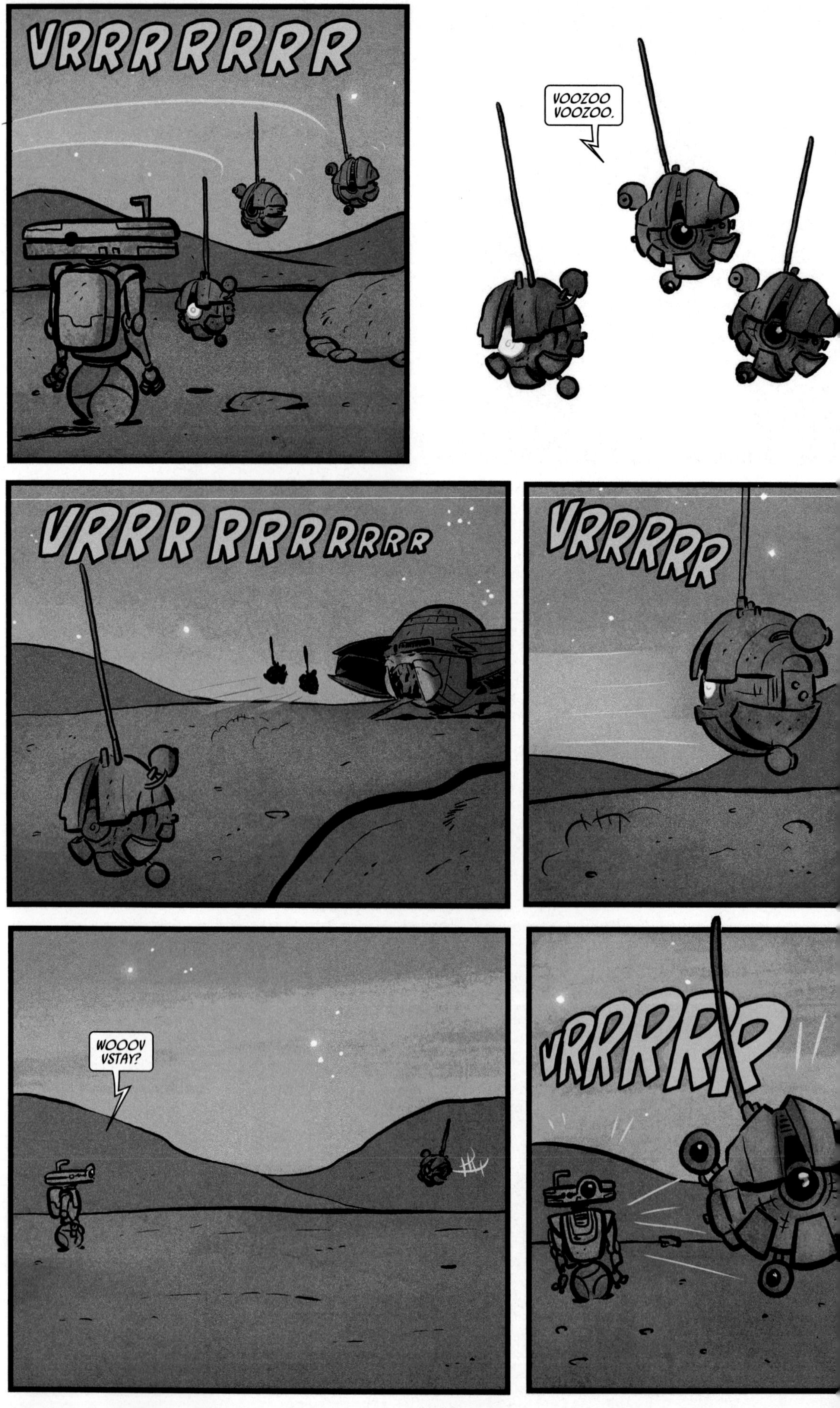
VRRRRRRR
VOOZOO
VOOZOO.
VRRRRRRRRRR
VRRRRR
WOOOV
VSTAY?
VRRRRP

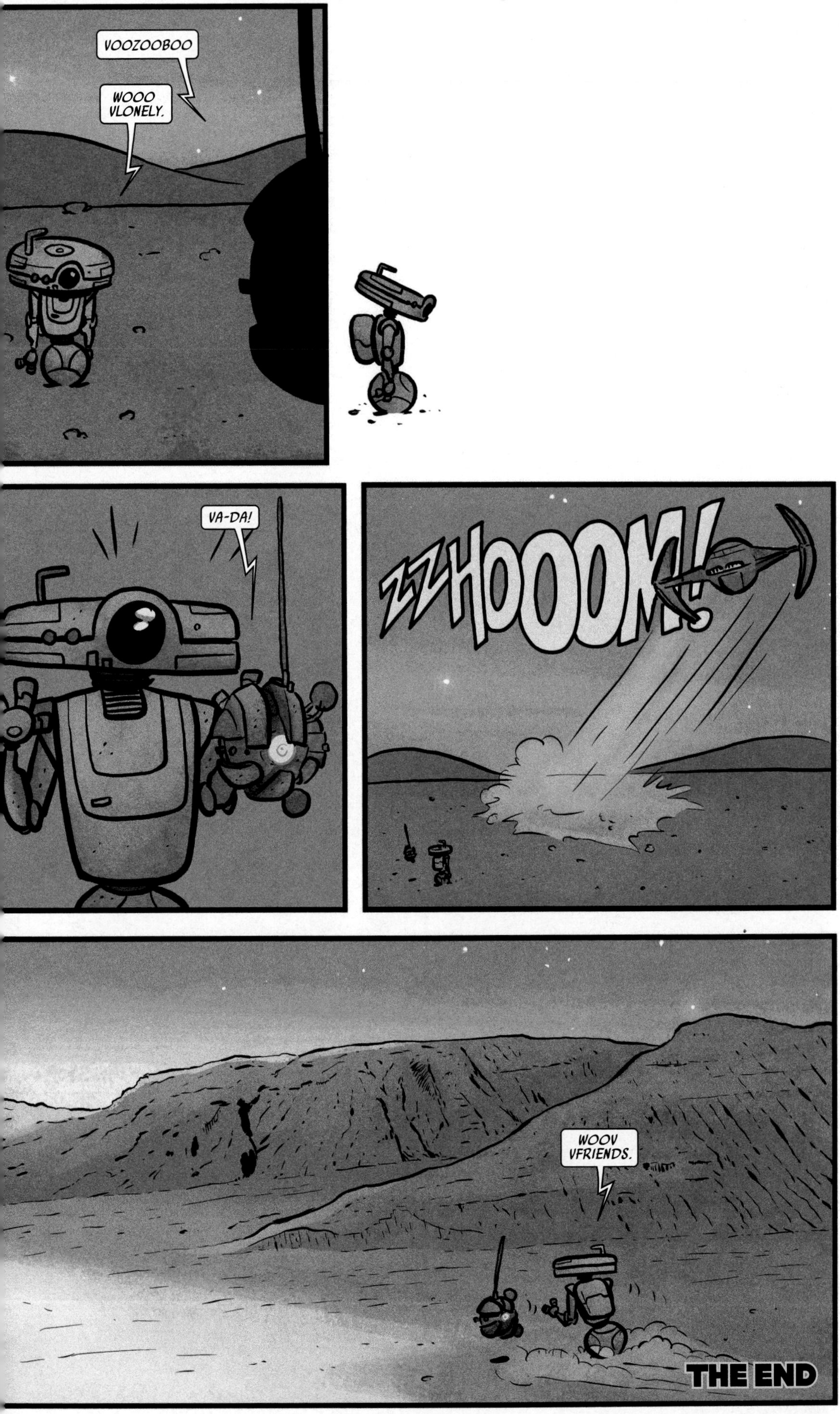
VOOZOOBOO
WOOO VLONELY.
VA-DA!
ZZHOOOM!
WOOV VFRIENDS.
THE END

Darth Maul 01
RATED T VARIANT
$4.99US EDITION
DIRECT EDITION
MARVEL.COM
STAR
WARS
Darth Maul

STAR WARS:
DARTH MAUL 1
ACTION FIGURE VARIANT BY
JOHN TYLER CHRISTOPHER

Darth Maul 01
MARVEL.COM
STAR
WARS
Darth Sidious

STAR WARS:
DARTH MAUL 1
ACTION FIGURE VARIANT BY
JOHN TYLER CHRISTOPHER

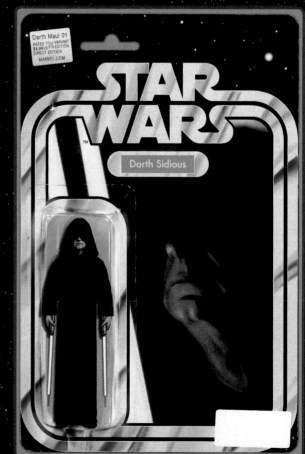

CHARACTERS YOU KNOW. STORIES YOU DON'T.

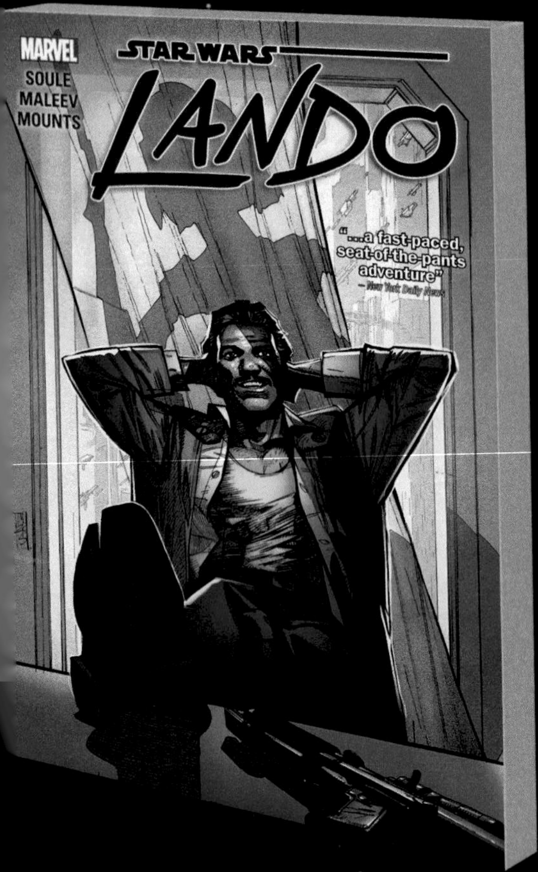
MARVEL
STAR WARS
SOULE
MALEEV
MOUNTS
LANDO
"...a fast-paced, seat-of-the-pants adventure"
– New York Daily News

STAR WARS: LANDO TPB

978-0-7851-9319-7 • $16.99

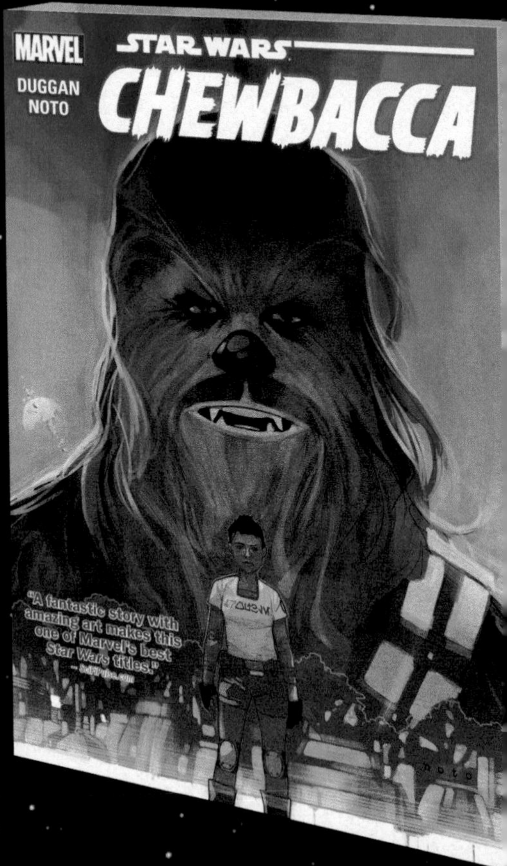
MARVEL
STAR WARS
DUGGAN
NOTO
CHEWBACCA
"A fantastic story with amazing art makes this one of Marvel's best Star Wars titles."

STAR WARS: CHEWBACCA TPB

978-0-7851-9320-3 • $16.99

ON SALE NOW

IN PRINT & DIGITAL WHEREVER BOOKS ARE SOLD.

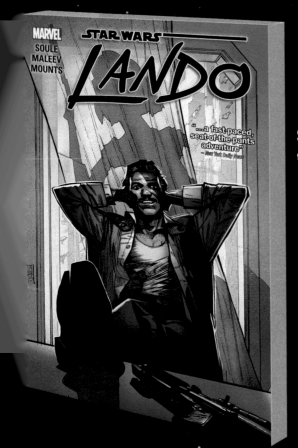

WHAT IS A PRINCESS WITHOUT A WORLD?

STAR WARS: PRINCESS LEIA TPB
978-0-7851-9317-3

ON SALE NOW!